CULTURE, PLACE, AND NATURE
STUDIES IN ANTHROPOLOGY AND ENVIRONMENT

K. Sivaramakrishnan, Series Editor

CULTURE, PLACE, AND NATURE

Centered in anthropology, the Culture, Place, and Nature series encompasses new interdisciplinary social science research on environmental issues, focusing on the intersection of culture, ecology, and politics in global, national, and local contexts. Contributors to the series view environmental knowledge and issues from the multiple and often conflicting perspectives of various cultural systems.

The Kuhls of Kangra: Community-Managed Irrigation in the Western Himalaya
by Mark Baker

The Earth's Blanket: Traditional Teachings for Sustainable Living
by Nancy Turner

Property and Politics in Sabah, Malaysia: Native Struggles over Land Rights
by Amity A. Doolittle

Border Landscapes: The Politics of Akha Land Use in China and Thailand
by Janet C. Sturgeon

From Enslavement to Environmentalism: Politics on a Southern African Frontier
by David McDermott Hughes

Ecological Nationalisms: Nature, Livelihood, and Identities in South Asia
edited by Gunnel Cederlöf and K. Sivaramakrishnan

Tropics and the Traveling Gaze: India, Landscape, and Science, 1800–1856
by David Arnold

Being and Place among the Tlingit
by Thomas F. Thornton

Forest Guardians, Forest Destroyers: The Politics of Environmental Knowledge in Northern Thailand
by Tim Forsyth and Andrew Walker

Nature Protests: The End of Ecology in Slovakia
by Edward Snajdr

Wild Sardinia: Indigeneity and the Global Dreamtimes of Environmentalism
by Tracey Heatherington

Tahiti Beyond the Postcard: Power, Place, and Everyday Life
by Miriam Kahn

TAHITI

BEYOND THE POSTCARD

Power, Place, and Everyday Life

Miriam Kahn

University of Washington Press

SEATTLE & LONDON

This publication is supported in part by the Donald R. Ellegood International Publications Endowment.

University of Washington Press
P.O. Box 50096, Seattle, WA 98145, U.S.A.
www.washington.edu/uwpress

Printed and bound in the United States of America / Designed by Ashley Saleeba Composed in Minion Pro and Meta

COVER: "Preparing Coconut *Monoi* Oil," painting by Bobby Holcomb; courtesy of Dorothy Levy.

LIBRARY OF CONGRESS
CATALOGING-IN-PUBLICATION DATA

Kahn, Miriam.
Tahiti beyond the postcard : power, place, and everyday life / Miriam Kahn.
p. cm. — (Culture, place, and nature)
Includes bibliographical references and index.
ISBN 978-0-295-99101-6 (hardback : alk. paper) — ISBN 978-0-295-99102-3 (pbk. : alk. paper)
1. Ethnology—French Polynesia—Tahiti (Island) 2. Human geography—French Polynesia—Tahiti (Island) 3. Culture and tourism—French Polynesia—Tahiti (Island) 4. Geographical perception—Tahiti (French Polynesia : Island) 5. Postcolonialism—French Polynesia—Tahiti (Island) 6. Tahiti (French Polynesia : Island)—Social life and customs. 7. Tahiti (French Polynesia : Island)—Foreign relations—France. 8. France—Foreign relations—Tahiti (French Polynesia : Island) I. Title.
GN671.S55KK34 2010
996.2'11—dc22
2010043123

To my parents,
Tatyana Uffner Kahn
and Ludwig Werner Kahn

Contents

Foreword

The imprint that places leave on the societies that inhabit and shape them has always been of great interest to environmental anthropology. In this study Miriam Kahn draws upon fieldwork and archival research conducted in both Tahiti and France to reflect on the basic question of how places and people form and change their identity in interconnected ways. She takes a historical view of the formation of modern Tahiti as an object of intense Euro-American interest and desire, and from that vantage point tells the story of how Tahitians and others have narrated their lives in this group of islands and in the island's necessary and elective relations with the rest of the world.

Colonized by France after several voyagers had already begun to represent Tahiti as a place of legendary beauty and comfort, French Polynesia offers a story that at one level resembles European arrivals in other parts of the Pacific and Polynesia. Those comparative lessons do not escape Kahn, but she is more interested in providing a careful account of how—in the experience of colonialism and cold war—residence, travel, interconnection, and the production of livelihood in Tahiti mark the landscape and thereby shape identity for those who live and travel there. Before the arrival of European explorers, Tahitian lives were already shaped by the travel and trade characteristic of Pacific Islander and Polynesian cultures. By focusing here on arrivals and departures in the era of European expansion and beyond, to the contemporary incorporation of Tahitian lives into the world of nuclear deterrence and tourism, Kahn traces the different modes and regimes of travel and, thereby, the history and power of place making that can be discerned in patterns of mobility and their artistic representation.

There is a larger body of work, mostly coming out of cultural and colonial history, that has examined how various tropical areas were shaped, imagined, depicted, and transformed by colonial encounter. Histories of conquest, exploration, natural resource mining, and migration have all done that work well, and the Pacific Islands have their share of such accounts. Kahn has engaged that body of work, but with a further ambition, appropriate to anthropology, to narrate these accounts from theoretical and ethnographic perspectives both Tahitian and European. The invention of Tahiti as a tourist paradise is continuously juxtaposed with its use for nuclear tests and the environmental destruction caused by both tourism and military industry.

Fabrication of beaches, environmental health hazards caused by nuclear testing, and conflicts over land and water between local agriculture and industry and the international tourist trade squarely raise the issues often couched in terms of political ecology. Kahn also weaves into her account, via the focus on place making, the struggles over representation of nature and the natural that are inseparable from struggles over natural resources. To this valuable theme in environmental anthropology she brings a new lens ground in theories of space, place, and identity and held over an underreported Pacific island. What she finds is then presented in limpid, evocative prose that refuses to meander or become dull even in its most theoretical passages. The result is a book astute in observation, kind and generous in tone, incisive in analysis, and elegant in exposition—indeed, a remarkable extension of environmental anthropology into the realm of humanistic inquiry.

K. SIVARAMAKRISHNAN
Yale University
May 2010

Acknowledgments

Although the task of putting words to paper can feel like the loneliest of endeavors, what lies behind the words has been a delightfully social, cooperative undertaking. Many people are within these pages. They have opened their worlds to me, helped me gather information, included me, patiently taught me, answered my endless questions, and discussed my ideas. They read what I wrote, commented, and read again. Without them, there would be no book.

I am profoundly grateful, humbled, and honored by the many people in French Polynesia who helped me. Our good friends Édouard and Kim Tai Piha, and their extended family, Poema and Billy, Rachelle and Philippe, Kiki and Moana, and Brigitte; as well as Jessica (my daughter's constant companion), Vaimiri, Tevaihau, and Haurai shared their lives and thoughts with us, fed us, and laughed with us. Many of them also visited us in Seattle. On Huahine, Édouard took my husband, Richard, under his wing, working in the *faa'apu*, going on midnight fishing trips, teaching him how to fertilize vanilla, and building new benches for the church.

Marietta and Atea Tefaataumarama opened their hearts and lives to us, inviting us to events that became some of my most memorable experiences. I learned much from Marietta, as I worked side by side with her in the Fare Pote'e and traveled with her and Atea with the *matahiapo* to Taha'a. One of my most memorable experiences was when she and Tamari'i Mata'ire'a, a troupe of eighteen dancers and musicians from Huahine, came to Seattle to perform at the Seattle International Children's Festival and at the Northwest Folklife Festival.

Many other friends couldn't have been more generous, inclusive, and helpful: Théophile and Huguette Ihorai, Heitiare and Willy Tereua, Kiki and Bianca Taupu, Jean Yves Teri'itapunui, Hiti and Turia Gooding, Tetua and Émile Piha, Georges Matauteute and Pauline Barff, Paul and Vatiana Atallah, Marty and Moe Temahahe, and (in Fetuna) Peto and Mariette Firuu and their children, Angéla and Arai.

Bruno Saura, professor at the Université de la Polynésie Française, a friend and mentor on Huahine, and constant supporter, painstakingly read my manuscript and provided enormously helpful feedback. Dr. Yosihiko Sinoto of the Bishop Museum in Hawai'i taught me about the complex history of Huahine, and included Richard (trained as an archaeologist) as a member of his archaeological team on Huahine.

It is an understatement to say that my research would not have been possible without the loyal friendship of Dorothy Levy, soul mate, facilitator, and sounding board for everything I did on Huahine. Dorothy also read my manuscript and provided supportive feedback. Her mother-in-law, Mama Rere Teururai, was profoundly helpful as I asked question after question. Dorothy's daughter, Sabrina Levy Birk, lawyer and artist, provided useful insight on the politics of French Polynesia.

I am particularly grateful to Teva Sylvain and Diane Commons for their willingness to talk to me about their postcard businesses and for the helpful insights these conversations provided. I also benefited greatly from conversations with Jan Prince, Dominique Wolton, Norbert Itchner, Richard Shamel, Etienne Faaeva, Henriette Colombanie, Jean-Pierre Amo, Etienne Ragivaru, Jean-Merry Delarue, Paulette Viénot, Karine Villa, Christel Bole, Brigitte Vanizette, Laurent Bessou, Louise Peltzer, Gilles Fuller, Christine Sauvagnac, and Suzanne Lau-Chonfont.

I am deeply gratified that Do Carlson (widow of Henri Hiro) and Chantal Spitz read parts of my text and provided valuable input.

Several students read the manuscript in earlier drafts and provided their honest, critical, and extraordinarily helpful feedback: Rochelle Tuitagava'a Fonoti, Karen Capuder, Jaye Sablan, Ellen Wohlford, Shumei Huang, and Hang Truong.

Anthropologists Setha Low, Lamont Lindstrom, and Stuart Kirsch offered discerning and meticulous feedback on drafts of my manuscript that was critical for improving its quality. Kalyanakrishnan Sivaramakrishnan, editor of the University of Washington's Culture, Place, and Nature series, also provided perceptive input.

At the University of Washington Press, Lorri Hagman moved my manuscript along with remarkable wisdom, care, and speed. Kerrie Maynes's copyediting was impeccable. I was fortunate, once again, to have Ashley Saleeba design the layout of my book. I thank Amir Sheikh for making the maps. I am grateful to Raoul Céré for providing me with high-quality images of the postcards.

I thank the government of French Polynesia for graciously granting me permission to carry out my research.

I thank the Fulbright Program, the American Philosophical Society, the Max and Lotte Heine Philanthropic Fund, and the Royalty Research Fund at the University of Washington for having provided the funds that made the research possible.

Finally, and underlying everything else, my family has been a tremendous support throughout the years.

My late parents, Tatyana Uffner Kahn and Ludwig Werner Kahn, always offered their loving understanding and encouragement during my far-flung adventures.

Being in Tahiti with my family was an incredible bonus in many respects. Having them with me deepened the experience in ways I couldn't anticipate. Our being there as a family allowed Tahitians to relate more personally to all of us. In addition, having shared the experience with them allows it to remain close to all of our hearts.

The presence of our daughter, Rachel, made it possible for me to learn about details of Tahitian life that otherwise would have remained elusive: the playful and disciplinary worlds of young children; the school experience, with its colonial curriculum; and parents' concerns for their children. Later, when she was a teenager, I learned much about Tahitian teenagers, including their creative tactics for sabotaging colonial spaces (and French teachers) within the school setting. Regardless of her age and her various feelings about being in Tahiti, Rachel was always a cheerful participant.

My husband, Richard L. Taylor, has been my constant companion on this journey. He accompanied me on every fieldtrip, assisted in the gathering of data, was instrumental in the formulation of my ideas, and helped enormously with the editing of the manuscript. As with our daughter, his presence allowed me to gain insight into wider Tahitian worlds, in this case the lives of men. My cultural understanding was greatly enriched when friends invited him to go fishing, work in the *faa'apu*, play *pétanque*, or share some *fafaru*.

Note to the Reader

PEOPLE'S NAMES

All individuals quoted, other than public figures, have read over the passages in which I quote them and have approved of the content as well as the use of their name. The way in which I refer to people (that is, first name, professional title, and so on) reflects the type of relationship I had with them.

TRANSLATIONS

Unless otherwise noted, all translations from French or Tahitian are my own.

PHOTOS

Unless otherwise noted, all photos are my own.

TAHITI BEYOND THE POSTCARD

Introduction

I n a darkened conference room of a sumptuous hotel in French Polynesia, the word "TAHITI" appeared—in large turquoise letters—on the screen in the front. The image grabbed my attention, and that of the other people in the room, most of whom worked in Tahiti's tourism industry. The speaker, the North American representative for Tahiti Tourism, brought his presentation to a close with that one slide, reminding us that the vision of Tahiti, evoked by its mere name, was powerful. "Like magic," he said. Leaving us with that thought, he flipped the lights back on. I rose from my seat, gathered my materials, and left the room. Yet the image of Tahiti lingered, not only on the screen but also in my mind. The word and everything about it—its power, its turquoise color, its ability to flaunt itself and seduce you, as well as its knack for fading under intense light—seemed to encapsulate everything I was trying to understand.

Why does "Tahiti" have such overwhelming power beyond its geographical borders? How does the mere name of a place become "like magic," capable of making people from all over the world pay high prices and travel endless hours to fulfill a lifelong dream? How do Tahitians, living their daily lives in a place others refer to as "paradise," experience Tahiti? How does the global circulation of this mediated imagery affect the people for whom Tahiti is home? How do these two perspectives—Tahitians' senses of their place and outsiders' visions of "Tahiti"—intersect, disrupt, and influence one another?

Several scholars have written about the "myth" of Tahiti and its history.[1] Even the government of French Polynesia realizes the value of *"le mythe de Tahiti"* and the need to perpetuate it consciously, cleverly, and with a large investment of funds. Less has been written, however, about the complexity of this myth today. Employing a theoretical lens of "place" helps shed light on this complexity. From a "place" perspective, one can see how power dynamics reinforce the creation and maintenance of this myth and affect the ways in which Westerners imagine and experience "Tahiti."

As an American anthropologist who does research in Tahiti/French Polynesia, I constantly find myself tangled in the far-flung web of this myth. Tahiti is a place that causes others to chuckle when I mention it as the location of my serious scholarly work. It's a place from which one of my colleagues has a postcard on the wall in her lab to remind her that, if her scientific experiments fail, there's always plan B, namely to escape to Bora Bora. It's a place that, when I recently was introduced at a professional gathering as someone who had just returned from doing research in Tahiti, made others in the room roll their eyes and ask, "Why did you come back?"

This tangled web that has created a place of unusual power (and in whose filaments I'm also caught) is the very reason that I chose to do research on the power of place in Tahiti. There are few locations that bring forth as many images of, and associations with, a particular place as this one does. Yet beyond the postcard image exists another, quite different, place—the one inhabited and experienced by *ta'ata ma'ohi*, as many Tahitians refer to themselves. For *ta'ata ma'ohi*, their land/place (*te fenua ma'ohi*) provides physical and spiritual nourishment as well as a profound sense of identity. Their lived reality also includes the fact that Tahiti is still a colony of France.[2] Over the centuries, the French government has appropriated these Polynesian islands as refueling stations for the French navy, mined one of them for phosphate, and destroyed others. Less well known to the public is that Tahiti's long history of colonial domination includes thirty years (1966–96) of nuclear testing by France in the air above and in the bedrock below Tahitian soil.

Although these different places—the imagined and the experienced— seem disconnected at first glance, they are deeply intertwined in both economic and political ways, emerging from the complex, nearly 250-year-long colonial relationship between France and French Polynesia. Romanticized accounts by the first European visitors to Tahiti in the eighteenth century led countless writers, artists, adventurers, missionaries, colonists, scientists, filmmakers, and tourism entrepreneurs to follow, searching for and creating a "Tahiti" of the imagination. Today the image endures as the bedrock of Tahiti's tourism industry, the largest private enterprise and leading source of foreign exchange in Tahiti. This mythical image (and the desire to understand the reality) propelled me, as well, to go there—with many questions on my mind. What motives—whether economic, political, or cultural—support this vision of "paradise"? How does colonialism feed into (and on) these images? How can nuclear weapons testing exist in a place that is promoted as a pristine paradise? How and why is "Tahiti" crafted by a complex tourism industry whose business is to create desire? And how is this fantasized product embraced, ignored, or perhaps even sabotaged by Tahitians who spend their lives in a colonial outpost in today's "postcolonial" world?

PLACING MYSELF AND MY INTEREST IN "PLACE"

When I think about my own sense of place, what comes to mind is a persistent feeling of having gone from being in place to being out of place. I'm also aware, although only recently more consciously so, of my lifelong search to again feel in-place. I spent my first seven years in (what I now idealize as) a multicultural utopia of sorts, into which my German-Jewish refugee parents, my sister, and I blended seamlessly. We lived in an area of Queens that was nicknamed the United Nations Village because the housing was mostly reserved for employees of the UN (even though my parents didn't work for the UN).[3] I felt at one with my physical and social surroundings, unaware of any discord between place and self. For each of my friends, home was a place where different languages were spoken and different aromas wafted from the kitchen. The scents of Mexican chili from the apartment below us and of Indian curry from across the hall mingled with the aromas of the pot roast and potatoes in our kitchen. It was only later when we moved to a homogeneous suburb of New York City that, although I now looked like everyone else, I suddenly felt out of place. For the first time I noticed—because friends told me—that my parents had strange accents and that my lunches of dense pumpernickel bread and hard cheese were peculiar. Ever since my awkward attempt at assimilation into suburbia, I have longed to return, however symbolically, to the harmonious place of my childhood where everyone belonged and played together happily (or so I remembered).

When I discovered anthropology in college in the late 1960s, it struck a chord. The discipline encourages one to embrace the whole world as one's home and, thus, made me feel at home in the world. I soon learned, however, that practicing anthropology ironically meant that I would have to put myself in situations where I would feel emphatically out of place. Whenever I conduct fieldwork, whether in Papua New Guinea, Tahiti, or elsewhere, my senses of self and place get rattled. I feel, as Foucault has said of ships, like "a floating piece of space, a place without a place" (Foucault 1986, 27). I am always the awkward outsider—observing, listening, learning, and responding from a place in between. Trying to feel at home in the home of someone else, I face my ultimate challenge—to go from feeling dislocated to feeling ensconced—a Sisyphean task that can never be accomplished. Indeed, I wouldn't be writing this particular book if I hadn't *always* been watching and noting from the interstices: being in-between cultures, in-between languages, in-between the indigenous and colonial spaces about which I was writing, and in-between the ruptures within myself caused by my very displacement. Strangely, I have found solace in the oddest things precisely because, for a fleeting moment, they allowed me to feel like less of an "other." When, on one of my early trips to Tahiti, my daughter and her friend were punished in school for giggling while the teacher was talking, I was ecstatic! Her friend (and her friend's mother) were humiliated that she had to stand in front of the class for thirty minutes as punishment, but I was overjoyed. For my "outsider" daughter to be singled out and disciplined like any ordinary misbehaving seven-year-old was a sign for me that she "fit in." Perhaps, in that moment, I unwittingly identified with her, seeing her—and me?—as that child feeling at home in the United Nations Village.

The experience of constantly uprooting oneself, living in different places, and then crafting new social relationships to learn and feel at home has provided the methodological base and theoretical springboard for anthropology for over a century. This legacy, however, entails a constant tension between feelings of being in and out of place. In this in-between state of "research" I am constantly exploring both my own homeland and those of others, searching for that feeling of being-at-home-in-the-world so that ultimately and paradoxically, "place" becomes less of an obstacle.

PLACE AND PLACE-BASED IDENTITY IN THE PACIFIC

Although my personal interest in "place" probably originated in my childhood, my academic interest in the topic was first piqued during three years of field research (on food symbolism and horticultural ritual) in the village of Wamira, Papua New Guinea, in the late 1970s and early 1980s (Kahn 1986).

One of the things I learned from people in Wamira was that their identities were generally deeply rooted in their sense of place (Kahn 1990, 1996). In Papua New Guinea, as elsewhere in the Pacific Islands, history is visible in the landscape. The past is commonly understood spatially rather than temporally.[4] Even my own experiences as an anthropologist in Papua New Guinea became embedded in the landscape. When I first had to say farewell to my friends in Wamira after having lived in their village for two years, the woman who had taken care of me as her "daughter" during that time wailed,

> My child, you stayed here and took care of us. You helped us and now you are leaving. Everywhere I go I will think of you, the places where we walked, the places where we sat. . . . You stayed in Wamira a long time and left your mark in many places. Under that breadfruit tree you first gave Osborne some tobacco . . . on that hill you helped us turn the sod in the garden . . . at that rock on the riverbank you washed your clothes . . . at that tree stump you rested to eat mangoes on the way home from market . . . and there is the banana garden where you sat on top of the fence, causing it to come tumbling down. (Alice Dobunaba, personal communication, 1978)

People would anchor personal narratives and communal histories to physical forms in the landscape—such as a breadfruit tree, a hill, a rock, a tree stump, or a banana garden—and these places then became important markers for recalling histories, whether of cultural heroes and heroines or of visiting anthropologists. Even now, thirty years later, my memory still lingers in specific places in Wamira, something I am reminded of each time I receive a letter from Alice or, more recently, an e-mail from her children or grandchildren.

Stones, in particular, play an important role in marking, recalling, and reconfiguring Pacific Island pasts and presents.[5] I learned this early on in Wamira, where there were several important cultural heroes and heroines who had turned into stone and who inhabited the landscape as daily reminders of history and morality. These stones, like histories, are still alive. They are known to walk around, especially at night, and even swim across the ocean, animating history as they travel. In one instance, my plan to map a group of stones in a neighboring village was agreed to only on condition that I would later print two dozen rugby shirts—which, I was told, had to be done in the United States—with my map of the stones prominently displayed on the front. These stones were indicators of a particular clan's power, and members of the clan's rugby team wanted to wear the shirts while playing against their rivals, to ward off jealousy (and sorcery) by reminding their rivals of the stones that anchored them to a place and gave them power. When I was back in the United States ordering the shirts, I contemplated the many layers of experiencing, inscribing, and demonstrating place and place-based identity. In this case, the clan's sense of identity, rooted in and visible upon the land, could be transcribed onto an anthropologist's map and then further reproduced on sports jerseys. These permutations seemed to enhance, rather than lessen, the sense of power embedded in the land, the stones, and the shirts. I was told that when the rugby players would scrimmage against their opponents—with the anthropologist's map on their chests—they would feel empowered through their place-based identity, all of which was intensified by the map's journey to another, and quite distant, place, namely "America."

With my interest in the meanings of place piqued by my research in Papua New Guinea, I later decided to broaden my horizons and become familiar with a second Pacific Island field site, and specifically one where I could focus more intently on ideas—and especially a complex multiplicity of ideas—about place. Thus, I began new work in Tahiti in the early 1990s, a choice based on several factors.[6] The main reason I decided to work in Tahiti, though, was because it seemed to combine multiple perspectives on place. With the divergent perceptions of Tahitians, colonists, tourists, and others, Tahiti appeared to be an excellent setting for exploring how various, seemingly conflicting, senses of place were entangled.[7]

Even the name itself—Tahiti—raises key issues about place. In a factual way, one could describe French Polynesia/Tahiti as a French territory of 118 islands in the Pacific Ocean. One could also recognize that the first European explorers misunderstood the language and applied the name of one island (Otaheite) to the whole region and its people, a misnomer that, ever since, has become a commodity of its own. For example, ask individuals in the United States what French Polynesia is or what it consists of and many would have some difficulty providing an answer. "Ask about Tahiti, however, and a vision of a beautiful tropical island rising from a deep-blue sea immediately materializes on the map" (Wheeler and Carillet 1997, 10), even though there may be no sense of exactly where "Tahiti" is. Moreover, French Polynesia, which spans an area more than twice the size of Western Europe, but with a total land area only a third that of Connecticut, is incredibly diverse. Differences in topography, history, and language are far greater than indicated in the early explorers' accounts or tourists' contemporary visions.

Likewise, using the word "Tahitian" as an identifier raises critical political issues about place-based identity.[8] Some Tahitians prefer to use the term "Ma'ohi," an ancient Tahitian word that means "indigenous" or "authentic" but was originally used for plants and animals, not human beings.[9] Over the past decades the term "Ma'ohi" has taken on new usage—first in the late 1940s by the supporters of Pouvana'a O'opa (Tahiti's most respected nationalist, who led a separatist movement at the time), then in the 1960s as a reaction to the changes brought about by France's nuclear testing program (Tevane 2000, 15), and again during the cultural revivalism of the 1970s. This new usage, in opposition to the word "Tahitian," had distinct political, anti-colonial, nationalist implications. Since the 1980s its use has become more widespread, with the word appearing in poems, songs, dance performances, political discourse, media advertisements, acronyms for groups and institutions, and even in the Ma'ohi Protestant Church (Saura 2004, 125). The goal in making this term widely used was to create an anti-French and inclusive identity for the inhabitants of French Polynesia.[10]

Here both "Tahitian" and "Ma'ohi" are used to refer to the inhabitants, and both "Tahiti" and "*te fenua ma'ohi*" to refer to the land/homeland/place—depending on the context. Tahiti/*te fenua ma'ohi*, like any place, does not have one fixed identity, but is multiple and shifting; it includes ancestral lands, personal narratives, shared histories, meaningful memories, economic imperatives, political entanglements, fantasized images, and saturated symbols. It was this complex multivocality and multilocality that I wanted to understand when I began research in Tahiti/*te fenua ma'ohi* in 1993.

ANTHROPOLOGY OF SPACE AND PLACE

An interest in "place" was energized by new anthropological scholarship on the topic in the 1980s and 1990s. Although anthropologists have long attended in one way or another to issues of place,[11] there has been a major shift to a more nuanced, critical, and indigenous understanding of place in recent years. Since the mid-1980s, social and cultural theories about human behavior have taken what is often referred to as a "spatial turn," where place has become a rallying cry for understanding social life in its fullest.[12] Before that, as Michel Foucault pointed out, "space was treated as the dead, the fixed, the undialectical, the immobile. Time, on the contrary, was richness, fecundity, life, dialectic" (1980, 70). Scholars began to rethink the relationship between space and time, and space gained a more central and critical role. People from various disciplines, especially geography, urban sociology, and cultural studies, began using spatial concepts and metaphors to think about the complex and differentiated world in which we live. This recent focus on space may have surfaced because "the anxiety of our era has to do fundamentally with space, no doubt a great deal more than with time" (Foucault 1986, 23).

In the late 1980s new consideration was given to the relationship between place and voice in anthropological theory (Appadurai 1988b). Anthropology was seen as always having been engaged with place because of "the culturally defined locations to which ethnographies refer" and the fact that "such named locations, which often come to be identified with the groups that inhabit them, constitute the landscape of anthropology" (Appadurai 1988a, 16). Anthropology's problems of place (speaking "from" and speaking "of") and voice (speaking "for" and speaking "to") became linked to issues of power, where the appearance of dialogue was seen as concealing the anthropologist's monologue. "Anthropology survives by its claim to capture other places (and other voices) through its special brand of ventriloquism" (Appadurai 1988a, 20). It is this tendency of anthropologists to speak from, of, for, and to that was examined critically at this time, resulting in an epic shift in anthropology's approaches to place.

In the early 1990s another wave of interest focused on space and place by examining how such topics as location, displacement, community, and identity help to reevaluate the idea of cultural difference (Gupta and Ferguson 1992). It was noted that for anthropology, a discipline "whose central rite of passage is fieldwork, whose romance has rested on its exploration of the remote . . . [and] whose critical function is seen to lie in its juxtaposition of radically different ways of being (located 'elsewhere') with that of the anthropologists' own, usually Western, culture," there has been surprisingly little reflection about the topic of place or development of insightful theories about it (Gupta and Ferguson 1992, 6). In rallying to this challenge, several anthropologists sought to reevaluate ideas about "culture" and "cultural difference" in terms of place rather than, as had previously been the case, to assume an isomorphism of place and culture (Gupta and Ferguson 1992).

Margaret Rodman called for the rethinking of place as an analytic construct to show "that place as an anthropological concept is as complex as voice" (1992, 641). She argued that "places are not inert containers. They are politicized, culturally relative, historically specific, local and multiple constructions" (1992, 641). She recommended that, in providing their academic analyses of place, anthropologists do so with greater consideration for the multiplicity of the inhabitants' voices (see also Low and Lawrence-Zúñiga 2003, 15). She used the term "multilocality" to indicate that places have many voices, perspectives, meanings, confluences and divergences, and multiple understandings.

Anthropological approaches to space and place have since branched out in many directions.[13] Some scholars have viewed place as culturally constructed or inscribed.[14] Others have viewed it as existing "in the bodies of people with feelings and desires" (Low and Lawrence-Zúñiga 2003, 29–30), as well as outside, beyond, and across political borders.[15] Place has been analyzed in terms of gender[16] and class.[17] It has been used as a lens to examine the ways in which "nature" has been constructed as separate from culture and to challenge the boundaries between the two.[18] Many have seen it as fraught and contested where, as Donald Moore (2005) shows, struggles are spatially situated, thus creating place as well as being about place.[19] Others have analyzed the complexities of place as they appear in global, transnational, and translocal forms.[20] The topic has also added important dimensions in discussions of power where, in addition to being understood in terms of its oppressive abilities, place can also be seen as a creative moment of transformation, a space for dialogue and critique (Mbembe 2001). In other words, "Places are in flux, sliding in and out of existence, and our discourse about place is also in flux, sliding between disciplines and uses" (Janz 2005, 87). Place has become a topic of study in geography, sociology, and anthropology, as well as in urban planning and medicine. There is, however, a surprising lack of communication about the topic across disciplinary boundaries. "It is as if place has to be discovered anew in each discipline" (Janz 2005, 89).

An understanding of place has benefitted especially from the contributions of indigenous (and other) scholars who draw attention to indigenous perspectives on place. For many indigenous peoples the landscape is animate and sentient, inseparable from the lives of human beings (Ball 2002; West 2005, 2006). "For indigenous peoples, interaction with the land is always defined by conceptions of the sacred, the spiritual, and the power of the land and the beings that live within and on it" (Ball 2002, 474). "American Indians hold their lands—places—as having the highest possible meaning, and all their statements are made with this reference point in mind" (Deloria 1994, 63). Similar perspectives have been described about place for Navajo, Salish, and other Native peoples.[21] For the indigenous people of Australia, "country" has its own agency. People are nurtured by, and caretakers of, the land, which they know as a living landscape with spiritual powers (Rose 1996).

Pacific Islanders, in general, share this same understanding about their relationship to land and its embodied ancestral presence and cultural values. In the novel *Potiki,* when property speculators in New Zealand started using Maori land to develop tourist attractions, golf courses, and apartment blocks, the community reacted strongly. The mother of the Maori family eloquently conveys this spiritual attachment. "Land does not belong to people, but . . . people belong to the land. We could not forget that it was land who, in the beginning, held the secret, who contained our very beginnings within herself. It was land that held the seed and who kept the root hidden for a time when it would be needed" (Grace 1986, 110). The Maori scholar Linda Tuhiwai Smith sums up not only this indigenous understanding of the land but also the ways in which this perspective clashes with, and is often engulfed by, Western conceptions:

> Spatial arrangements are an important part of social life. Western classifications of space include such notions as architectural space, physical space, psychological space, theoretical space and so forth. Foucault's metaphor of the cultural archive is an architectural image. The archive not only contains artefacts of culture, but is itself an artefact and a construct of culture. For the indigenous world, Western conceptions of space, of arrangements and display, of the relationship between people and the landscape, of culture as an object of study, have meant that not only has the indigenous world been represented in particular ways back to the West, but the indigenous world view, the land and the people, have been radically transformed in the spatial image of the West. In other words, indigenous space has been colonized. (L. T. Smith 1999, 51)

GAINING INSIGHT FROM CONTRADICTIONS

Inspired by much of the place-related work mentioned above, I embarked on my research in Tahiti.[22] While living there, however, no matter how much I tried to encourage conversations about "place," I soon realized that place was not something Tahitians talked about in ways that I could understand. My most insightful moments occurred when I perceived what appeared to be jarring contradictions, several of which are described below.

On my first research trip to French Polynesia (for six months in 1994), my husband, daughter, and I lived in the village of Fetuna (population about 500) at the southern tip of the island of Raiatea, which is the largest and most populous island (population about 8,600) in the Leeward group of the

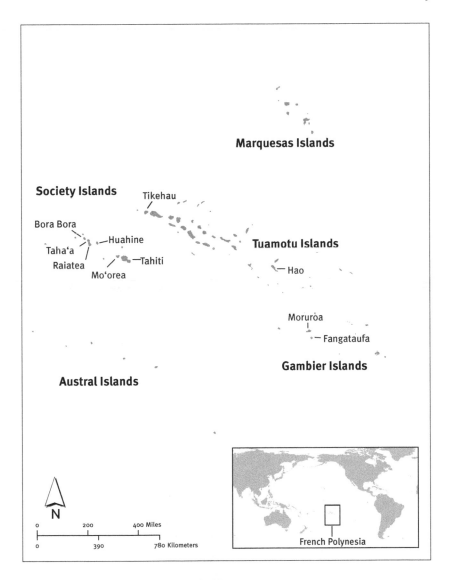

Map 1   French Polynesia. Map by Amir Sheikh.

Society Islands, one of the five archipelagoes in French Polynesia (map 1).
Although we lived in Fetuna, I visited the main town of Uturoa at the north
end of the island once or twice a week, accompanying Tahitian friends when
they drove (via either the ten-mile interior mountain road or the twenty-five-
mile winding coastal road) to shop for groceries, pick up their children at the

high school, or attend special church functions. Each time I made the trip between the village and the town, I was reminded of the psychological distance and political disconnection between them. Fetuna was a picturesque seaside village with its houses arranged along an unpaved, poorly maintained road made of crushed coral and shell that had been dredged from the sea. Because of its distance from Uturoa, the government provided no garbage collection services in Fetuna. One day the *mara'amu* trade winds blew fiercely in Fetuna, whipping the sea against the coast and washing water over the road. As the sea swelled and retreated with each wave, it left behind scattered trash—rusty tin cans, plastic bottles, plastic bags, torn clothes, and broken rubber sandals. Several days later, when the winds had calmed down, government employees responsible for road maintenance arrived from Uturoa. Sitting on top of their yellow road graders, they cleared the road by methodically plowing the garbage back into the sea. That same road, but wider, paved, and more heavily traveled, became the main thoroughfare through Uturoa, where it was flanked by shops selling food, clothing, jewelry, pharmaceuticals, stationery goods, and fishing gear. The first thing people saw when they entered the shops in town were piles of calendars with pictures of sandy white beaches under stunning blue skies, racks of postcards of coquettish, bare-breasted women, and magazines with glossy photos of multicolored fish darting through sparkling lagoons. Each time I entered the shops and saw these images I wondered: why is there such an immense chasm between the Tahiti of daily village life, where garbage disposal consisted of the government plowing it into the ocean, and the Tahiti of the glossy tourist material with images of crystal clear lagoons?

On my next trip (for five months in 1995) I lived in Faie, a small village (population about 400), on the less populous island of Huahine (population about 6,000). Being in French Polynesia in 1995—a time when nuclear testing was resumed after a three-year hiatus, accompanied by intense local protesting—serendipitously provided me with an opportunity for better understanding connections between the seductive imagery portrayed on postcards and calendars and the lived realities of Tahitians. This time I was struck by a glaring discrepancy between two types of images and the purposes they served. On the one hand were images of seductive landscapes and people, most of which the French Polynesian government produced to promote tourism. On the other hand were images that Tahitians generated and disseminated (with the help of the international media) to protest the nuclear testing. These images—of angry Tahitians demonstrating, looting, and burning buildings—were a clear bottom-up challenge to the government's top-down control. The government was visibly shaken by the worldwide dissemination of what it called "ugly" images. Noticing the government's discomfort, I began to wonder: could it be that violence was lodged not only in the exploding bombs and antinuclear testing riots but also in the idealized images of a peaceful paradise? Had these images, for the past three decades, distracted attention from nuclear testing and its consequences? If so, for how long had they quietly distracted attention from other things?

When I next visited French Polynesia in September of 1996, it was because a Tahitian family, with whom we were close friends and who had visited us in Seattle a few months before, invited my family and me to Huahine. This invitation was extended so that I could attend the opening of the local museum because I had helped with its development the previous year. The highlight of the festivities was a kite-flying contest, an ancient Maʻohi tradition that had disappeared decades before and, through concerted research efforts (in which I had participated), had been resurrected specifically for this occasion. For days in advance, many people were busy making these enormous kites (up to seven feet by ten feet), which, in their shapes, resembled sea turtles and manta rays. The revival of this tradition was so significant that an oral historian from the Musée de Tahiti et ses Îles (Museum of Tahiti and Her Islands) on Tahiti had been sent to Huahine. The contest was held on a white-sand beach adjacent to one of the most luxurious hotels on the island. Yet none of the hotel guests were told about it. As I accompanied friends to the beach with their kites, we passed a number of air-conditioned vans filled with tourists who were being shuttled to the standard points of interest on tours for which they had signed up and paid: a vanilla plantation, the local fish traps, a panoramic view, and a murky stream that was home to several huge blue-eyed eels that the tourists could feed with canned mackerel. Clearly Tahitians never considered that what they were doing—by and for themselves—might be of interest to others. Nor did the hotel think of altering their program to include this perhaps once-in-a-lifetime kite-flying attraction. Why, I wondered, did only certain activities and images define "Tahiti" to outsiders? These two groups—Tahitians and tourists—seemed to operate in two parallel, but disconnected, worlds.

Two years later, in the spring of 1998, I waited anxiously at the Seattle-Tacoma International airport for a group of eighteen dancers and musicians from Huahine who had been invited to perform in Seattle at two different cultural festivals. Like many Tahitians, they had dreamed of traveling, and especially to the United States, so that they could experience places they previously had only imagined. In true Tahitian style, they used dance as their ticket to see the world (see Kahn 2011). While in Seattle the dancers were invited for an evening at the waterfront home of a Tahitian family on Lake Washington. Within minutes of their arrival, the dancers connected with their hosts through shared genealogies and connections to land on Huahine. As the evening progressed I found myself sitting on the sprawling lawn that sloped down to the lake, surrounded by Tahitians and Tahitian food, music, dance, language, and laughter—and having to look across the lake at the Seattle skyline to remind myself of where I was. The visitors seemed completely oblivious to their physical surroundings. Although their collective dream had been to experience Seattle, on this one evening they had spontaneously recreated their Tahitian "home" around them. Many of them told me later that the evening they spent with the Tahitian family was the most memorable experience of their trip—because they felt so much at home. Why, I wondered, is it so common for people who travel with the intent of being "elsewhere" to want to feel at home? What is it about feeling out of place that makes people gravitate to situations in which they feel in place?

In 2001 my family and I again went to Tahiti, and this time we rented a house just outside the town of Fare[23] on Huahine. Each time I went into town I noticed a few tourists strolling on the main waterfront street and was always struck by how uncomfortable they looked as they wandered around, seeming unsure of where to go or what to do. I enjoyed Fare, in part because it made few attempts to cater to tourists. It was simply there, an organic space in which local residents went about their daily lives. Amid all this regular activity, tourists wandered around, poked their heads into stores, purchased a few postcards, and often ended up at the outdoor café at one of the small hotels, where they passed the time sipping cold drinks and talking to other tourists. On these occasions the divergence I noticed was between daily life, as lived in Fare, and the staged setting that I knew so well at the hotels where the tourists were staying and to which they would soon return. There, for a price, they were offered "authentic" Tahitian activities in which they could participate, such as weaving coconut leaves into hats, watching food being cooked in an earth oven, learning how to wear the sarong-like *pareu,* or mastering some Tahitian dance techniques. Why were the tourists slightly uncomfortable mingling in a truly authentic place, yet seemed to be at ease in a place where an ersatz Tahiti was staged for their benefit? And why was "Tahitian culture" even staged for them when just outside the door it was going on all around them?

What these seemingly jarring encounters all have in common are conflicting ways of experiencing, imagining, depicting, valuing, and managing place. In trying to make sense of these nuanced realities encountered in Tahiti, the work of two individuals—Henri Lefebvre and Henri Hiro—has been especially helpful. More than any one perspective, it is the synergy between the two that helps shed light on the current realities of Tahiti. These realities, after all, are themselves the products of the historical and ongoing intertwining of beliefs, values, and encounters that are synergistically indigenous and colonial, Tahitian and Euro-American. Bringing Lefebvre's and Hiro's ideas into dialogue has inspired me to think about these many disjunctions in ways that move beyond the blinding binaries and instead embrace complex totalities about place.

HENRI LEFEBVRE UNITES THEORIES IN THE ACADEMY WITH EVENTS ON THE STREET

Henri Lefebvre (1901–1991) was a French philosopher who has been credited as being "one of the most original Marxist thinkers of the twentieth century" (Merrifield 2000, 170). The geographer Edward Soja has called Lefebvre "the most persistent, insistent, and consistent" voice in the area of space and place (Soja 1989, 16). As a political activist and a popularizer of Marxist ideas, Lefebvre relished contradictions. He rebuffed fragmented realities and instead sought out totalities, knowing that comprehending these was best accomplished by embracing the conflicts and contradictions within them. For example, he wanted to grapple not only with the quality of daily life but also with the ways in which people's appropriation of space could crystallize into an overwhelming political force (D. Harvey 1974, 248). Lefebvre's life, as the title of his biography by Rémi Hess (1988) suggests—*Henri Lefebvre et l'aventure du siècle*—spanned nearly all of the twentieth century and its myriad political events.

Three important events from Lefebvre's youth and early adulthood—the first World War, the Russian revolution with the subsequent rise of communism, and the fight against Hitler and fascist Germany—greatly affected his scholarship on urbanism, everyday life, and space. They shattered Lefebvre's innocent faith in common sense and drew his attention instead to the power of politics. Later, his experience as a taxi driver in Paris for two years, as well as the urban unrest he witnessed, caused him to think deeply about the relationship between politics and urban space. He developed many of his most seminal ideas while involved in the political debates and struggles of the French left during the 1960s. In particular, the sweeping events of May 1968 fueled his growing understanding of the connections between political theories in the academy and daily life on the street. Leftist students at the University of Paris, Nanterre (a hotbed of Marxist activity and the institution at which Lefebvre taught at the time), carried their protest (of a threatened expulsion of a German-Jewish undergraduate from France) into the Latin Quarter, where they clashed with right-wing students at the Sorbonne. Riots erupted when the Sorbonne's administration summoned the police. Within a few days most of Paris was affected, causing daily life in the capital to come to a halt. As Mavis Gallant wrote from France for the *New Yorker*,

> Paris became a city where it was impossible to buy a newspaper, go to school, mail a letter, send a telegram, cash a check, ride in a bus, take the Métro, use a private car, find cigarettes, sugar, canned goods, or salad oil, watch television or, towards the end, listen to a news bulletin. No garbage was collected; no trains left the city; there was no time signal, no weather report. Teachers stopped teaching; actors stopped acting. (Gallant 1968, 2–3)

Living through, and participating in, the Paris riots caused Lefebvre to turn his full attention to the politics and complex social processes of space. By appropriating and redefining public spaces, people could transform them, which in turn could affect every aspect of social life. For Lefebvre, the May riots provided awareness of what was humanly possible; namely that actions on the street could alter the dynamics of power. From that point on, he sought to locate the transformative and revolutionary potential that lay within spaces and places. In the six years following 1968 he wrote seven books, all on the subject of space, the last of which, *La production de l'espace* (1974), is his undisputed *chef-d'oeuvre*. The English translation, *The Production of Space*, appeared in 1991, thus bringing his ideas about space to Anglophone audiences.

In this powerful treatise Lefebvre laid out his ideas about space and its transformations. His ideas developed in reaction to what he saw as a growing gulf between spaces that people imagined and those in which people lived. He proposed a "science of space" (what he called "spatiology") to overcome the "abyss between the mental sphere on one side and the physical and social spheres on the other" (Lefebvre 1991, 6). Wanting to move beyond previous

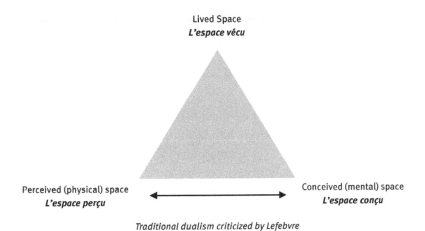

Fig. 1.1 Lefebvre's spatial trialectics.

approaches to space, which tended to be either lofty philosophical discourses or concrete material descriptions, his aim was to develop a method for analyzing space and its transformations. His object of study became the *process* by which space is generated. His emphasis on the *production* of space echoes Marx's focus on the social relations of production. For Lefebvre, dialectics was essential because it placed the emphasis on process and transformation and—what I kept noticing in French Polynesia—contradictions.

Concerned with the unity that embraces oppositions within it, Lefebvre—following Marxist tenets—divided space for analytical purposes into opposing dyads. He argued that there was, on the one hand, perceived space (*l'espace perçu*)—physical, tangible, material reality—and, on the other hand, conceived space (*l'espace conçu*)—mental space composed of representations, signs, symbols, codes, abstractions, ideas, and depictions. He saw their interrelationship as creating an overarching triad, or "thirdspace" (fig. 1.1).[24] This thirdspace (*l'espace vécu*) is the fully lived space of both physical and imagined engagement, the dynamic space of everyday experience.[25]

Although *l'espace perçu* and *l'espace conçu* can be separated for analytical purposes, the reality of *l'espace vécu* is that it is never simply one or the other, but is simultaneously and interpenetratingly both, where each element within a relationship supports and undermines the others (Ollman 1993). Places are always filled with a multitude of interactions, and especially with interactions motivated by the power in whose grip people are caught. "Space thus produced also serves as a tool of thought and of action; that in addition to being a means of production it is also a means of control, and hence of domination, of power" (Lefebvre 1991, 26).

Although Lefebvre never used the term thirdspace, Soja later took up the phrase, suggesting it was prefigured in Lefebvre's work.[26] Soja proposed it as "an alternative envisioning of spatiality, as illustrated in the heterotopologies of Foucault, the trialectics and thirdings of Lefebvre, the marginality and radical openness of bell hooks, the hybridities of Homi Bhabha" (Soja 1996, 163). For him, thirdspaces were not simply other spaces but rather other ways of thinking about space. The intention was to challenge all conventional modes of spatial thinking by detonating and deconstructing ideas, not by comfortably pouring them back into the same old containers (Soja 1996, 163).[27]

Lefebvrian scholars, on the whole, have tended to engage with his work more by offering intellectual interpretations and critiques of his ideas than by applying them to everyday life.[28] Recently this has been changing. Applied explorations of Lefebvre's ideas are now enjoying a renaissance (see Goonewardena et al. 2008). Yet, in general, Lefebvre's work, although embraced by geographers, sociologists, and urban planners, has received less attention from anthropologists.[29]

HENRI HIRO RECONNECTS THROUGH THE ANCESTRAL CORD

Henri Hiro (1944–1990) was a Ma'ohi poet, orator, writer, dramatist, filmmaker, pastor, and political activist. He grew up on the island of Tahiti in a family that spoke only Tahitian, their mother tongue.[30] He learned that Ma'ohi must listen to the land and the sea as the source of all physical and spiritual nourishment. Dan Taulapapa McMullin, a Samoan painter, writer, and filmmaker, noted that in all of Hiro's poems, "We see his close relationship with the world around him in all its flourishing forms, as an artist, as a family man, and as a fisherman" (McMullin 2005, 344).

McMullin also contrasts Western and Polynesian ways of thinking about "nature." In the West, nature is seen as separate from human beings — something that originated from "darkness" and within which human beings have been cast to wrestle with moral concepts of light and darkness, good and evil. From a Polynesian way of thinking, land originates from its own essential being. Human beings and other animals are seen as coming from the land, a belief that is reflected in Polynesian polytheism. A vast difference exists

between, on the one hand, the Ma'ohi term *te tumu* (which can be translated as "foundation," "essence," "base," origin," "underlying principle," or
"source") from which all life and thought spring and, on the other hand, the
Western concept of "nature" as something that exists in contradistinction to
human life (McMullin 2005, 346).

Recalling his childhood and the profound knowledge of, and respect for,
te tumu, Hiro wrote,

> Among us, to be a fisherman or farmer was not seen as a profession. It was the
> art of living. To be a fisherman, for example, was not to pillage the bottom of
> the ocean in order to fill up freezers or to export canned fish; it was first and
> foremost to possess a deep knowledge of the fish and their environment. We
> didn't say, "I'm going fishing." We said, "I will get *'i'ihi* [a type of swordfish]
> from the lagoon in the *haone* [sandy crevices of the reef] during the *oharaa
> 'ava'e* [when the moon will be just above the horizon]. Knowing the exact
> details about the environment was critical. (Hiro 2004, 7)

A deeply religious young man, Hiro spent time in France to attend the
seminary in Montpellier. His stay in the *métropole* became a time of new
awareness and self-reflection. He began to question Christianity and the status of Tahitians as colonized people. He also became aware of the importance
of Ma'ohi language and spirituality for recognizing one's place in the world.

> When you go far away, you see in a new light the things that have been clos-
> est to you. Isn't that so? For me, it was my culture, my country, my people, my
> own situation, the activities of the church and its contribution. In short, the
> big questions. It was my time of soul searching, a very propitious time, since
> we were emerging from May 1968. (Hiro 2004, 82)[31]

When Hiro returned to Tahiti, he said it was with "disturbing questions
weighing on [my] mind. And the first collision between the church and
myself was, of course, my protests against nuclear testing" (Hiro 2004, 82).[32]
Exiled from the church because of his antinuclear stance, he found a new
spiritual home at the Maison de la Culture in Tahiti, an organization whose
mission is to encourage the production and dissemination of Tahitian culture. It was during this time that he founded the political party Ia Mana te
Nuna'a (Power to the People) and began directing his energy toward a new
project, namely eradicating what he saw as Tahitians' often blind acceptance

of colonial exploitation of their land and people. For this enormous task, he focused on rekindling the source of Maʻohi identity through knowledge of language and land. With his goal of "reviving the light of the past in order to shed light on the future" (Pambrun 2005), Hiro emerged as the voice of the Maʻohi independence movement in the 1960s and 1970s.

The task of reclaiming Maʻohi cosmology, and of speaking out and writing about it, is more than just an introspective and restorative act. It is also an act of resistance because it underscores the vast difference between European and Maʻohi ways of thinking, knowing, and theorizing about one's place in the world. "The violent historical and political reality in which [Hiro and other poets] found themselves means that as political beings they produced both poetry and praxis. Their art inevitably reflected a whole range of social, economic, political, and cultural issues affecting their land and people" (Nicole 2001, 179). For example, they objected to being left out of decision-making about ownership of land. They resented being diminished to colonized French men and women. Most importantly, "They were also motivated to write by the threat of institutional forgetting, which is sponsored by the educational system of the colonial state and that encourages a lack of knowledge about being Maʻohi, the past, language, and culture. Their efforts were intended to acquire visibility, identity, and self-respect" (Nicole 2001, 179).

Language and land were at the core of the Maʻohi revival movement. Through language the revivalists attempted "to establish an initial dialogue not with the colonizer but with fellow Maʻohi" (Nicole 1999, 274). As Hiro said, "To know one's own language is to feel good inside and with others. This language is threatened, words are getting lost, expressions forgotten. With every word that is lost, a social treasure disappears" (Hiro 2000, 5). Hiro and other Tahitian poets (for example, Turo Raapoto, Hubert Brémond, and Charles Manutahi) were at the forefront of the Tahitian indigenous literary movement in the 1960s and 1970s. Later, much of the creative literary energy came from Tahitian female writers, such as Titaua Peu, Taaria Walker, Vaitiare (a pseudonym for Flora Devatine), Michou Chaze, Chantal Spitz, and Louise Peltzer. Through their writing, they created a dialogue between peoples of the Pacific (Mateata-Allain 2005, 270). Although there has been disagreement about the language in which one should write (for example, Maʻohi linguist, poet, academic, and theologian Turo Raapoto has refused to translate his work from reo maʻohi into other languages), there was agreement about transforming what previously was an oral tradition into what would also become a literary form. Hiro was adamant about this early on, saying, "For this renewal to continue, Polynesians must write . . . they now must write and express themselves. It doesn't matter what language they use, whether it's *reo ma'ohi,* French, or English.[33] The important thing is that they write, that they *do it!*" (Hiro 2004, 80).[34]

Land was the other foundation upon which to build a Ma'ohi consciousness. "To rediscover and renew this heritage, *land,* the symbol of life and bearer of those who built the Ma'ohi past, must be reclaimed, reappropriated" (Raapoto 1980, 4). In 1985, to put this spiritual link between people and land into practice, Hiro moved his wife and children to Huahine to live on family land in a Ma'ohi style. In his poem "To'u fare au" (My native house), he writes about the intimate connection between his sense of self and his house—with its roof, walls, and floor all made of materials from the land. He describes the protective warmth the materials give his dreams (*hi'i pumahana no ta'u moemoe*), and how they are the root of his dwelling (*noho'a tumu no to'u hiro'a*) and the source of his identity (*ma'ohi no to'u ma'ohira'a;* Hiro 2004, 30).

He underscored the bond between language, land, and identity when he lamented the relocation of Tahitians to urban housing developments:

> When we greet one another we say, *haere mai ra,* which means to come to one another without pretense. This phrase makes sense within the framework of our customs, but in urban settings it no longer has meaning. If you take a Tahitian away from the land and put him in urban housing he no longer has the vocabulary to greet his neighbor. And a human being who can no longer communicate with his neighbor is a human being whose soul is withering away. (Hiro 2004, 8)

An important Polynesian custom that occurs after the birth of a child is the planting of the placenta and umbilical cord in the ground. Although the details vary about who does the planting (mother, father, or grandparent), what is planted (just the placenta, just the cord, or both), and where the planting takes place (under the house, under a tree, or at the family's sacred *marae*), the custom was—and still is—widely practiced in Tahiti as well as in other parts of Polynesia.[35]

The ethnologist Bruno Saura has written in some detail about this custom, saying that in Tahiti the placenta is "a vital territory or universe to which people are intrinsically attached, like an infant is attached to its mother's flesh" (Saura 2002a, 129). The name for placenta—*pu fenua*—

translates as "core/heart/essence of the earth." It is the origin of life, a point of anchorage, and the source of nourishment. "Polynesian infants are born attached by their navel to a parcel of land, *pu fenua*, and islands also have a navel" (Saura 2002a, 133). Polynesian mythology maintains that the islands were fished out of the ocean and were later stabilized by cultural heroes and deities (although nowadays Tahitians tend to say that their islands are volcanoes and/or were created by God). In this light, the placenta can be seen as land, an island, and a source of life, within the uterine water (Saura 2002a, 130). In Polynesia, islands that share a lagoon are likened to twins who share a placenta.

If the placenta is the source and force of nurture, the umbilical cord—*pito* (navel)—is the canal through which this force is transmitted (Saura 2002a, 136). It is the cord of knowledge, of mutual attachment and belonging, and the transmitter of life, in all its physical and spiritual forms. To return the placenta and umbilical cord to the earth is to recognize several essential connections: between child and family, between place of birth and place of planting, and between one's island and one's cultural knowledge.

Much of what Hiro reveals in his poetry about a general Ma'ohi vision of the world and about relations between land, people, plants, and nourishment emerges from this belief that the placenta is the "flourishing source" and that the umbilical cord is the connection to one's culture. Hiro's poem "Ho mai na" (The gift) explores these relationships. The land and the mother—or the land's children and Ma'ohi people—are seen as so deeply intertwined that they are referred to as one and the same. It is through understanding and asserting these connections that Ma'ohi people feel a sense of place and identity.[36] Elaborating on the poem, Hiro said,

> *Ho mai na* means giving everything, the way a mother gives everything she possesses to her son. The mother gives, and when she has given everything possible, the son can go on from there. He will always have his mother near him; his mother connects him to the source of everything: his roots, his blood, his ancestral lineage. . . . The child is made whole because of these connections and can proceed. The mother is the symbol of the direct link, the parental link; the land is the mother. That genealogical linkage is the umbilical cord, the *pu fenua,* the placenta. (Hiro 2004, 86)[37]

Another of Hiro's poems, "Fero" (The cord), beautifully conveys this spiritual and genealogical oneness of land and its people.[38]

FERO

E fero e, fero e, fero e!
E fero ana'e na i te taura o te iho tumu!
Ei hono vai tamau no te mau u'i.

E nana'o e, nana'o e, nana'o e!
E nana'o manava ana'e na i te hiro'a tumu ma'ohi,
'ei te tau fa'aara no e mau ui.

Maeva! Maeva hua i te taura ma'ohi!
Manava hu'a ia 'outou e to teie naho'a tini, i roto i te arofa tupuna ra!
Manava hua i te farereiraa!

Haere ra!
Haere e 'ia vai a ra!
E 'ia vai a!

THE CORD

Attach, attach, attach ourselves!
Attach firmly to our traditions!
Create a cord in which our children can wrap themselves.

Tattoo, tattoo, tattoo ourselves!
Tattoo our souls with the imprint of Ma'ohi culture,
As a sign of future promise for the coming generations.

Greetings! And welcome, oh Ma'ohi people!
Embrace the love of our ancestors!
Our souls rejoice at this reunion!

Now go!
Yes, go,
But always preserve the cord!
(Hiro 2004, 41)

Similarly, in one of his plays, *Te aroha e pehepehe na te metua vahine i tana tama* (Love poetry from a mother to her son), Hiro writes,

E te tama e, e fano!
A fano! A fano ra!
A fano ra mai te faura'o atu i to'u
Pu fenua ia fenua te fenua i to tipaeraa ra
Te pu fenua i hii ia o'e e'i tama.
. . .
O vau nei a to vaa, o vau nei a to tau'ati,
I taraihia i to'u hiro'a tumu,
I paepaehia i to'u arofa metua,
I ferohia i to'u manava nana'o, i 'iatohia i to'u pito, te tihi ahi ra,
Na to'u aho nei a te mata'i e puhi hau i to 'ie.
I tuia, e i patuia, i te hi'u rouru putii ra o to metua vahine.

My son, you must go now,
Go on your journey!
Go, but take my placenta with you
The essence of our land that nourished you
So that the land will be here when you return.
. . .
I am your canoe, I am your double-hulled canoe,
Lashed according to the customs of my ancestors,
Connected by the umbilical cord of my maternal love,
Attached to my soul that created you,
Held by my cord, your first connection
My breath inflated your sail
Sewn and re-sewn with your hair that your mother combed.
(Hiro 2004, 70–71)

The message of the poems (child, go away but stay attached/connected to the land, traditions, language, and so on) bespeaks a profound sense of liberation that comes from this specific form of spiritual attachment. If you let go of the cord, you will find yourself confused and adrift, faltering on a foreign sea, charmed by distractions such as money, commercialism, and vanity (about which Hiro has written in other poems). These Western forms of nourishment, anchorage, and identity, however, will only deceive you.

UNITING INTERPRETIVE FRAMEWORKS

Henri Lefebvre and Henri Hiro, living oceans apart, had something in common. Both sought wholeness and unity instead of fragmentation and detachment—whether this takes the form of synergy between *l'espace perçu* and *l'espace conçu*, or a rekindling of Ma'ohi language, land, people, spirituality, and genealogy. Both were social activists who championed a more just future. Bringing their ideas into dialogue with one another has helped me understand the entangling of the beliefs and behaviors of the colonizers and the colonized.

Combining the philosophical and theoretical perspectives on place of both Lefebvre (as well as other Western thinkers) and Hiro (as well as other Tahitians) illuminates a situation that itself is the result of the intertwining of indigenous and colonial histories, beliefs, visions, and values. The expressions of these different perspectives take distinct cultural forms, ranging from scientific theorizing to poetry, songs, and story telling. Both also take the form of political action. It is important to remember that just as Lefebvre is not the average Frenchman, thinking and philosophizing about the dynamics of space and place, so too Hiro is not necessarily representative of all Tahitians, searching for and writing poetry about deeper connections to place and self. Both can be seen as spokespeople—intellectuals, theoreticians, and philosophers—who thought deeply about pressing issues of their time. Combining these diverse perspectives provides an understanding of place that might escape us if we viewed it solely from a Western or a Tahitian point of view.[39]

THE CHAPTERS AHEAD

In general, the narrative moves from a broad historical background to material that is more ethnographic, contemporary, and personal. Chapter 1 explores the colonial history of French Polynesia by focusing on the spaces in which the French *métropole* and *te fenua ma'ohi* meet and intertwine. In the eighteenth and nineteenth centuries European visions, moral dilemmas, "scientific" ideas, and later notions of urban planning were played out in the colony. Throughout this period "Tahiti" also penetrated the European imagination through various forms of representation such as exhibits at worlds' fairs, picture postcards, Pierre Loti's steamy novels, and Paul Gauguin's colorful canvases.

Chapter 2 brings the entangled history between *métropole* and colony into the present by examining current competing Western and Tahitian understandings of place. Whereas Tahitians see *te fenua* as a nourishing mother, the French government has (since the 1960s) viewed it as a site for the French nuclear weapons testing program, which has brought massive destruction to *te fenua* and threatened the wellbeing of its inhabitants. Tourism and its images, which intensified in tandem with the beginning of nuclear testing, conveniently served to distract attention from the nuclear testing program and its less-than-picturesque consequences.

The myth of Tahiti as "paradise" is perpetuated through consciously crafted commercial imagery. Chapter 3 presents several critical aspects of imagery production: the importance of redundancy, the calculated decisions about the branding of Tahiti, and the ways in which synthetic arrangements of images are organized to target specific audiences. The ways in which these images travel to, and come to reside in, the *métropole* further illustrate the entangled political economies of *métropole* and colony.

Tourist "cocoons," explored in Chapter 4, offer a highly effective strategy for coping with the disjuncture between what people imagine about Tahiti and what exists in reality. This is illustrated through several aspects of the luxury hotel experience (chosen by 90 percent of tourists in Tahiti): the language and imagery used to promote hotels, their neo-Polynesian architecture, and the engineering feats involved in creating their "natural" setting. The many players involved—architects, hotel directors, hotel employees, dancers at hotel floorshows, and guests themselves—contribute to constructing the kind of experience that "Tahiti" promises.

Chapter 5 explores the local politics of place by examining the Fare Pote'e, a traditional-style building on the island of Huahine. In the past century it has been transformed from a village meetinghouse into a building dismissed by missionaries and then abandoned by local residents in favor of a new church, into an income-producing cultural center, and, most recently, into a "scientific information center" that the government decided to turn into a tourist destination. Various interpretive codes have continually assigned, dissolved, and reassigned meaning to the Fare Pote'e.

The relationship between *métropole* and colony is not simply one of unilateral domination but rather one that is always in a delicate balance of power. Chapter 6 examines some of the many ways in which Tahitians spontaneously create their own counter-spaces through creative uses of music, dance, food, language, and humor. They do so in ways that are primarily visible and audible only to other Tahitians. These discourses become all the more transgressive precisely because they are invisible to those in power.

Chapter 7 offers some concluding thoughts about place in French Polynesia, new possibilities for the anthropology of place more generally, and what these insights might tell us about the world beyond Tahiti.

CHAPTER ONE

New Geographies in the Wake of Colonialism

The colonial history of French Polynesia reveals itself in numerous place-related ways. Places are moments of intersecting social relations. Some of these are "contained within the place; others stretch beyond it, tying any particular locality into wider relations and processes in which other places are implicated" (Massey 1994, 120). Pape'ete, the capital city of French Polynesia, provides an example. Before European explorers arrived in the late 1700s, Pape'ete was a spot in a sheltered bay known for its supply of fresh water.[1] Today, with a population of about 130,000 (about half the total population of French Polynesia), it is a lively town with many urban features, each of which hints at a complex history of intersecting social relations. Among these features are the Tahiti Manava Visitors Bureau near the quay; a tree-lined esplanade that runs the length of town along the waterfront; the Marché Municipale, with fish, fruits, vegetables, and other food for sale on the main floor and crafts on the second floor; Parc Bougainville (named after the first French explorer to land in Tahiti); the Catholic Cathédrale Notre-Dame de Pape'ete; the Protestant Temple de Paofai; nearly a dozen hotels; numerous banks; Place Tarahoi (the governmental center that houses the Territorial Assembly and the High Commissioner's Office, located on what was once the site of the palace of Tahiti's last queen, Pomare IV); a monument to Pouvana'a O'opa (a leader of the independence movement); elegant shopping centers; squatters' settlements; the Brasserie de Tahiti brewery; small shops with postcard racks spilling out onto the sidewalks; the school Lycée Paul Gauguin; numerous restaurants and snack bars; taxi stands; cruise ships in the harbor; and the recently built Place To'ata, an outdoor amphitheater used for major performance events, such as the annual Heiva festival.

History—as observable in Pape'ete—leaves its traces, both conspicuous and subtle, in the landscape. "A landscape is the most solid appearance in which a history can declare itself. . . . There it is, the past in the present, constantly changing and renewing itself as the present rewrites the past" (Inglis 1977, 489). In colonial situations, space is constantly erased and redesigned as territory is invaded, land possessed, borders established or obliterated, terrain altered, and new names assigned to places, creating a new geography in the process.[2] Indeed, the social construction of space is one of the main elements in the machinery of imperialism (Jacobs 1996, 158). As Edward Said remarked, "Imperialism, after all, is an act of geographical violence through which virtually every space in the world is explored, charted, and finally brought under control" (Said 1993, 225). Imperial expansions establish specific spatial arrangements in which the imagined geographies of the colonists' desires are changed into material realities, which in turn inform us about colonial notions of race, class, gender, and nationhood (Jacobs 1996, 2).

In Tahiti, as in other places affected by imperialism and colonialism, one sees the "mutually constitutive processes, practices, and forms of power through which *métropoles* and (post) colonies make and remake one another" (Hart 2006, 981). Lefebvre's dyad of *l'espace perçu* (physical, tangible, material reality) and *l'espace conçu* (mental space composed of representations, signs, symbols, codes, abstractions) is apparent in the wake of Tahiti's colonial history. European imperial and colonial actions and activities created new places in Tahiti. A newly imagined Tahiti then emerged in Europe, first through the production and circulation of explorers' accounts, and later through art, literature, exhibits, photographs, postcards, films, and commodities.

The European Renaissance, with its revolutionary concepts of space and time, set the stage for the Enlightenment, which focused on the conquest and rational ordering of space as an integral part of the modernizing project. David Harvey has described this spatial transition with great clarity. During the Enlightenment, no longer were space and time organized to reflect the glory of God "but to celebrate and facilitate the liberation of Man as a free and active individual, endowed with consciousness and will." Many different modern landscapes emerged across the globe. These included new urban areas that unified the world through innovative systems of transportation and communication, new ideas about city planning, new institutions for social regulation, and new styles of architecture. More attention was now also paid to land surveys, the drawing of maps, boundary definitions, and the creation of administrative domains. These ideas and practices allowed Europeans to locate the entire population of the earth within a single spatial frame. As a consequence, a European conception of "otherness" began to flourish. These ideas hinged on a notion of "others" having a specific place in a spatial order "that was ethnocentrically conceived to have homogeneous and absolute qualities."[3] This "totalizing vision of the map allowed strong senses of national, local, and personal identities to be constructed in the midst of geographical differences" (D. Harvey 1989, 249–50, 252).

FANTASIES MADE REAL

By the mid-1700s, France and England, both facing the imminent loss of their colonies in North America, began to explore the Pacific Ocean.[4] Many Europeans, intimately familiar with biblical references to an earthly paradise, grew nostalgic for a life that they envisioned as more pleasant than their daily existence, and where they could live freely and simply, in harmony with nature. This utopia took different forms: a golden age in the past; a divined future; or, more tantalizing and perhaps more feasible, a distant, as yet undiscovered land.

Although these utopian visions were the subject of many writers, poets, and painters, it was the French philosopher Jean-Jacques Rousseau whose ideas about human nature reached the widest audience. He wrote *Discours sur l'origine de l'inégalité parmi les hommes* (Discourse on the Origin of Inequality among Men), his much-acclaimed treatise on the "noble savage" and the origins of social corruption (Rousseau 1754). He presented an idyllic picture of the origin of mankind, where everyone was equal and lived in balance with nature. Only later, Rousseau claimed, as mankind began to form families, build houses, cultivate land, and develop social needs, did the problems of inequality, jealousy, and hostility arise. Rousseau's arguments motivated Europeans to search for a place where they could test his philosophical and moral speculations.

Two years after the appearance of Rousseau's discourse, the French magistrate and scholar Charles de Brosses wrote *Histoire des navigations aux terres australes* (History of Navigation to the Southern Lands),[5] which chronicled in exacting detail every voyage of exploration from the mid-1500s to the mid-1700s and enabled French navigators and explorers to envision searching for the utopia Rousseau had described. The book "was not just a history of what had been done. It was an argument for what ought to be done" (Thomas 2003, 16). Indeed, the book was a companion for many later explorers, including Louis-Antoine de Bougainville and Captain James Cook (Ryan 2002, 177, 181).

It was with these aspirations for a replenished empire, visions of a terrestrial paradise, and confirmations of navigational feats that European explorers set out to discover "new" lands. The earliest images of Tahiti were deeply influenced by imperialist ambitions and philosophical speculation long before any European had ever set foot on the island.

The first European to land on the island of Tahiti was British captain Samuel Wallis, while searching for *terra australis incognita.*[6] The HMS *Dolphin* set anchor at Matavai Bay on the northern tip of Tahiti in 1767. Wallis and his men bartered beads, mirrors, and nails (which Tahitians especially coveted for making fishhooks) in exchange for food and sex. When Wallis's crew later returned to England, they added new excitement to Rousseau's "noble savage" myth by circulating greatly embellished stories, the most popular being that the HMS *Dolphin* nearly fell apart as sailors pulled nails from the ship.

By the time French explorer Louis-Antoine de Bougainville arrived in Tahiti the following year (not yet aware of Wallis's earlier landing), Tahitian leaders had adopted a strategy for "taming" foreign ships by sending women out in canoes to offer themselves to the sailors. Bougainville immediately named the island Nouvelle Cythère (New Cytheria) after the birthplace of Aphrodite, the Greek goddess of love. To aestheticize Tahiti and Tahitians through classical references was a common practice at the time (Despoix 1996, 5).

After Bougainville returned to France with stories of beautiful, uninhibited women of classical proportions, visions of a paradise of sexual abandon swept like wildfire through Europe. The publication of Bougainville's *Voyage autour du monde,* in 1771, followed by the English translation, *A Voyage Around the World,* in 1772, provided European men with an unambiguous vision of earthly paradise—the "Garden of Eden" Bougainville claimed to have discovered. One of the book's most popular passages tells of sending women out to the ships.

> They pressed us to choose a woman, and to come on shore with her; and their
> gestures . . . denoted in what manner we should form an acquaintance with

her. It was difficult . . . to keep at their work four hundred young French sailors, who had seen no women for six months. In spite of all our precautions, a young girl came on board, and placed herself upon the quarterdeck near one of the hatchways, which was open in order to give air to those who were heaving at the capstan below it. The girl carelessly dropped a cloth, which covered her, and appeared to the eyes of all beholders, such as Venus showed herself to the Phrygian Shepherd, having, indeed, the celestial form of that goddess. (Bougainville 1772, 218–19)

A closer examination of *Voyage autour du monde* reveals that what Bougainville described for his European audience was tremendously exaggerated. Wanting to adapt his narratives to the tastes of the European public, he embellished his writing with stylistic flourishes and details taken from other people's writings, as well as references to goddesses, nymphs, and noble savages (Claessen 1994, 23). Comparing *Voyage autour du monde* with Bougainville's original journal indicates even more clearly the extent to which his encounters and impressions were rewritten in a way that would be more appealing to his European audience (Taillemite 1977; Vibart 1987, 96).[7]

Captain James Cook visited Tahiti on each of his three voyages (1768–71, 1772–75, and 1776–79). The first was organized by the Royal Society of London as principally a scientific mission to observe the transit of Venus.[8] Like his predecessors, Cook also aestheticized Tahitians with classical references. Unable to master Tahitian names, he and his crew bestowed Greek pseudonyms upon individuals. For example, they named one man Hercules because of his strength, another Ajax for his dour face, one Epicurus for his appetite, and another Lycurgus because of his sense of justice in returning a snuffbox that had been taken from Joseph Banks (Banks 1896, 79).

In addition to taking along astronomers, botanists, and cartographers, Cook also took several artists, whose drawings and paintings helped to further the fantasies of the "noble savage." In keeping with Rousseau's beliefs about mankind living harmoniously in nature, these artists depicted the landscape as one of Arcadian peacefulness and luminous beauty. One such example is William Hodges's 1776 landscape painting *Oaitepeha Bay, Tahiti*,[9] with nude women lounging in the foliage at the water's edge (fig. 1.1). Another is John Webber's 1777 *Portrait of Poedua, the Daughter of Orio*, the first visual summation of the Pacific muse, a bare-breasted Tahitian woman Webber rendered classical by draping a white cloth around her waist and placing her in an idealized landscape under a sultry sky (fig. 1.2). Less known is that, much

Fig. 1.1 William Hodges, *Oaitepeha Bay, Tahiti*, 1776. Oil on canvas, 36 x 54 in. National Maritime Museum, Greenwich, London.

to the Tahitians' anger, Webber produced the painting while holding Poedua captive for five days (O'Brien 2006a, 85). Both paintings were reproduced endlessly, helping to impose a combination of eighteenth-century classical idealism and scientific realism on the Tahitian landscape, conflating images of Tahitian nature, women, and fecundity with this newly discovered island (B. Smith 1985, 62–63). These paintings, and others like them, became tabula rasa for depicting European moral conundrums. Some artists included what they interpreted as symbols of native mysticism lurking in the shadows, often in the form of a dark ancestral carving, as a reminder of moral dilemmas about civility and bestiality. In Hodges's painting, this icon appears as a large ancestral figure perched on a rock in the foreground.

The projection of European romantic fantasies and their consequent moral dilemmas onto "Tahiti" occurred in more embodied ways when Tahitian men were brought to Europe. On his return voyage to Paris in 1769, Bougainville brought along Aotourou, the first Tahitian to visit Europe. Portrayed as the embodiment of the noble savage from paradise, he created quite a sensation

Fig. 1.2 John Webber, *Poedua, the Daughter of Orio*, 1777. Oil on canvas, 57 x 38 in. National Maritime Museum, Greenwich, London.

by adapting effortlessly to Parisian life, where he navigated the streets like a Frenchman. Aotourou was introduced to Louis XV and his court and was known to be especially fond of the opera. In 1771, Marion du Fresne set sail with Aotourou to return him to Tahiti. Unfortunately, Aotourou died from smallpox en route. Three years after this, in 1774, Cook took Omai, a young man from the island of Huahine, to England, an experience that became the subject of a London theatrical performance (O'Keefe and Shield 1785) and a novel (Baston 1790), and more recently the topic of several books (Clark 1941; McCormick 1977) and two art exhibits (Auckland City Art Gallery 1977;

National Library of Australia 2001). Omai became a darling of English society. His British benefactors, one of whom was Cook's botanist, Joseph Banks, dressed him in London's latest fashions, including silk shirts and velvet jackets. Omai took English lessons, met the king and queen, dined in London's best homes, and learned to ride horses, hunt, and ice skate. After spending three years in London, Omai returned with Cook, who left Omai on Huahine with a supply of pistols and muskets (Newbury 1980, 9). Cook later learned that Omai died only two years after returning home.

The transportation—and imagined transformation—of these men (notably, never women) meshed well with prevailing ideas at the time about geography, climate, human adaptability, and stages of civilization. Because Tahiti and Europe were seen as emblematic of different geographies, climates, historical periods, and civilizing potential, these ideas were put to the test in the Pacific (and with Pacific Islanders in Europe). European colonies in the tropics became laboratories of Western rationality and experimentation (Morton 2000). Bringing Aotourou or Omai from Tahiti to Europe was an opportunity to see if "savages" could become "civilized." An equally compelling possibility was to see if "savageness" would emerge in Europeans when they went to Tahiti.

With the celebrity of Aotourou and Omai in Europe, as well as the exhibition of Cook's collection of Pacific artifacts in London, Polynesian themes became fashionable in Europe. These novelties allowed Europeans to further experiment—while remaining in Europe—with being Polynesian. "'Tahitian' verandas were designed for country houses, 'Polynesian' wallpaper became fashionable, and 'South Seas' lakes were built into landscaped vistas" (Daws 1980, 11). In these ways, Tahiti—as described in Bougainville's and Cook's journals, depicted in Hodges's and Webber's paintings, and brought to life by the appearance of Aotourou and Omai in Paris and London—was not only molded by Europe but in turn could also penetrate and influence European space. As Anna Tsing so correctly said, "Places are made through their connections with each other, not their isolation" (Tsing 2000, 330).

Images of the Pacific Islands as a utopia were further fixed in the minds of Europeans with the mutiny on the HMS *Bounty* in 1789, one of the most notorious uprisings in British naval history. Captain William Bligh, the commander of the ship, had brought his crew to Tahiti to collect young breadfruit seedlings. The crew planned to transport these to the West Indies to be grown as food for African slaves. Bligh's crew lived among Tahitians for five months while the breadfruit seedlings took root, before setting out for the

West Indies with the young plants. Due in part to Bligh's tyrannical treatment of his crew, and in part to the crew members' desires to return to Tahiti and the Tahitian women with whom they had fallen in love, the crew mutinied soon after leaving Tahiti. The leader of the mutiny, Fletcher Christian, set Captain Bligh out to sea in a small boat and returned to Tahiti with the HMS *Bounty*, eventually sailing the ship accompanied by several Tahitian men and women to the uninhabited Pacific island of Pitcairn. Ever since, the name "Bounty" has reverberated with a sense of male adventure and freedom, with breaking the shackles of oppressive government on the high seas, and finding sexual pleasures under the tropical palms.

During this same period, several French literary luminaries (for example, Voltaire, Chateaubriand, and Joubert), although never visiting Tahiti themselves, further embellished and perpetuated the image of Tahiti as paradise. These literary texts demonstrate the intensity with which images of a fantasized utopia had entered and dominated the European imagination. For example, French moralist and essayist Joseph Joubert, a candidate for an academic prize on the eve of the French revolution, celebrated Tahiti when he wrote,

> O-Taheiti, how beautiful are your women and how gentle are your men. Ever since we got to know you the sun sets more beautifully on the mountains of Europe. . . . Your discovery, charming island, will not be wasted on the happiness of the world. The golden age is in your wooded groves. I sleep turned towards you. (quoted in Rennie 1995, 136–37)

Ironically, once Europeans had "discovered" (that is, created, and realized, their vision of) Tahiti, there was no longer a yet-undiscovered place for them to imagine, no longer a blank slate upon which they could project their longings, fears, and dilemmas. Victor Segalen, a nineteenth-century French naval officer, later wrote that the first voyage around the world was disenchanting because, from that point on, there was no longer a remoteness in the world, no longer an unknown place to imagine (Segalen 1890, 64).

STRATEGICALLY EXPANDING THE EMPIRE

The exotic images and ideas about Tahiti that circulated in Europe, fueling the fantasies of many, conflicted directly with Christian beliefs. When French Catholic and British Protestant missionaries arrived in Tahiti in 1797, they were determined to change a way of life that was portrayed, and that they interpreted, as immoral. The missionaries' efforts led to the banning of customs such as singing, dancing, and the worship of Tahitian ancestral deities on the *marae*. "*Marae* were the sanctity and glory of the land . . . the pride of the people . . . the ornaments of the land . . . [and] the palaces presented to the gods" (Henry 1928, 150). Human sacrifice was sometimes performed on the *marae* as a necessary part of declaring war and proclaiming victory. Missionaries, however, saw the *marae* as "hideous dens and dungeons of idolatry" where "rites of blood and the orgies of darkness were celebrated" (Tyerman 1831, 114) and immediately banned their use.[10] The missionaries also disapproved of the Tahitians' hierarchical sociopolitical system, which was reflected in practices associated with land tenure, village settlement, religion, and warfare (Ellis 1829; Oliver 1974). In particular, they took issue with the communal ownership of land, although they misunderstood how this system actually worked (Newbury 1980, 24; Oliver 1981, 435),[11] and tried to convert Tahitians to a land tenure system that was more compatible with the idea of a Christian nuclear family.

The presence of the missionaries in the islands, and their efforts (and success) in changing the behavior of the Tahitians, directly paved the way for a firmer colonial foothold. It was the tension between French Catholic and English Protestant missionaries, and competition between the French and British governments over the possession of new colonies, that eventually resulted in the establishment of Tahiti as a French Protectorate (see Pritchard 1983). In the 1820s and 1830s, the English and French consuls competed for the support of Tahiti's Queen Pomare IV (who ruled from 1827 to 1877).[12] In 1842, while the Queen was away, pro-French chiefs signed a petition,[13] drawn up by the French consul, Jacques-Antoine Moerenhout, asking to be brought under French protection. The Queen's flag was lowered, the French flag was raised, and Tahiti became a French Protectorate.

Resistance to French rule was fierce, with three years of armed guerrilla warfare (1844–47). From the island of Tahiti, Queen Pomare fled to Raiatea when her palace was surrounded. The fighting continued until the last stronghold was captured and the remaining rebels retreated to Tahiti Iti, the island's southeastern peninsula. Giving up the struggle in 1847, the Queen returned to Pape'ete and ruled as a figurehead until her death in 1877. Today, there is a monument to the fallen Tahitians near the airport at Faa'a, the village noted for its pro-independence sentiment. In 1880, King Pomare V abdicated, allowing France to annex Tahiti, and to change its status from a protectorate to a colony. The people of Huahine resisted longer than those on other islands and did not become part of the French Protectorate until 1898. The remains of stone fortifications can be seen in the underbrush near the *marae* complex in Maeva, reminders of Huahine's valiant struggle.

A nation-state expands its influence and control over a new colony by a variety of means, most of which produce new spatial arrangements. Examples include the construction of transportation infrastructures such as roads, wharves, and airports; the production and management of energy resources such as electricity and nuclear power; the establishment of educational institutions; and "the planning, construction, and reconfiguration of urban built environments to enable the reproduction of both labor-power and capital" (Brenner 1997, 148). As a colonial power, France altered the geography of Tahiti to suit its needs for national security and economic growth.

The mid-nineteenth century was a period of intense competition between the great colonial powers, resulting in France's development of a more deliberate policy for expansion. The same year that Tahiti became a French Protectorate, François Guizot, the chief minister for King Louis-Philippe, described his plans for a new vision of the world to the French National Assembly, arguing that it would be imperative for France to possess maritime stations at strategic points around the globe, which would serve as both safe harbors for the French fleet and centers of commerce (J. Martin 1987, 291). At this same time, C.A. Vincendon-Dumoulin and C. Desgraz, a French navy commissioner and hydrographic engineer, respectively, produced an important plan for developing French ports and naval bases in the Pacific (Vincendon-Dumoulin and Desgraz 1844).

> [The islands] can extend France's trade and assure her a good commercial position in the event that the archipelagoes of the South Seas take on any importance or if new commercial relations are established between China and America. The passage of ships through these archipelagoes assures these colonies precious resources; if ever the isthmus of Panama is canalized, the importance of our establishments as military bases will be great, and our colonists will be able to extract great advantages, even though Tahiti will profit only indirectly from the newly opened commercial routes. (quoted in Aldrich 1990, 239)

As outlined in Guizot's plans for maritime stations, and detailed in Vincendon-Dumoulin and Desgraz's hopes for a canal linking the oceans, France

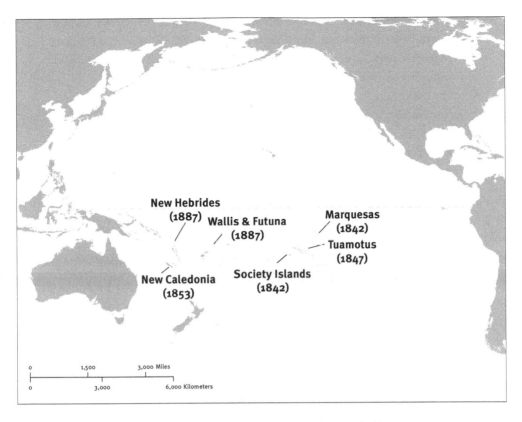

Map 2   France's Pacific Overseas Territories (1840–80). Map by Amir Sheikh.

soon developed a network of refueling stations for its sailing fleet. Between 1840 and 1880 Tahiti and other Pacific islands served as places for French military and commercial vessels to be refueled and resupplied. The islands proved relatively easy for France to acquire and maintain because they were small and the local chiefs were relatively compliant. France gradually established a suite of colonies in the Pacific that were collectively called Territoires d'Outre-Mer (TOM).[14] These comprised the Marquesas, the Society Islands (including Tahiti), the Tuamotus, New Caledonia, Wallis and Futuna, and the New Hebrides (now Vanuatu; map 2).

The building of a canal between the Atlantic and Pacific oceans was the feat extraordinaire of engineering in the nineteenth century. From the early 1800s, French engineers had been contemplating schemes that would join the world's oceans and, thus, realize their dreams of a more accessible world. The Suez Canal, which connected the Mediterranean with the Red Sea, had opened in 1869. The plan to connect the Atlantic and the Pacific by a canal through Panama, however, was even more ambitious. Work on the Panama Canal, after decades of planning, was begun by the French in the 1870s and eventually completed by the Americans in 1914.

In 1880 King Pomare V (the successor to Queen Pomare IV) "was persuaded to sign a proclamation donating 'Tahiti and dependences' to France with 'all the guarantees of property and liberty' for Tahitians." In January 1881 Tahitians learned that the French Parliament had ratified the annexation (Newbury 1980, 201–2). The former protectorate was given the new name of Établissements Français d'Océanie (EFO), and Tahiti (including all of its five archipelagoes: the Society, Austral, Tuamotu, Gambier, and Marquesas islands) became the French colony as it is administered today.

With the refueling stations secured, the Panama Canal under construction, and Tahiti firmly in France's grip, the moment had arrived for France to safeguard her imperial future. The politician Paul Deschanel, who in 1920 became the eleventh president of the French Republic, wrote a two-volume treatise on Oceania and the Panama Canal (Deschanel 1884). It was the first comprehensive study of French Oceania and a statement of French colonial ambitions in the South Pacific. Deschanel's work, which focused on the global economic and political revolution that would result from the completion of the Panama Canal, continued to influence others for decades. He described how great merchant and military fleets would move from France's Atlantic coast through the canal to the South Pacific, and eventually on to Australia and China. "The canal would make a 'French Pacific' through a masterstroke not of conquest or territorial expansion but by integrating, relaying, and connecting a set of disparate points into a tenuous web of empire" (quoted in Matsuda 2005, 47). The idea was for the great military and commercial routes meeting at Panama to be "linked with well-placed French stepping-stones: Martinique, Guadeloupe, the Marquesas, Tahiti, New Caledonia, Cochinchine" (Bionne 1880, 275). To help realize this goal, people in France needed to become more aware of Tahiti and its strategic importance (see Aldrich 1990, 242–44).

Other French colonies, such as Algeria and Indochina, had their own raisons d'être, as a settler colony and a trade hub, respectively. In the case of the Pacific Islands, with their small landmasses and limited resources, however, the French government needed to create a rationale for possessing them. In the *métropole* it was necessary to constantly reinvent the image of the colonies, design new development strategies, and reconnect the value of the islands to changing international conditions, all in an effort to win the support of the French citizenry (Aldrich 1990, 334). Colonial expansion, although embraced by the majority of traders, missionaries, scientists, and politicians, was far from universally popular in nineteenth-century France. Thus, the *parti colonial*, a lobby whose job was to stir up popular interest at home, played an important role. It was comprised of a number of separate committees and organizations that issued periodicals, held meetings, and tried to sway legislators to support its cause. The *parti colonial* greatly helped the French government by its dissemination of propaganda asserting the importance of France's overseas possessions. The promotion and maintenance of a national policy of colonization relies as much on images, myths, and pseudo-knowledge as it does on objective assessments of the local resources, economic opportunities, and military importance.

PAPE'ETE AS A COLONIAL CITY

"Cities are the products of history, both of the urban forms and functions inherited from the past, and of the new urban meaning assigned to them by conflictive historical change" (Castells 1983, 331). The Pape'ete that one sees today can be "read" as such a historical product. After annexation in 1880, Tahiti—and especially its capital city of Pape'ete—became shaped more and more by activities and policies that were dictated from the *métropole*. A favorite argument for the value of French colonialism "proclaimed the outre-mer [overseas territories] as a terrain for working out solutions to some of the political, social, and aesthetic problems which plagued France" (Wright 1991, 3). Colonies were even referred to as *champs d'expérience* or experimental terrains. "The colonies provided more than the ideal laboratory setting so often invoked. . . . They functioned like a magnifying glass, revealing with startling clarity the ambitions and fears, the techniques and policies that pertained at home, here carried out almost without restraints." In the late 1800s, colonial cities in particular became sites for the strategic production of material and symbolic values. They provided "appealing visions of social hierarchy, orderly growth, a thriving economy, and effective political authority" (Wright 1991, 306, 3).[15]

In the late nineteenth century, the metropolitan movement in Europe examined the relationship between metropolitan centers and their peripheries. Its proponents sought to re-envision and redesign imperial cities at home, a scheme that depended on capital produced by colonial economies

(Rotenberg 2001). The urban areas of both Paris and Papeʻete were undergoing major—and sometimes parallel—changes, albeit on different scales, necessitated by massive population growth in both centers. Between 1851 and 1901, the population of Paris and its suburbs had quadrupled (Rabinow 1989, 253). In the 1860s Baron Georges Haussmann directed the transformation of Paris from a medieval city, densely populated and unsanitary, to what he hoped would serve as a modern capital in tune with contemporary needs for transportation, health, and political control. "It has been noted time and again that Haussmann shattered the historical space of Paris in order to impose a space that was strategic—and hence planned and demarcated according to the viewpoint of strategy" (Lefebvre 1991, 312). Much of what one sees in Paris today was based on Haussmann's ideas of a modern city. Rail networks and stations were designed to connect rural areas to the urban core, circular routes were built around the city, and wide avenues were designed for the movement of the military. To further emphasize this new spatial structure, façades of apartment buildings were made uniform and building heights were determined by the width of the avenue on which they were located. Haussmann also built new urban markets, bridges across the Seine, public parks, and cultural buildings and palaces, giving the city a "visible ability to produce both symbols and space" (Zukin 1995, 2).

This type of nineteenth-century organization of space was heavily influenced by new ideas about visual perception. It constructed a quintessentially modern experience by creating ways of seeing and being seen (Berman 1983). In contrast to what they experienced negotiating the narrow, twisting, and trash-filled streets of the "medieval" city, Parisians now could see into the distance, and could perceive where they had come from and where they were going. The new boulevards, lined with shops and cafés, brought people together in new ways (Urry 1990, 137). "After centuries of life as a cluster of isolated cells, Paris was becoming a unified physical and human space" (Berman 1983, 151). Haussmann's Paris, carefully planned according to ideas about space and vision, also became a feast for the eyes of photographers and impressionist painters.

At the same time that Paris was undergoing these changes, Papeʻete, with its growing population of French immigrants and the concentration of French economic and political power, was being fashioned into the Territory's political and commercial center. The French colonial administration inhabited and redefined space in Papeʻete as part of its strategy of expansion and production of capital. It linked transportation networks, established sites of capital accumulation, invested in urbanization projects, and orchestrated everyday life. Each such form commanded space to serve its purposes.

In Pape'ete, modern ideas about city planning and architecture were used to demonstrate—to both the Tahitians and the French—the authority of the state. "Urban design was an integral part of colonial domination, especially after the end of the nineteenth century. It provided one of the means to establish military control, regulate activities, separate populations, and establish a comprehensive order, on both an aesthetic and political level" (Rabinow 1982, 267). Pape'ete, like most colonial cities, was a distinctly colonial phenomenon—a place where the *métropole* and colony intersected, and a site for the *métropole* to reproduce itself in the colony (Prochaska 1990a). In this process, colonial settlers became important agents of change.

After Tahiti became a French colony in 1880, immigration from France and elsewhere increased dramatically. By 1890, French citizens made up the majority of the foreign population (a group Gauguin would join the following year). By 1907, Pape'ete had about 2,000 French settlers of a total population of about 12,000 (Newbury 1980, 271–72). Life for the colonists, however, was anything but easy. What they found upon arrival contrasted starkly with what they had anticipated based on the idyllic images and romantic stories that often were the principal catalysts for their voyages. The difficulties they faced were many. They were exhausted from the lengthy voyage; they experienced older settlers' resentment toward newcomers; many became bankrupt; and almost a third of them would be convicted of acts of public disorder such as drunkenness or fighting. In general, the French who were drawn to Tahiti were mainly young, single men of modest backgrounds from French urban areas. Most had been soldiers or sailors lacking both savings and marketable skills, and for whom Tahiti was part of a long, meandering journey. Most stayed an average of about ten years and some ended up living with, or marrying, Polynesian women. On the whole, they also continued to have great difficulties making a living—much less a fortune—in the Pacific.

Eventually, in spite of these challenges, a small French elite emerged to dominate and influence commerce and politics. Most of these individuals gained their influence from being government employees, small property owners, shopkeepers, artisans, bakers, butchers, tailors, or café owners (Aldrich 1990, 141–43). Most consequential, however, were those who married into prominent Tahitian families and soon established dynasty-like privileges with their inherited wealth, land, and chiefly titles (Krizancic 2009; Newbury 1980, 174).

Pape'ete began serving important colonial functions for France, as seen in the many emblems of French modernity and power that were built—mansions, churches, government buildings, a post office, banks, plazas, cafés, naval ship yards, waterfront promenades, military barracks, and broad boulevards for the movement of troops. Pape'ete, a place originally chosen by missionaries in the 1820s as a tranquil escape from the *mara'amu,* the cool southerly winds of the tropical winter, was now anything but calm. Modern ideas about urban planning and architecture (echoing those in the *métropole*) guided the incorporation of Pape'ete's periphery and the organization of its space. Its street plan and building architecture were becoming increasingly French. Outlying Tahitian neighborhoods such as Paofai, Tarahoi, and Vaininiore were overlaid with a grid of streets and boulevards, many of which were given names of places in Paris. Rue de la Petite Pologne, for example (fig. 1.3), was named after an area in Paris that had been a slum enclave prior to Haussmann's overhaul.[16] Many streets in Pape'ete were given names that imbued the city with markers of French visions, exploits, and conquests: allée Pierre Loti, rue Paul Gauguin, rue Wallis, rue Cook, rue Jacques-Antoine Moerenhout, and the broad, tree-lined avenue Bruat, which was named after the French Admiral who convinced Queen Pomare to cede Tahiti to France.[17] As several scholars have noted, the built environment in which people live not only results from but also influences how people think (King 1980, 27; Lewandowski 1984, 237). After all, "spatial relations are also social relations" (Lefebvre 1979, 290). Living in, or visiting, these new urban spaces, Tahitians became increasingly more influenced by French ways of thinking and behaving. They were incorporated into the French colonial economy, converted to European religions, and affected by French laws, language, and food (Aldrich 1990, 336). Tahitians were also taught to use open spaces to engage in French leisure activities, such as playing *pétanque* (also known as *boules*), still quite popular today.

The reorganization of space, of course, was not unique to Tahiti but was also occurring in other French colonies. At its height in the late 1800s, the French empire encompassed more than six million square miles of territory (roughly thirty times the size of France) and included more than 100 million people, giving France the second-largest empire after Britain. France's possessions included tropical jungles in Africa and South America; sun-

Fig. 1.3 *Rue de la Petite Pologne à Pape'ete.* 1880s postcard.

drenched islands in the Caribbean, the Indian Ocean, and the Pacific; and vast expanses of Saharan desert and Antarctic ice. It included "enormous colonies such as Indochina and Madagascar, remote little-known outposts such as Wallis and Kerguelen, and toeholds in India and on the Red Sea. The French tricolor flag flew over the fabled city of Tombouctou and the legendary island of Tahiti" (Aldrich 1996, 1).

In the overall scheme of French colonialism, however, the legendary island of Tahiti (as well as other French possessions in the Pacific) played an insignificant role. Most of its other colonies provided France with a much greater array of benefits, including agricultural products (rubber, hardwoods, palm oil, coffee, cocoa, nuts, and spices); mineral resources (gold and oil); animal products (animal hides, ivory, and feathers); human laborers and slaves; strategic military outposts; and penal colonies. In contrast, Tahiti offered little. There was neither enough land for plantations or settlement nor sufficient mineral resources for extraction (other than phosphate on the small island of Makatea), and its distance halfway around the world from France made Tahiti impractical as a viable settler colony. Moreover, the many attempts to grow commercial crops (oranges, coffee, and cotton) failed.

PSEUDO-KNOWLEDGE OF THE COLONY IN THE *MÉTROPOLE*

What Tahiti did provide for the *métropole,* however, was an endless source of dreams and fantasies. It served as a tropical looking glass for philosophical musings about the nature of mankind and for fantasy escapes from the perceived drudgery of growing industrialization in Europe. The main resources exported to Europe were visions and illusions—of lush landscapes and seductive women, which many saw as a veritable paradise on earth. Being a source of dreams was not the raison d'être of Tahiti remaining a colony; but ideas about this imagined place provided a strong foundation for France to initiate and undertake numerous economic and political schemes.

At the same time that images portraying a Pacific paradise were circulating throughout the Western world, daily life in Papeʻete was changing rapidly. French rule in Tahiti, after a century of widely disseminated romantic images, encouraged a number of European and American writers and artists to make their way to the colony to live out, write about, and paint their dreams, further adding to the repertoire of narratives and images that portrayed Tahiti as a paradise on earth. This body of work often interlaced colonial notions of sex, race, and domination, indicating that the colonial gaze was fixed on the Europeans as much as it was on the colonized. These narratives of colonial expansion, couched within the framework of sexual adventures, indicated that "European manhood in the colonies, whether measured by 'character' and civility or by position and class, was largely independent of the presence of European women" and instead was contingent on sexual conventions and racial categorizations (Stoler 2002, 1–2).

The list of writers who produced these evocative images of Tahiti during the early colonial period is extensive. It includes, most notably, the American authors Herman Melville, whose risqué (for the time) autobiographical book *Typee* (1846) was the first novel about a love affair between a white man and a Polynesian woman, and Robert Louis Stevenson, who spent six years traveling in the South Seas and wrote about his attraction to the islands in his journal, which later appeared as a book, *In the South Seas* (1896). The French author Pierre Loti (the pseudonym of Louis-Marie Julien Viaud) was among the most prolific. Recalling memories from his early childhood, he wrote,

Oh! What magic and mental turmoil there was during my childhood in the simple word "the colonies," which, at that time, denoted in my mind every far-off tropical land with its palm trees, enormous flowers, Negroes, animals and adventures. . . . Oh, "the colonies!" How can I describe everything that stirred in my head at the very sound of that word! (Loti 1891, 71–72)

As a midshipman in the French navy, Loti traveled extensively throughout the French colonial empire. Everywhere he went he gathered material for his books, which eventually won him election to l'Académie française. While in Tahiti, he fell in love with Rarahu, a fifteen-year-old Tahitian girl from Bora Bora, and in 1880 wrote about his affair with her in *Le mariage de Loti* (The Marriage of Loti). This book, with its vivid portrayal of adventures in the colonies, made him one of France's most popular authors. He depicted his life as one of rough, virile escapades and sexual pleasures, all framed by a racist and cavalier spirit of empire. French readers were captivated by passages such as the following, in which Loti describes every inch of Rarahu (and, like Bougainville, Hodges, Webber, and others before him, occasionally drapes his descriptions in classical imagery).

> Rarahu's eyes were of a tawny black, full of exotic languor and coaxing softness, like those of a kitten when it is stroked; her eyelashes so long and so black that you might have taken them for painted feathers. Her nose was short and delicate, like the nose in some Arab faces; her mouth, rather too thick and too wide for a classic model, had deep corners deliciously dimpled. When she laughed she showed all her teeth . . . of brilliantly white enamel. . . . Her hair, scented with sandalwood oil, was long, straight and rather harsh, falling in heavy locks on her bare shoulders. Her skin was of the same hue all over, from her forehead to the tips of her toes; a dusky brown, verging on brick-red, like that of old Etruscan terra-cotta pottery. Rarahu was small, beautiful in proportion and mould; her bosom was purely formed and polished; her arms as perfect as an antique. (Loti 1880, 16)[18]

It's not difficult to imagine the effect that passages like this had on readers who were looking out of their windows onto a cold, rainy, and soot-stained Paris.

When Loti first arrived in Pape'ete in 1872, he found the islands to be very different from what he had imagined. Missionaries had been in the islands for almost a century, and Tahitians were "suffering from the physical, social and spiritual maladies [of] a culture in decline and distress." In response, "Loti edited, embellished and manipulated material for dramatic effect when writing his novels" (O'Connor 1986, x, xi). Rarahu, evocatively described in his novel, was a composite of several Tahitian women. He was able to sweep aside his initial misgivings, saying, "I, too, am under the spell . . . I fancy I see it . . . through the same transfiguring prism. It is already two months since I first set foot on the island, and already I am bewitched. The disappointment of the first few days is now a thing of the past" (Loti 1880, 37–38).

The success of *Le mariage de Loti,* so popular that there were several print-ings, is thought to be due in large part to its "accurate reflection of the atti-tudes to the colonies that prevailed in his day" (O'Connor 1986, xiii). Loti's writings, along with those of others, ratified France's "civilizing" mission by promoting notions of European racial superiority, and by portraying Tahi-tians as exotic playthings who are easily seduced and then abandoned. Loti's popularity was due, in part, to the romantic fantasies and amorous triumphs in which he indulged his readers. "More generally, Loti's works help to sus-tain gratifying images of cultural superiority among his European readers. To enjoy reading Loti is to enjoy the personal and cultural complacency on which the colonial venture thrived" (Hargreaves 1981, 84).

During the late 1800s France displayed this feeling of cultural superiority in several visually dramatic and politically powerful ways, all of which were part of its efforts to gain support for its colonial projects. These representa-tions played a crucial role in maintaining the fantasy and keeping reality at bay in the *métropole.* By celebrating and validating the colonial experience, they also allowed the government to bring the Tahiti of *l'espace conçu* and *l'espace perçu* into alignment. Through creative constructions, such as exhib-its, models, and visual representations, places are reduced to an endless suc-cession of symbols wherein any part of the construction can pass itself off as a coherent whole, and where seemingly innocent knowledge can be used to further political goals (Lefebvre 1991, 311). Represented places masquerade as scientific realities despite the fact that they are embellishments of the truth and can be manipulated for political gain.

France was host to several Expositions Universelles from the second half of the nineteenth century to the early decades of the twentieth. These exhibi-tions occurred in Paris in 1855, 1867, 1878, 1889, 1900, and 1931, with many other fairs taking place in other French cities during other years.[19] These fairs, many of which drew crowds that numbered in the millions, presented France's colonial possessions as an endless procession of monuments, build-ings, exhibits, and performers. By bringing the far-flung colonies within reach of French citizens, these representations were designed to commu-nicate a positive message about the logic, convenience, and economic usefulness of France's empire, as well as to entice France's youth with colonial vocations.[20] The broad expanse of the French colonial world, already linked through militarization and commerce, was further united and celebrated in the symbolic space of the exhibition. The focus was not only on the glories of empire but also on economic values resulting from a new world of spatial interconnections facilitated by modern networks of communication and materialized through commodity exchange (D. Harvey 2003, 114).

The grandest of all the fairs—marking the centennial of the French Revolution—was the 1889 exhibition in Paris. This was the occasion for which the Eiffel Tower was built, thus marking an important moment for the triumph of science and industry by signaling the end of the use of stone and the beginning of the age of iron. The tower's unique lattice structure, which gave the illusion of grace and transparency, was also seen as oppressive in its demonstration of industrial might. It was visible from everywhere; it also allowed people on the tower to see everywhere. They could ascend to heights heretofore unachievable to observe Paris in all its glory and, in scanning the layers of history below them, to "contemplate the centuries in tranquility" (Loyrette 1992, 364). Looking down, one could also see pavilions exhibiting curiosities from the many colonies of France. The view from above was that of an orderly world of French possessions that elicited French pride and nationalism (see T. Mitchell 1988).

The transformation of colonial subjects into objects of curiosity was especially noticeable when native inhabitants of French colonies were put on view at the fairs. Pacific Islanders were put into fabricated, "authentic" villages and were asked to re-enact their customs. These efforts were intended to provide European viewers with a mock experience of being in another world, where they could come face to face with both noble and ignoble "savages" (Breckenridge 1989; Greenhalgh 1988).[21]

Photography, a relatively new art and technique, was well suited to promoting colonial ideologies. During the mid-nineteenth century, French newspapers and magazines, such as *Le tour du monde* and *l'Illustration*, specialized in the publication of photographic images from the colonies. These images shed light on French colonial life by showing exotic vegetation, indigenous people, and military action. The advent of photography allowed many people to regard the distant world as one of choreographed scenes viewed through a camera, a technology that divided people into spectators and spectacles, or colonizers and colonized.

PICTURE POSTCARDS

By the late 1800s photography was put to a new use to produce images for postcards. The development of reliable postal services and new printing techniques allowed travelers to communicate inexpensively with friends and family by sending postcards with images of distant places. After the introduction of postcards, "the world rapidly became encircled by a network of exchanges that bombarded reciprocally illustrated messages at reduced tariffs" (O'Reilly 1975, 8). As Europeans began to travel more widely, postcards played a crucial role in validating a sense of place by capturing firsthand impressions, authenticating the experience of "being there," and then conveying these "impressions" to family and friends back home. Postcards became exemplary souvenirs in that they recall an "other" place. They do not arise out of need or use value, but "out of the necessarily insatiable demands of nostalgia" (S. Stewart 1984, 135).

Postcards soon became the most ubiquitous and widely distributed images of colonial life (Aldrich 1996, 258). Like the exhibits at the fairs, postcards allowed images of exotic "human types" and faraway places to be brought closer to home and within the colonial grip.[22] At the same time that colonized labor and products were penetrating into and circulating within European economies, the images on postcards traveled on parallel paths to visually entangle colonial resources, capital, and power. By moving effortlessly across borders, postcards reinforced the emerging spatial interconnection and political reorganization of the world.

Postcards met with instant and universal success. At a time when images were otherwise available only in the less portable (and more expensive) forms of books and paintings, and when the use of photography in magazines and newspapers was still new, postcards were truly revolutionary. The first decades of the twentieth century were the heyday of the picture postcard (MacDougall 2006, 195). In France alone it is estimated that, while eight million postcards were printed in 1899, the number increased to sixty million in 1902, and to 123 million in 1910 (Prochaska 1990b, 375).

The period from 1890 to 1918 was a maelstrom of postcard activity, "a period in which postcards were produced, collected and circulated with an energy that remains historically unmatched" (Mathur 1999, 95). Postcard collecting, which was a predominantly female activity (DeRoo 2002), became the latest vogue. Postcard albums appeared in many forms. Exchange clubs

became especially popular. One such organization was the Société Cartophile de France et des Colonies (Society for French and Colonial Postcard
Enthusiasts). Several journals about postcard collecting appeared, with one
of them — *La Gazette Cartophile* — designed specifically to cater to female
collectors.

The popularity of postcards meshed perfectly with fin de siècle ideologies
in which colonized peoples were made "manageable" through what Foucault
has referred to as "a certain policy of the body, a certain way of rendering
a group of men docile and useful . . . [which] required the involvement of
definite relations of power; it called for a technique of overlapping subjec-
tion and objectification" (Foucault 1979, 305). It is difficult to imagine a more
effective way to validate such an ideology than this one, where the images of
landscapes were charged with signs of French civilizing infrastructures in
distant lands, and those of "exotic" bodies were transformed into workers
and consumers, and to then circulate these images around the world, as they
traveled from hand to hand, open to the nostalgic view of others. As Malek
Alloula has stated so graphically,

> The postcard . . . becomes the poor man's phantasm: for a few pennies, display
> racks full of dreams. The postcard is everywhere, covering all the colonial
> space, immediately available to the tourist, the soldier, the colonist. It is at once
> their poetry and their glory captured for the ages; it is also their pseudo-knowl-
> edge of the colony. It produces stereotypes in the manner of great seabirds pro-
> ducing guano. It is the fertilizer of the colonial vision. (Alloula 1986, 4)

Images of Tahiti from this golden age of postcards also represented
these fin de siècle visions of "civilizing" colonized subjects. Many postcards
depicted displays of French colonial infrastructure, power, and pride, such as
a historic flag raising when land was possessed or the celebration of Bastille
Day half a world away. They showed French mission stations, hospitals, and
churches, or the taming of the tropical jungle by turning it into neatly plowed
sugarcane plantations or mining it for phosphate. Other images showed the
successful results of these "civilizing" ventures when native bodies were disciplined by French customs and institutions. Among these were images of
Tahitians in various settings: sporting European clothing and ruffled para-
sols; wearing French military attire with tasseled epaulettes and brass but-
tons; sitting obediently in school; reading the Bible in church; or mastering

Le Quai du Commerce, Papeete – TAHITI. – The Quay of Commerce, Papeete

Fig. 1.4 *Le Quai de Commerce, Pape'ete, Tahiti.* 1920s postcard.

European musical instruments or dance steps as French flags waved in the background. Postcards with images of wharves crowded with boats, bulging bags of copra (dried coconut), and hardworking Tahitians were "proof" of industrious native (male) labor and bustling commerce (fig. 1.4). "Photographs of Native bodies provided visual referents to the expansion of an imperial body politic" by signaling a frontier to be crossed and illustrating the extent of what could be assimilated into the nation (Rafael 2000, 81).

Still other postcards highlighted the comforts of home that were available for French settlers in a foreign land, communicating that one of the outcomes of native labor was French comfort and leisure. These depicted the civilized amenities of Tahiti under French rule: the arrival of the mail steamer; the mansard-roofed, veranda-encircled post office; tree-lined streets with names like rue de Rivoli; manicured public parks with benches and music pavilions; tennis courts; or fashionably dressed French men and women enjoying an outing on the beach with a horse-drawn cart.[23]

Postcards that included images of romantic scenery were especially useful for maintaining French support for the colonial enterprise. Landscape postcards focused on dramatic waterfalls, deep gorges, or lush valleys

OCÉANIE FRANÇAISE   TAHITI. - Rivière de Tautira

Fig. 1.5 *Tahiti—Rivière de Tautira,* F. Homes. 1920s postcard.

capped by the mountain peaks of Tahiti's interior. A particularly popular postcard image (produced in various versions by different photographers) was a view of *Rivière de Tautira* (fig. 1.5), modeled on Hodges's 1776 painting of *Oaitepeha Bay, Tahiti.* This endlessly replicated suite of Arcadian images etched the illusions of a Tahitian paradise ever more deeply into the minds of Europeans.

Among the many postcard images produced, those of Tahitian women were by far the most popular (O'Reilly 1975, 9). These were always posed studio portraits. Lucien Gauthier, who arrived in the colony in 1904 and soon became the best-known photographer of the time, created a particularly popular series of portraits of individual women in various poses set against black backgrounds. He grouped these together under the title *Beautés Polynésiennes,* hoping that postcard collectors would purchase the entire set.

The images chosen for use on postage stamps, like those on the postcards to which they were affixed, bore witness to the same colonialist and nationalist ideologies. In 1913, the Établissements Français d'Océanie (EFO) produced its first stamp featuring a Polynesian (rather than a French) theme—a Tahitian woman with a crown of flowers on her head and a hibiscus flower behind her ear. As these images on postcards and stamps traveled around the world, the visual message—that Tahiti was beautiful, seductive, and feminine, but securely under French control—circulated to the world at large.

PAUL GAUGUIN

Although there were many writers, exposition designers, photographers, postcard producers, and others who created the images that helped fabricate a certain mythical Tahiti, no one played as powerful a role in creating an enduring idyllic vision of Tahiti as did Paul Gauguin. The time he spent painting in French Polynesia is viewed as "one of the most mythologically potent episodes in the history of Western art," and his paintings from that era became the "very pivot of modernism" (Shackelford and Frèches-Thory 2004, book cover). Gauguin himself was seduced by this Tahiti of the imagination. His interest was first piqued when he visited the 1889 Exposition Universelle in Paris and when he read in one of its guidebooks about the typical Tahitian woman, who "is usually a perfect model for a sculptor . . . her large, dark eyes, so lovely and pure, her almost excessively full lips, and her magnificently white and regular teeth, make her look so sweet and innocently voluptuous that it is impossible not to succumb to the admiration she inspires" (Henrique 1889, 25).

This romantic vision was reinforced when Gauguin read *Le mariage de Loti,* with its steamy passages about Loti's affair with Rarahu. In letters Gauguin wrote to friends, he reported his affairs with women brought from the colonies to the Exposition Universelle, described his desire to "buy a hut of the kind you saw at the Universal Exhibition . . . this would cost almost nothing," and expressed his longing to "do something like what one finds in Pierre Loti's book" (Gauguin 1949, 118, 142; Druick and Zegers 2001, 333). Reading Loti's book while working as a stockbroker and living in poverty in cold, gray France with a wife he no longer loved, Gauguin's imagination took flight. Wanting to pursue his own creative rebirth in the tropics of the South Seas, he embarked on a journey that would allow him to recreate these fantasies in his own life, and to reproduce them for others through his art. He sailed to Tahiti in 1891, where he could live inexpensively while advancing his career and fulfilling his dreams, setting canvases colorfully ablaze with his impressions of Tahiti and, especially, of Tahitian women.[24]

Gauguin's journey to Tahiti was made possible because he was a French citizen and Tahiti was a French colony. In his application for passage to Tahiti (a trip that, for a French citizen, would cost nothing), he stated that he would record daily life as part of a French government-sponsored "scientific mission," one of the intellectual by-products of colonialist expansion (Druick and Zegers 2001, 337). Although Gauguin's artistic accomplishments in Tahiti were complex expressions of the convergence of European decadence and French colonialism (Perloff 1995), he was—and continues to be—regarded as a symbol of the rejection of European civilization and the embrace of South Seas "primitivism." Having left his wife and five children in France (and having taken up residence with a fifteen-year-old Tahitian girl, Teha'amana, and fathering at least four children during his time in Tahiti),[25] he was viewed as "a figure of scandal and envy among the bourgeois collectors who bought his sensual visions of escape" (Schjeldahl 2002, 82). Because of what people continue to read into his art and the opinions they form about his life choices, Gauguin has achieved a notoriety in the popular imagination that is independent of his artistic achievements.

Gauguin's penchant for imaginative embellishments on canvas is now well known.[26] Tahitians, too, have begun voicing their own, usually critical, opinion about Gauguin and his art at international conferences (for example, at the Université de la Polynésie française in 2003), in speeches (Spitz 2003), and in writing (Pambrun 2003). Ironically, more than a century after the first European explorers traveled to Tahiti, Gauguin—enticed by the very images the explorers and their followers had created—encountered a very different place than the one in his imagination. As was the case for Loti and others, "What the artist experienced there from the outset was a cruel disappointment. The actual Tahiti that he began to witness in the capital was a far cry from the one of his dreams" (Shackelford and Frèches-Thory 2004, 25). Upon arriving in Tahiti, Gauguin wrote in a letter to a friend, "Tahiti is becoming completely French. Little by little, all the ancient ways of doing things will disappear" (Druick and Zegers 2001, 337; Mancoff 2001, 69). What is most telling, however, is that although Gauguin's expectations of Tahiti were at odds with what he found upon arrival, he continued to depict the mythic fantasy, rather than what he saw, on his canvases. He was left to invent, in his mind and with his paints, the "savage" culture he had hoped to find. At one point he said that he could no longer record Tahitian life for the colonial government, declaring that he was no longer a painter from nature because everything took place in his wildest imagination.

To enhance his creative endeavors, he brought along a portable "museum" of images that included postcards and other reproductions of Egyptian,

Greek, Japanese, Indonesian, and European art. Although he was looking at Tahiti while composing his paintings, he nonetheless synthetically borrowed, juxtaposed, and superimposed images from Egyptian frescoes, men and horses from the Greek Parthenon, elements from Hokusai's block prints, stone reliefs from Borobudur, and Giotto's scenic compositions in order to create the artistic effect he desired. Only through painting in this inventive way was he able to preserve his fantasies and create a "dream of hope" for himself (Druick and Zegers 2001, 340).

Although Gauguin moved to French Polynesia in part to escape what he perceived as the expense and boredom of living in France, his artistic efforts were still directed toward capturing the attention of the art world in Paris. He was acutely aware that painting in a foreign land would lend his works "an exotic air when they were sent to Paris for exhibition" (Mancoff 2001, 69) and that by painting what he perceived as the unconventional beauty and mysteriousness of Tahitian women, the novelty of his subjects "would attract attention in the market" (Druick and Zegers 2001, 338). He traveled to Paris in 1893 to sell his paintings, but failed to meet with much success. He then began to write *Noa noa* (Sweet Fragrance), a romanticized journal about his life in Tahiti, as part of an intense campaign to promote his Tahitian art to a French audience.

Because of Gauguin's achievements and consequent fame, many other European and American painters have since gone to Tahiti to recreate Gauguin-inspired images on canvases of their own (artists such as Octave Morillot, François Ravello, Jacques Boullaire, Pierre Heyman, Yves de Saint-Font, and many, many more).

COLONIAL ROLE-PLAYING IN THE *MÉTROPOLE*

Images of colonized places and people also appeared in French schools and homes (Deroo, Deroo, and de Taillac 1992, 26). Classroom walls were decorated with colorful maps of France and its colonies, and schoolbooks featured stories from the colonies. At home children could role-play at colonialism with decks of cards that displayed "native types" or colonial-themed board games in which, by moving their pieces across the board, they could conquer countries, establish order among unruly natives, and plan further expansion (Marscille 1986, 12, 16–17). Jigsaw puzzles with pictures of "natives" from different colonies were also popular. By joining the pieces, players could reconfigure the fragments of empire into a unified whole, while also making them seem closer to home.

Representations of the French colonies infiltrated almost every domestic space. Cocoa, coffee, and soap were packaged in containers decorated with colonial imagery. Some of the most popular images appeared on wrappers of chocolates produced by companies such as Nestlé, Suchard, Chocolat Cémoi, and La Chocolaterie d'Annecy. These wrappers, depicting the people and landscapes of all the French colonies, were designed to be collected and put into albums produced by the chocolate companies. By simply buying and eating chocolates, and then putting the wrappers in their assigned spots in the albums, Europeans could collect and organize these miniature representations of Tahiti and other colonies, all of which fed their fantasies about these faraway places and people. "The miniature . . . became the realm not of fact but of reverie . . . [and] frequently served as a realm of the cultural other" (S. Stewart 1984, 43).

People living in France during the late nineteenth and early twentieth centuries learned everything they knew about Tahiti or Tahitians from representations—passages in Loti's book, exhibits at the colonial fairs, postcards, paintings by Gauguin, games, or colorful chocolate wrappers. This particular Tahiti existed purely in the imagination. It was seen as exotic, feminine, distant, orderly, and very much part of France—a reverie, a spectacle, a game, a hobby, or a sweet morsel to be gratifyingly devoured.

THE PAST LEAVES ITS TRACES

The chasm between the fantasy and reality of Tahiti—*l'espace conçu* and *l'espace perçu*—is vast, but the two places are intricately intertwined. The eighteenth-century European vision of a Rousseau-inspired utopia with people living in harmony with nature was nothing like the Tahiti that Wallis, Bougainville, and Cook encountered. The simulacra of colonial worlds neatly laid out at the expositions in Paris were a far cry from daily life as it was experienced in the colonies. These romantic images of Tahiti also failed to prepare writers and artists such as Loti and Gauguin for the "cruel disappointment" when they arrived at their dreamed-of destination.

Every place is a complex result of the ongoing relationship between its physical reality and what outsiders imagine about it, and of the intersecting social relations in which these two are brought together. As the physical and the imagined interlace, they render historical process and product almost impossible to differentiate. European scientific projects and utopian visions, from the eighteenth century on, have greatly affected how Tahiti evolved as a physical place. Likewise, as visual and textual images of Tahiti made their way back to Europe, new ideas and fashions emerged in the *métropole*. As the economic and political interests of the *métropole* and its colony grew increasingly more entangled, new geographies materialized, leaving their marks both on the ground and in the imagination. "One must continually move back and forth between the past and the present. . . . The historical and its consequences . . . the 'etymology' of locations in the sense of what happened at a particular spot or place and thereby changed it—all of this becomes inscribed in space. The past leaves its traces; time has its own script" (Lefebvre 1991, 37). Tahiti's history continually weaves itself into "place," and these movements back and forth across the seas leave new geographies in their wake.

CHAPTER TWO

Placentas in the Land, Bombs in the Bedrock

The idyllic images of "Tahiti," fueled by Western imaginations for two centuries, were put to new use in the early 1960s when two transformative events occurred in the Territory. The first was the relocation of France's nuclear testing program from Algeria to French Polynesia. The second was the worldwide intensification of mass tourism. These contradictory phenomena—which created destruction and nightmares on the one hand, and dreams and fantasies on the other—became deeply intertwined in French Polynesia's political economy. Now representations of a seductive paradise served new purposes. Those images of blue lagoons and attractive people could divert attention from the nuclear testing program by creating a veil behind which the dire consequences of the testing could be hidden.[1]

Neither of these—exploding nuclear weapons in the atmosphere above and in the bedrock of an island, or altering the environment to create artificial "paradises" for tourists—was a way in which Tahitians would behave toward the land. The result was an ongoing struggle about how place is understood, sensed, used, abused, respected, and represented. In such situations, "the battle becomes the moment of struggle between conceiving space through representation and living place through actual sensual experience" (Merrifield 1993, 525). This struggle captures what has been transpiring in Tahiti since the arrival of Europeans in the 1760s and that greatly intensified with the arrival of the nuclear testing program and tourism. The escalating tension is between Tahitians' sensual and spiritual experiences of their place, as noted by Hiro, and the French state's (and others') representation of it, in accord with Lefebvre's *l'espace conçu*.

Lefebvre has argued that every state is born from violence and that its power survives by further directing that violence. "Nationhood implies *violence* . . . a political power controlling and exploiting the resources of the market or the growth of the productive forces in order to maintain and further its rule." This violence is spatial in appearance. "Without the concepts of space and of its production, the framework of power simply cannot be realized. We are speaking of a space where centralized power sets itself above other power and eliminates it" (Lefebvre 1991, 112, 281). The violence of the state is transformed into a rationality of accumulation, bureaucracy, and military authority. Resources from colonial spaces (vanilla beans, dried coconut, human labor, and alluring images) are combined with those of the *métropole* (banks, post offices, ships, planes, and military complexes) and are ultimately linked to aggressive military endeavors (for example, nuclear testing).

It is essential that state violence not be viewed in isolation; it permeates everything and infiltrates every possible space, both material and imagined. It can be embedded in the most common, everyday things (for example, Hollywood films, candy bars, and postcard images), which many people fail to consider critically. Noncritical thought simply registers and accepts the resultant "reality," consenting to what Pierre Bourdieu has termed "symbolic violence" (Bourdieu 1988, 1990). Bourdieu describes this as an unconscious mode of domination that maintains its power precisely because people fail to recognize it as violence. Indeed, the more it is employed and "works," the more it becomes a "habitualized" part of the subconscious. Symbolic violence can be more powerful than overt physical violence because it is subtly embedded in everyday thought and action. This is "gentle, invisible violence, unrecognized as such, chosen as much as undergone [and present in] trust, obligation, personal loyalty, hospitality, gifts, debts, piety" (Bourdieu 1990, 127).

LAND ALIVE WITH MEANING

Ma'ohi notions of place, which lie at the heart of this struggle over place, are rooted in beliefs about the origin of the islands and the relationship between people and the land. In Polynesia, "land figures as equivalent to one's own body and family rather than as an inanimate object" (Teaiwa 2006, 74, referring to Trask 1987). This understanding is reflected in Polynesian languages, which differentiate between possessive pronouns for things one treats with deference and respect (such as land, one's house, one's blood relatives, or one's body) and those one can influence or dominate (such as a car, a computer, a fishnet, or even one's spouse). Ma'ohi ideas about the importance and inviolability of land are similar to those anthropologist Deborah Rose has described for the Aboriginal peoples of Australia, where "there is no place without a history; there is no place that has not been imaginatively grasped through song, dance, and design, no place where traditional owners cannot see the imprint of sacred creation" (Rose 1996, 18). As is the case for most Pacific Islanders, a Tahitian's sense of cultural identity is rooted in land.[2] Tahitians experience their land, with its precipitous mountains, lush valleys, and verdant vegetation, as alive with procreative powers and nurturing abilities. In the Ma'ohi cosmology, gods and goddesses gave birth to the islands, which then embodied their deities' procreative powers. The name of the island Huahine, for example, consists of a joining of the words for genitals or seeds (*hua*) and woman (*hine*). For Tahitians the island reverberates with godly fertility. Every time I crossed the bridge between the two islands that make up Huahine, my friends would point out the form of the pregnant woman in the outline of the mountains across the bay. They showed me how she lay on her back with her head, breasts, and womb bulging toward the sky (fig. 2.1), her legs hidden behind a mountain in the foreground.

They had me follow a straight line from the place where her vagina would have been to a nearby peak, which, they explained, was the gigantic phallus of Hiro, the god who split Huahine in two with his canoe (fig. 2.2). These topographical features were favorites of the tour guides, who enjoyed titillating tourists with the sudden view of "Hiro's phallus" as their tour van rounded a bend in the road. This narrative about the meaning of the landscape was the basis for a local joke: A tourist, who was hard of hearing, kept asking her husband, "What is the tour guide saying about that peak?" Her husband answered, loudly enough for his wife (and everyone else in the van) to hear, "I'll show you tonight."

Tahitians see these topographical features as maps of the ancestral wanderings that connect today's inhabitants to their past. The association between people, the land, genealogy, and history is nowhere more evident than in the many *marae* in the landscape. *Marae* are sacred temples dedicated to individual deities, and serve as portals for the deities when they descend to earth. Today usually all that remains of a *marae* is a rectangular area covered with paving stones, sometimes surrounded by low walls, with a line of

Fig. 2.1 Reclining woman in Huahine (from left to right: forehead, nose, neck, breast, and womb).

Fig. 2.2 Hiro's phallus, Huahine.

Fig. 2.3 *Marae Rauhuru* with altar of stones, Huahine.

upright stones, referred to as an altar, at one end (fig. 2.3). Upright stones in front of the altar, or sometimes elsewhere on the *marae*, indicate the genealogies of the *marae*'s creators. *Marae* are no longer used for religious rituals as they once were (see Ellis 1829; Tyerman 1831), but they continue to be deeply respected as sacred spaces. They mark the presence of deities and signify the history of the ancestors as they settled in new locations and established new *marae*. Ta'aroa, the Tahitian god of creation, for example, is present and visible in *marae* on different islands—his upper jaw is a *marae* on Bora Bora, his lower jaw is a *marae* on Huahine, and his throat and belly are a *marae* on Raiatea (Salmon 1904, 3).

Because the land provides Tahitians with the most basic needs for their survival and for the care of their children, it is seen as the mother who nourishes them. As mentioned, Tahitian beliefs about the nurturing properties of the land are revealed most poignantly by the custom of planting children's placentas (*pu fenua*, "core," "heart," "essence of the earth") and umbilical cords (*pito*, "navel") in the belly of the bountiful mother. Marama Teiho, a woman from Huahine who had given birth in her home to twenty-four children, explained this practice to me:

> The placenta is always replanted in the earth. When a child is in the womb the
> mother takes care of the child, but when it is born the mother asks the land
> to take care of her child. The land will give life to the child by providing food.
> There are lots of *pu fenua* here because I had many children, plus my children
> bring their children's placentas. You can bury the placenta and then move
> away. It doesn't matter where you live because you are still connected to your
> family's land.[3]

The placenta can also be buried on land that one doesn't own. As a Tahitian woman living in urban Papeʻete told me, "When I asked the doctor for the placenta he had no trouble giving it to me because everyone does that. I had to stay in the hospital five days, so the placenta was put in a plastic bag and refrigerated. Later I put it in the ground next to the house I rent in Papeʻete."[4]

The practice of planting the placenta in the land is a recurring theme in the novel *Island of Shattered Dreams*[5] by Tahitian writer/poet Chantal Spitz. When Tematua (a main character) is born, his father, Maevarua, plants Tematua's placenta. Spitz's description of the event indicates the syncretism of ancient Tahitian customs and contemporary Christian beliefs:

> On the day of his son's birth, Maevarua took the placenta and went alone
> to Toʻerauroa, the headland where even today stands proud the majestic
> Manunu, *marae* of the old order. He prayed to the heavens, asking for the
> protection of the spirits of the Fathers who still watch over the village, and the
> protection of the minister's God, who is only there on Sunday, the Lord's day.

> Benevolent spirits of the *marae,*
> You who have always protected our Fathers
> And who still watch over us today,
> I entrust to you the life of my son
> Newly arrived in our world.
> May your benevolence always be with him.
> May your light shine upon him.
> May your love enfold him.
> For in you is the source

Of our strength and our wisdom,
Since without you we are nothing.
I ask you humbly,
Help me to lead him in your light
Along the path of his life's journey,
And if I am weak, forgive me.

> Then as he has been taught, he finishes with the real prayer to the real God:
> *Our Father, which art in Heaven . . .*
> Tematua is now doubly protected, by the old order and the new world.
> (Spitz 2007, 23–24)

Spitz then describes the rites that Maevarua performs. He opens up the belly of the bountiful mother, places the placenta tenderly within it, plants a *tumu ʻuru* (breadfruit sapling) on top of the placenta, and replaces the soil.

> The placenta nourished Tematua inside Teuira [his mother], the *tumu ʻuru* will nourish him through his life as a man. This is the union of man with the earth into which he thrusts his roots, the union of the earth with man who makes his food spring forth from her belly. (Spitz 2007, 24)

Years later, when Tematua goes to France to serve in the French army, his mother gives him a bamboo container with earth from his motherland to carry with him. As Tematua leaves, his father says,

Tematua my son,
On the day of your birth,
I entrusted your *pito* [umbilical cord] to your land,
And now on this day
I entrust your body and your spirit
To the limitless ocean,
The sacred *marae* of our people,
With its many caresses,
Its thousand faces,
Its bottomless deeps.
. . .
Remember, Tematua,
That the land is here, eternally,

And that we keep it for your return.
(Spitz 2007, 30)

When Tematua returns to Tahiti five years later, he longs to reconnect with his land. As he walks on Tahitian soil, he feels the strength of the land flowing back into him through the soles of his feet and suddenly understands why France had always felt foreign to him. It was because "he spent the whole time wearing shoes, cramping his feet, too wide from their long freedom, into those coarse and heavy instruments of torture which prevent the land from communicating with those it carries" (Spitz 2007, 34).

Still later, when Tematua becomes a father, he in turn repeats the timeless act of uniting his children with their land. When his daughter is born, "he takes her with him and speaks to her before he unites her with her Land. . . . He joins to her placenta an 'ora [which refers to a banyan tree, but also means "life" or "health"] with many meanings and implications" (Spitz 2007, 61).

The relationship between people and land, exemplified by the act of planting the placenta, is *always* reciprocal. People must care for the land because the land, in turn, nourishes people by providing the foods and other materials they need. A person's health and well-being are dependent on the land and, in fact, can be seen as extensions of it. The traditional medicines for curing illnesses are made from products of the land, another reflection of the interdependence of the land with its people.

Because the land embodies such deep meaning (spirituality, ancestral connections, family history, and cultural identity) as well as providing nourishment, medicine, and shelter, Tahitians are known to respond passionately when their land is threatened.[6] For example, in 2000, the Sheraton Moʻorea Lagoon Resort and Spa (then the Outrigger Hotel) announced plans to create an artificial beach and build thirty-one overwater bungalows—actions that would chase away the fish and disturb the coral ecosystem. Local residents responded with a three-month protest. Fishermen in canoes surrounded the dredge that would suck up the sand used to create the new beach. On shore, families set up a camp and placed signs by the road alerting tourists and others to the social and environmental injustice occurring as a result of this tourism development. Eventually the hotel was ordered to remove the dredge.[7]

Protests can also be more indirect, yet equally effective; they can be as subtle as a pothole in the road. On Huahine, the French manager of one of the most luxurious hotels (built on prized land that included a *marae* and access to fishing grounds) routinely ignored the concerns and complaints of local residents. When he wanted to import staff from France, food from Pape'ete, and souvenir shell necklaces from the Philippines, local residents spoke quietly but effectively through their respect for and use of the land. Tourists being taken to the hotel and their $500-per-night overwater bungalows had an uncomfortable journey as their van had to slow down and weave a path through the many large potholes in the dirt road to the hotel—because the Tahitian owners of the land refused to allow it to be maintained.

Although land provides Tahitians with a sense of place and identity, most Tahitians also believe that there is a spiritual and complementary association between land and sea. As I was told by more than one person, "We need both. From the land we get taro, yams, and breadfruit. From the sea we get fish and seafood." This belief in the complementarity of land and sea is reflected in the Tahitian practice of bringing large pieces of coral to add to the stones at a *marae*.[8]

BUILDUP AND FALLOUT OF NUCLEAR TESTING

Always present during the colonial history of Tahiti were conflicts between Tahitian ideas about land as nurturing mother and Western ideas about land as expendable resource. These tensions were greatly exacerbated by the arrival of the nuclear testing program and the increase in international tourism—events that were to be more destructive of the environment and dangerous to human health than anything that had occurred previously.

In 1958 a referendum was held to determine if the Territory should maintain its ties to France. Many Polynesians, influenced by threats of losing French financial and technical assistance, were persuaded to vote in favor of continued ties (Aldrich 1993, 176). This coincided with the change in the colony's name from Établissements Français d'Océanie (EFO) to La Polynésie Française (French Polynesia) in 1957 and became one of the most critical turning points in Tahitian colonial history (see Aldrich 1996, 302). Along with this new name and status came several changes in France's relationship to its Territory. France had been conducting its nuclear testing program in Algeria, which in 1954 had begun what became a successful eight-year struggle for independence. Realizing that it would need to find another testing site, the French government cast its eye toward La Polynésie Française, no doubt influenced by the United States, which had been testing in the Pacific (in the Marshall Islands) since 1946. Implementing these new plans, France deepened its political and military entanglement with its colony, transforming Tahiti from a peaceful island to a site of massive military installations.

To facilitate the movement of military personnel and equipment needed for the nuclear testing program, an airport capable of landing large jet aircraft was built at Faaʻa, about three miles southwest of Papeʻete. A large part of the lagoon was filled in to create the land needed for the runway. The new airport—L'Aéroport International Tahiti Faaʻa—opened in 1960. Soon thereafter, headquarters and support facilities for the nuclear testing program were built in Papeʻete. To expand the port, another large area of lagoon was filled in adjacent to Motu Uta, which had once been a small island belonging to Queen Pomare. These expansions included new docks to shelter and service the numerous ships that would be required to sustain and supply the nuclear testing program. A causeway was also built to connect Motu Uta to the mainland, creating a large area that was used for a French naval base, an arsenal, customs offices, and other administrative services.

In 1963 (the year after Algeria's independence), with the new infrastructure in place in Tahiti, president Charles de Gaulle established the Centre d'Expérimentations du Pacifique (CEP), the organization responsible for conducting the nuclear tests. A year later, ignoring the Territorial Assembly and without a popular vote, President de Gaulle claimed sovereignty over Moruroa and Fangataufa (map 3), two uninhabited atolls about 700 miles east of Tahiti in the Tuamotu Archipelago (Aldrich and Connell 1998, 185; Firth and Von Strokirch 1997, 343). Moruroa was chosen because it had a wide pass into the lagoon that could accommodate large ships. He announced that these atolls would become the new test sites, specifying that, should the nuclear testing program be discontinued, the atolls would be returned to the Territory along with the buildings and other "material" left on the site.[9]

A support base was built on Hao atoll, 550 miles east of Papeʻete and 280 miles from Moruroa and Fangataufa. The work on Hao included an airport, a large naval port, military installations, and housing for the roughly 700 people who were involved in the testing. Hao served as the main staging area for the testing program, as it was deemed prudent for personnel to spend as little time as possible on Moruroa or Fangataufa, especially during the period of atmospheric testing.

Attracted by high salaries, as well as free food and housing, about 3,000 Tahitian men signed on to work at the test sites on Moruroa and Fangataufa, initially building airstrips, blockhouses, and other military facilities. This infusion of large amounts of cash led to an unprecedented economic boom

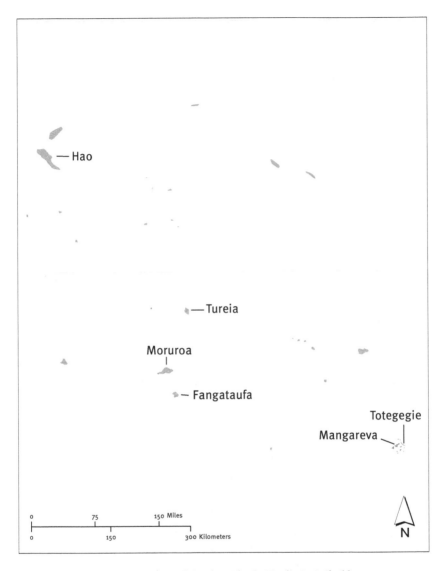

— Hao

— Tureia

Moruroa

— Fangataufa

Totegegie

Mangareva

0   75   150 Miles

0   150   300 Kilometers

N

Map 3   The Southeastern Tuamotu and Gambier Islands. Map by Amir Sheikh.

in the Territory. "Contractors were swamped with orders, hardware shops did land office business, homes were built by the hundreds, and the standard (and cost) of living was given a sharp boost upwards" (Covit 1968, 181).

In 1966 France began atmospheric testing on Moruroa, refusing to agree to the 1963 agreement (by the United States, the Soviet Union, and Britain) to halt atmospheric tests and instead to shift to underground testing (it was not until 1974 that France moved its tests below ground).[10] In response, on September 7, 1966, deputy of Polynesia John Teariki "pronounced a very virulent indictment against the nuclear tests in front of General de Gaulle, who came to [French Polynesia to] 'push the button' for the next blast over Moruroa" (Barrillot and Doom 2005, 373).[11]

Less well known were the installations in the Gambier Archipelago, where in 1968 construction began on the inhabited main island of Mangareva and the outlying islet of Totegegie. The activity there was fraudulently described to Tahitians as creating a test site for rockets, not nuclear bombs (Barrillot 2002, 115). The facilities on Totegegie included an airstrip, a port, a desalinization plant, water reservoirs, radio and meteorological stations, supply hangars, cement dikes, and a radiation analysis station (*Le journal de Tahiti*, March 8, 1969). On the island of Mangareva a bunker with meter-thick walls was built for sheltering the military and the island's inhabitants from radioactive fallout during the nuclear tests (Barrillot 2002, 113).

Ironically, the Tahitian name for the island on which most of the testing occurred—*moruroa*—means "big lies." Moruroa, which the French renamed Mururoa, became shrouded in secrecy. It was off-limits to everyone except authorized personnel. The French government claimed that the testing posed absolutely no environmental or health dangers. Tahitians I knew who had worked on Moruroa, however, told me about local bans on the consumption of fish from the lagoon and food from the land, and about people being sick after disregarding the prohibitions. I also learned that it was mandatory for visitors to carry Geiger counters and to wear special anti-radiation suits while there (Constance Cody, personal communication, 1995). One man, who had worked at Moruroa, recalled that during the tests the French workers were ensconced in thick cement bunkers, whereas the Tahitians were often left on open-air platforms. "We were given masks to protect ourselves, but the masks were so small and useless that we rolled them up and played volleyball with them" (Maitititi Faatau, personal communication, 2010). In spite of the government's policy of making local health statistics top secret (B. and M.-T. Danielsson 1986, 307), it has been well documented that the incidence of health problems had skyrocketed. Within a decade after testing began, such typically radiation-induced diseases as leukemia, thyroid cancers, brain tumors, and eye cataracts began to appear in alarming numbers (B. and M. Danielsson 1993, 649; Tetiarahi 2005, 379).[12] Tureia, the atoll closest to Moruroa (about seventy-five miles to the north), buried one-third of its adult population between 1997 and 2002, all victims of cancer (Ista 2002,

34). By 2010 30 percent of the people who worked at Moruroa had become ill with cancer (Bruno Barriott, personal communication, 2010).

The land, too, was destroyed. Radiation leaked, fissures opened, and in some places the land sank below sea level. There was permanent damage to the food-producing trees and plants. One man, who had worked on Moruroa, recalled his experience:

> I remember how once, three days after an explosion, we returned to Moruroa. But what a shock! The vegetation was all razed to the ground. All that remained were some burned trees. The spot where we had been before was completely wiped out. The little island with the barrier reef had disappeared. The metal tower behind the bunker had melted at its base and was lying flat in the sun. We were forbidden from walking wherever we wanted, and could only go in the concrete zones, which, we were told, had been decontaminated. (quoted in Barrillot 2003, 190–91)

The land/*te fenua*, otherwise seen as Tahitians' main source of nourishment, was poisoned. Vaihere Bordes (the coordinator of women's activities at the Tahitian human rights NGO, Hiti Tau) referred to the custom of mothers planting placentas in the earth when she said, "It is the same thing the French Government is doing with the bomb. They plant it in the motherland—but they plant poison" (Fitzpatrick 1995, 42).

By the time nuclear tests were finally stopped in January 1996—after thirty years of nearly uninterrupted testing—France had conducted a total of 192 tests (46 atmospheric and 146 subterranean) in French Polynesia (Barrillot 2002).[13] Some of the bombs held yields of up to two hundred kilotons, more than ten times the size of the bomb that destroyed Hiroshima, with each test costing an average of US$20 million (Sancton 1995, 23).

The testing activities had profound effects that reverberated throughout French Polynesia. A "cash" economy was one of the most significant. Tahitians, who previously farmed and fished and had little need for money, now had jobs with salaries that allowed them to purchase food and shelter. The large influx of money created a booming economy.[14] Many other changes followed. The number of metropolitan French, attracted by salaries much larger than they would receive in France,[15] increased greatly. French and old-line demi families (families of mixed Tahitian and European ancestry) began amassing large incomes from their control of land and commerce. Mass migration from the outer islands to the island of Tahiti occurred as people sought employment in the new cash economy. All of this rapidly transformed Pape'ete. This included an increase in amenities that made the French population feel at home (for example, bakeries for the production of baguettes and supermarkets that stocked imported French foods like butter, cheese, and truffles). Between 1960 and 1970 the population of Pape'ete almost doubled, creating a demand for housing that was not met, and resulting in a number of squatter settlements within the city. The Territory was now importing most of its food, with only a small number of people (mainly those living on the outer islands) still relying on gardening and fishing. In a few short years, many Tahitians had become almost completely dependent on the money that France pumped into the Territory, through both the Centre d'Expérimentations du Pacifique (CEP) and the resulting increase in administrative costs to cope with a growing urban population of Tahitians and French immigrants.

Because of this increasing dependence on a cash economy, today many Tahitians have developed creative solutions that allow them to maximize their economic options at the local level (see Lockwood 1993). For example, a friend on Huahine explained how his family had to augment their subsistence farming:

> It's like having a water tank. You can't rely on just one faucet. You need to have many faucets so that you can tap into them at different times. The garden is just one. But you don't just have a garden, or you don't just plant one thing. You plant yams to eat. You plant melons to sell in the market. You plant flowers to sell to the hotel. You plant vanilla to sell to tourists. You also bake cakes for people who need a cake to celebrate a birthday. You cook food to sell in the market. You sew clothes and sell these too. If you have a water tank, you don't just put a faucet at the top. You have to put many faucets on the tank: one at the top, one lower down, one over here, one over there. That's how you do it. (Édouard Piha, personal communication, 2001)

After the establishment of the CEP, land, too, gradually slipped from Tahitians' control when some people took advantage of opportunities to earn money by selling their land. Between 1971 and 1983 the price of land multiplied eightfold (Toullelan and Gille 1992, 138). Those who purchased the land were primarily real estate agents who then sold the land to French, Chinese, and other nonindigenous buyers (Tetiarahi 1987, 54). One friend described her view of this spiraling descent into dependency and the related loss of land:

> Before CEP, Tahitians lived well. They worked in their gardens. They went fishing. They built their houses. After the first test in 1966 Tahitians became dependent on money. Now they need money in order to live. They buy their food. They buy cement and sheet metal to build their houses. Tahitians buy more and more things but how can they pay for everything? They can't. They go to the bank and get a loan. Then how can they pay back the bank? They can't. After a while the bank comes and takes their land and sells it. Who buys the land? Foreigners. Later where do the Tahitians live? They have no land. No house. They end up living in a tiny shack. Tahitians have gotten lazy. They don't grow their own food anymore. They buy it in the store. If they want Tahitian food they buy it in the market. I go to the market every Sunday to sell my Tahitian food. Do you know who buys it? Tahitians. Every week I get sad when I see that. (Kim Tai Piha, personal communication, 1995)

ARRIVAL OF TOURISM AND ITS IMAGERY

With the nuclear testing program firmly under way, and all of its accompanying ramifications and transformations, another new project began—the French Polynesian government's investment in tourism. The airport, which had been built to support the nuclear testing program, made it much easier for Western tourists to come in search of the paradise they had been dreaming about but which had previously been too difficult and expensive to visit (see Kahn 2000). As supplies and personnel for the CEP were channeled through the airport and harbor en route to the outer islands of Moruroa, Fangataufa, and Hao, tourists began arriving in increasing numbers. Before the construction of the international airport there was very little in the way of an organized tourism industry. Traveling to Tahiti was time-intensive, and the market was restricted to the most wealthy and adventurous. If tourists wanted to travel by ship, there were only a few luxury liners that traveled to Tahiti.[16] To reach Tahiti by plane was even more difficult. Before 1959 a tourist had only two such options: to fly with the New Zealand airline Tasman Empires Air Lines by way of Fiji over the "coral route" or to go by seaplane through Western Samoa and the Cook Islands. Either route required a journey of several days from Europe or the United States.[17] In 1959 the French airline Transports Aériens Intercontinentaux established a route via the World War II landing strip on Bora Bora. From there, tourists still had to travel to the island of Tahiti by boat. Once they were on Tahiti, the very few hotels that existed were only in Pape'ete and did not cater to tourists.

The opening of the Faa'a international airport brought dramatic changes to tourism. Fewer than 1,500 tourists had come to Tahiti in 1959.[18] A year later, after the airport was in operation, more than 4,000 arrived, and by the following year there were close to 9,000 (Covit 1968, 113). Each succeeding year witnessed significant increases in the number of tourists (most of whom were Americans), and several luxury hotels were built to accommodate them. The creation of "authentic"-looking hotel décor became a booming business, some of which was contracted out to commercial firms in the United States.[19] In 1966, L'Office de Développement du Tourisme was created. Also, for the first time, an official guidebook, *Official Directory and Guide Book: Tahiti,* was produced so that (as stated in its forward) tourists—unlike Wallis, Bougainville, and Cook two hundred years earlier—did not have to do the discovering on their own (Covit 1968, 5). "From that time on, a tourist policy was progressively elaborated and tourism was promoted to the rank of the great pillars on which the Territory's economy was to repose" (Robineau 1975, 63).[20]

It was also at this time that a young French woman, Paulette Viénot, established Agence Tahiti Nui Travel in Pape'ete, the first, and still the largest and most successful, of Tahiti's travel agencies. Viénot—later to become known as Tahiti's "queen of tourism"—was there in person to meet many of the tourists when they arrived at the new airport, present them with flower garlands, and escort them to their hotels.

One of the most popular forms of tourist entertainment in Tahiti has always been dance, an activity that has helped create the image of Tahiti as an exotic and erotic destination. It was Viénot who first introduced dance as an essential aspect of entertainment. She arranged bus tours around the island so tourists could see more of Tahiti and, while they were on the bus, gave them flower garlands, champagne, and cashews. The end of each tour culminated with a dance performance. As she explained, "When we got to Tautira at the other end of Tahiti we took a canoe to a small island, to which I had sent all my dancers ahead. That way when the tourists stepped from the canoes onto the island they heard dancing and music and were very surprised. It was very popular" (Paulette Viénot, personal communication, 2001).

Soon thereafter, in addition to becoming the most popular form of tourist entertainment, dance also became the main aspect of Tahitian culture that was chosen to represent and promote Tahiti in other countries. Dance became, and remains, integral to the promotion of tourism, with government-sponsored dance troupes traveling to tourism trade shows in Europe and the United States.[21] At her waterfront home in Pape'ete, Viénot held many dance events that were organized to promote tourism. In fact, tourists' fascination with dance led her to establish Tahiti Nui, the first official dance troupe, which stayed together for thirty-five years, touring the United States for several months at a time (Paulette Viénot, personal communication, 2001). Through her tour groups, dance troupes, and details such as flower garlands and champagne, Viénot helped align the Tahiti of the tourists' imaginations with the Tahiti they were experiencing. Her proactive undertakings were excellent examples within Tahiti's early tourism industry of the interplay between *l'espace perçu* and *l'espace conçu*.

The myth of Tahiti, ever present in the Western imagination, is the fuel that propels Tahiti's tourism industry. Today tourism is the largest private industry and the main source of foreign exchange for the Territory, generating roughly US$250 million annually (see Kahn 2003).[22] Consequently, the production of imagery that reinforces and validates the myth is critically important to the economy of French Polynesia. The challenge that Tahiti faces is how to maintain the myth, especially in the face of growing global influences. The greatest test for Tahiti's tourism marketing is that it must respond directly to the gulf between what actually exists and what tourists (inspired by the images) expect. As the reality of how life is lived in Tahiti today diverges further from the Tahiti of the imagination, the need for the myth becomes ever more crucial for the economy.

As the tourism industry has grown, images portraying a romantic and increasingly accessible Tahiti have appeared in new, more mediated forms, targeted to an audience that is ever more global. The 1789 mutiny on the HMS *Bounty* provides one example. A year after the airport opened, Hollywood crews arrived in Tahiti to portray these events in the film *Mutiny on the Bounty*, a production that took ten months, employed 10,000 local people, and cost US$27 million (Robineau 1975, 62). The result was a three-hour color film starring Marlon Brando (as Fletcher Christian) and Tarita Teri'ipaia, a Tahitian woman (who played Christian's lover and, later, his wife). In contrast to the 1935 black-and-white version filmed in Hawai'i, the 1962 film was shot on location on Tahiti and Bora Bora, bringing Tahiti—in vivid Technicolor—into movie theaters around the world. Highlighting the

Fig. 2.4 Bounty Bar Wrapper, 2006 (Mars Incorporated).

natural beauty of the islands and the physical attraction of Tahitians, the film reinforced the myth and its tantalizing promise of an earthly paradise. Later Marlon Brando married his costar Tarita Teri'ipaia and purchased for his private home Tetiaroa, a picture-perfect atoll twenty-five miles north of Tahiti. For many, this conflation of the myth and reality charged their imaginations and intensified their longings for an escape to "paradise." Indeed, an eco-resort, called The Brando, is currently being built on Tetiaroa, with completion scheduled for 2011. It will have forty-seven deluxe bungalows, each with its own private plunge pool, as well as a spa and fitness center.[23]

In 1952, the European subsidiary of the Mars Company produced a chocolate-covered, coconut-filled candy bar named Bounty, evoking not only the mutiny but also the idea of a trophy. On the original wrapper was an image of an island with coconut palms, and the tag line "a taste of paradise" (see fig. 2.4 for the contemporary version). For nearly a half century (1951–97) advertisements for the Bounty bar (often filmed in countries such as Mexico and Sierra Leone, but never French Polynesia) blurred the lines between biting into the candy bar, finding oneself on a tropical island, and discovering the "bounty" of sexual liaisons under coconut palms on the beach (Musée National des Arts d'Afrique et d'Océanie 2001–2). This promotion became one of the most famous and enduring in the history of confectionary advertising. Although not everyone eating the candy bar will recognize or ponder the source of the name, people do often associate it with a tropical paradise. As one Bounty enthusiast stated on a Bounty Hunter Web site, "Advertising for this chocolate must be very effective. . . . I get carried away with dreams of sun, sea, sand and bronzed muscle men feeding me chocolate-covered coconut with their teeth . . . when I see the bars on the shelf in the shop."[24]

By the late 1960s many coordinated forces had been set in motion to respond to tourists and their dreams and expectations—the new airport, L'Office de Développement du Tourisme, Agence Tahiti Nui Travel, guidebooks, hotels, and dance groups. In addition, the film *Mutiny on the Bounty* and the advertisements for the Bounty candy bar fired people's fantasies, which could potentially become "realities" with the purchase of an airline ticket. These series of events remind us that state power cannot be viewed in isolation or only in its most obvious forms but that it also permeates everything and infiltrates every space, both material and imagined. The subtlest everyday items, such as a Hollywood movie or a candy bar, weave themselves into the unconscious, as indicated by the Bounty customer who, upon seeing the candy bar in the shop, was instantly transported to the "reality" in her mind.

STAYING IN THE POSTCARD

Ironically, as tourists were arriving in increasing numbers in search of Gauguin's paradise, Tahiti was becoming radically transformed, diverging further from the imagined Tahiti that had caused them to visit. Mass migration of people from the outer islands to Pape'ete resulted in previously unknown phenomena, such as squatter settlements, unemployment, and poverty. Increased commerce meant that traffic started choking the streets of the city. The participation by more people in a cash-based economy led to greater dependence on imported foods. Instead of spending their time fishing and gardening in ways that tourists would have anticipated, and would have found picturesque, Tahitians were now walking out of stores with bags of imported groceries. Television was also introduced into French Polynesia at this time, and stores sprang up selling televisions and radios. An evening walk in a remote village, which prior to this time would have been lit mainly by moonlight, was now illuminated by the flickering glow of household televisions. The more Tahiti changed as a result of a cash economy, the greater was the effort needed to maintain its mythical image. The new weight given to tourism as the economic backbone of the Territory meant that representing Tahiti as a pristine paradise was of paramount importance. Thus, it is not surprising that the production of images and other representations designed to support and enhance the myth became a major undertaking.

Postcards provide a wonderful example of how the myth has been maintained.[25] Whereas the postcards of the pre-tourist period of the early 1900s featured images that glorified and validated French colonial endeavors, images produced during this second period of postcard efflorescence, which arose in the 1960s and 1970s, served a different purpose. Rather than validate

French colonial practices, images used on postcards now sought to camou-
flage their consequences. To fuel the myth, postcard producers employed
many of the usual photographic techniques. Shots were framed to eliminate
items that were inconsistent with the myth. Settings were staged with "traditional" props. When necessary, original images would be altered to erase
discrepancies. The images produced were, and for the most part continue to
be, of seemingly pristine landscapes, luxury hotels, folkloric activities, and
attractive Tahitian women. Postcards from both periods—whether valoriz-
ing or camouflaging colonial activities—have been an integral and strategic aspect of France's economic and political agenda for the Territory. Two
people have played especially prominent roles in the post-1960s production
of postcards in French Polynesia. One is Teva Sylvain, the son of a renowned
French photographer and a Tahitian mother, who, as the founder and chief
executive of Pacific Promotion Tahiti, began producing postcards in 1974.
The other is Diane Commons, an American who moved to Tahiti in 1995 and
created a company called Blu for the production of her postcards.

Teva is best known for his images of seductive *vahine* and idyllic scenery, which appear not only on postcards but also on calendars, posters, place
mats, coasters, address book covers, rulers, cigarette lighters, ashtrays, playing cards, stationery, books, and screen savers for computer monitors. He
said, "I create images that I think people want to buy. I come up with an idea
and then test it on the market. If an image sells well, I produce more. If it
doesn't sell, I take it off the market" (Teva Sylvain, personal communication,
1995). He explained his marketing strategies for his popular *vahine* images,
for which he uses professional models.[26] "Most of the women are not fully
Tahitian because the men who visit Tahiti want a woman they already possess in their head or in their libido. They want one who looks like women
they are used to. They don't want her skin to be too dark, her nose too broad,
or her thighs too strong." As a result, the women on the postcards have an
assortment of ethnic backgrounds.[27] As Teva pulled a postcard off the top of
a stack on his desk (fig. 2.5), he said,

Look at #911. She is one hundred percent French. But I put the crown of leaves
on her head, a garland of flowers around her neck, and a coconut-leaf basket
in her hands to give her a Tahitian look. That's all it takes. Other than those
props, there's nothing Tahitian about her. (Teva Sylvain, personal communication, 1995)

Fig. 2.5 Postcard
#911, 1994. Photo by
Teva Sylvain, Pacific
Promotion, Tahiti.
Photo courtesy of
Pacific Promotion.

Although rationalizing that he was only manipulating the market, he seemed very aware that, in doing so, he was also reconfiguring the very image of Tahiti and Tahitian women. He admitted that "the women of one's dreams that one admires in my lascivious poses are not found on every street corner" (Sylvain 1994, 64).

Diane Commons began to produce postcards because she objected to the sexist character of Teva Sylvain's portrayal of women. She thought that postcard images could be produced that broadened the way Tahiti was portrayed, beyond women and beaches. She soon realized, however, that she was unable to influence the market. As she explained,

Fig. 2.6   Pristine Polynesian afternoon, Diane Commons, 2002. Photo courtesy of Diane Commons.

I started producing postcards because I thought that what was on the market was inadequate. From an artistic perspective, there wasn't enough choice. Everything seemed to be Teva Sylvain's images. From a female perspective, I found his images offensive. I tried to do something more elegant that would focus on the folkloric side of Tahiti. I wanted to produce images of things like old homes, older women, the church environment, and the different colors that are here. But I quickly found out that the images I wanted to project to the world no one else wanted. (Diane Commons, personal communication, 2001)

She also came to the realization that for her business to survive she, like Teva, needed to be guided by sales statistics. As she explained, "This business is costly so the postcards need to sell. I knew people wanted pictures of the white-sand beaches and coconut palms, but I didn't know it would be that exaggerated. I no longer produce what I want. Instead, I need to produce what sells." For example, she explained that one of her paradise-like images of Bora Bora's lagoon sells fifty times more than the folkloric image of the fish traps still used by the people on Huahine.

Ironically, Diane, who started her business with the idea of providing an alternative to the existing repertoire of postcards, soon began to construct her postcard images with as much of a strategic eye to detail as Teva Sylvain. Diane explained the lengths to which she had to go to edit visually what has turned out to be one of her most popular blue lagoon images (fig. 2.6), musing about the irony of the situation and her own complicity in it:

> On the one hand, these beautiful postcard images really do exist. French Poly-
> nesia is very diverse and there are places, like the Tuamotu Islands, that really
> look like this with the beautiful white-sand beaches. But, on the other hand,
> the images on the postcards don't represent a reality. They're just an image, a
> dream. I try to create only beautiful images. That's the challenge. And, believe
> me, sometimes it's a big challenge. See this image of the blue lagoon. I had to
> walk through filth and stand in piles of trash in marijuana fields to take this
> picture. It was so ironic. If anyone had seen what I was doing they would have
> been amazed. I had to walk through a very impoverished area to get there, with
> dirty diapers and garbage all around, and people in really poor health. Imag-
> ine! I was trying to set up my tripod in the middle of the trash, surrounded by
> young men guarding their marijuana fields, just to get that beautiful image.
> What I saw through my lens was so majestic, so serene, and so beautiful. And
> there I was standing in the trash. Those two extremes really do exist in Tahiti.
> But, for my postcards, I have to focus on only one. Tourists want to stay in the
> postcard. (Diane Commons, personal communication, 2001)

RATTLING THE LID OF THE CAULDRON

Pristine postcard images serve, among other things, to conceal more contentious realities. Beneath the seemingly calm surface a political storm can be
brewing—fueled by opposing understandings of land/*te fenua*. As a friend
from Huahine told me during a period of nuclear testing,

> I am so angry all the time that I cannot sleep at night. Tahitians are angry
> about the nuclear testing and the way it is obscured. Tahitians may appear
> calm and not show their anger for a long time. But it is like a cyclone. Things
> are calm at first. Then suddenly there will be a storm and everything will
> shake and rattle. There will always be some people who sit quietly on the side
> with their eyes closed and say that nothing is happening. Tahitians feel the
> most anger towards these people on the sidelines—their fellow Tahitians who

have been bought and bribed by the government. I predict that there will be a revolution one day. It won't simply be Tahitians against the French; it will be Tahitians fighting against Tahitian traitors as well as against the French. (Norbert Itchner, personal communication, 1995)

Lefebvre uses the apt phrase "rattling the lid of the cauldron" in discussing this confrontational energy. In colonized spaces there are "forces on the boil" because the rationality of the state, its techniques, and programs provoke opposition. Whenever these negative forces emerge, they do so explosively. "These seething forces are still capable of rattling the lid of the cauldron of the state and its space, for differences can never be totally quieted. Though defeated, they live on, and from time to time they begin fighting ferociously to reassert themselves and transform themselves through struggle" (Lefebvre 1991, 23).

During my fieldwork in 1995, the lid of the cauldron was indeed rattling furiously. On June 13, 1995, French president Jacques Chirac ended former president François Mitterrand's three-year moratorium on nuclear testing in French Polynesia by declaring that testing would resume within a few months. The rationale was that these additional tests would allow for the perfection of simulations and computer modeling techniques that would make future testing unnecessary. As Gabriel Tetiarahi (delegate of Te Hui Ti'ama and president of the Human Rights League at the time) has written,

> His irrevocable decision caused concern and dismay. Without bothering at all to first consult the Polynesian people, he committed an act of gratuitous violence. . . . It felt like a planned assassination of the child—all the future generations carried by the mothers in their wombs, their *pu fenua*—by the new occupant of the Elysée. (Tetiarahi 2005, 378)

Typically, the international media tend to ignore political events in far-flung French Polynesia. The announcement that nuclear testing was to resume, however, caused a worldwide uproar. Resumption of testing was seen as further evidence of France's unwillingness to join with the rest of the international community to end nuclear testing of any kind. In anticipation, journalists and television reporters from all over the world came to Tahiti. Greenpeace, an organization dedicated to the elimination of all nuclear weapons, arrived with its ship, the *Rainbow Warrior II* (with a crew representing ten countries). This was seen as a very provocative act, given that the original *Rainbow Warrior* was blown up, killing one person, by French agents of the Direction Générale de la Sécurité Extérieure in Auckland, New Zealand, in 1985.

Within days of President Chirac's announcement, antinuclear protests began on a scale unprecedented in the history of French Polynesia.[28] On June 29, a crowd estimated to be between 15,000 and 20,000 people took to the streets of Pape'ete, demanding a referendum on whether nuclear testing should resume. Oscar Temaru, then mayor of Faa'a and the leader of Tavini Huira'atira (the pro-independence party), led the demonstrations. Blockades were set up along the main roads into the city. People sat down in the streets and played their ukuleles. Traffic came to a halt. The protests lasted until July 2, the twenty-ninth anniversary of the first nuclear test at Moruroa. In the words of one member of the crew of the *Rainbow Warrior II*, "The commitment of the people is amazing—sitting all day through thirty-five degree [centigrade] heat, and then sleeping on hard asphalt all night" (Leney 1995). Protests began again on July 14, the French national holiday of Bastille Day and the height of Tahiti's annual Heiva (a month-long, interisland festival that features dance competitions, art displays, beauty contests, sport competitions, feasting, and partying). The protests were so disruptive that the Heiva festivities had to be postponed for a week.

As a result of the media's comprehensive coverage of the protests, as well as the near-universal moral opposition to nuclear testing, the entire world was suddenly listening, watching, and responding. People burned croissants and stomped on French bread in the United States, picketed French restaurants in Hong Kong, bombed one French consulate and delivered a truckload of manure to another in Australia, demonstrated in Chile, and held an antinuclear testing rock concert in Belgium (Gluckman 1995). Even in France, two-thirds of the population was opposed to the resumption of testing (Lewis 2005), and former President Mitterrand publicly condemned President Chirac's decision. Yet, in spite of these local and global protests, the governments of both France and French Polynesia remained committed to resumption of the testing.

These two governments continued to assert that the testing caused no harm to people or the environment. To demonstrate this, the president of French Polynesia, Gaston Flosse, invited political leaders, including Oscar Temaru (who declined the invitation), to a "picnic" on Moruroa. A few days later, *La dépêche de Tahiti* (the Territory's principal newspaper, which, although privately owned, is strongly supportive of the government's views) published a two-page article about Moruroa and Fangataufa with the headline "Les poissons étaient bien du lagon!" (Fish in the lagoon are fine; *La dépêche de Tahiti* 1995a, 16). The article included photos of government officials drinking from coconuts, catching fish, and posing in front of fifty barbecued lobsters. Prominent was a photo of President Flosse relaxing in Moruroa's lagoon.

In August, there were several more (but smaller) peaceful protest marches in Pape'ete. The largest was organized by l'Église Évangélique de Polynésie Française (the Protestant Church), the dominant church in French Polynesia. Their president, Jacques Ihorai, prayed for an end to the testing. As September approached (the month in which the nuclear tests were scheduled to resume), a large number of journalists from around the world returned to French Polynesia.

At 11:30 on the morning of September 5, 1995, with no warning to the public, Operation Thetis was carried out at Moruroa—an explosion with a power that was only slightly less than that at Hiroshima. It generated temperatures of several hundred million degrees and pressures of several million atmospheres. The instruments that recorded the explosion transmitted data for only a billionth of a second before they were destroyed by the blast (Sancton 1995, 27). That night, as friends and I watched the television news, we saw a crowd of reporters as they fired questions at the director of CEP, Admiral Jean Lichère, who appeared in his crisp white naval uniform bedecked with medals. He explained matter-of-factly that at 11:30 they had received orders from Paris to push the button. He said that there had been no noise, just a minor shaking of the ground for three seconds, some slight agitation in the sea with waves and geysers, and then everything was calm and "back to normal." The test was "for the stability of the world, to insure security for everyone," he declared. "It will have no significant impact on the environment." When reporters pressed him about why he didn't test the bomb in France, he responded with the standard phrase, "Mais, c'est la France!" (But this is France!). He then deflected further inquiries by claiming, "One can't even call this a bomb. It's nuclear physics."

Although the Moruroa lagoon had quieted down, the explosion sent loud waves of rage and indignation throughout French Polynesia and the world. In Pape'ete in the following thirty-six hours, rioting, burning, and looting took place. About thirty Tahitian women began an antinuclear testing sit-in on the airport runway (literally and symbolically the tourism gateway), which gathered strength when several hundred Tahitian men joined them (Strokirch 1997, 228). Provoked by tear gas fired into the crowd, some protestors seized a bulldozer and drove it into the terminal building, demolishing walls and shattering windows, before setting the terminal on fire, making it impossible for planes to land or take off. After wrecking the airport terminal, the demonstrators moved into downtown Papeʻete, torching buildings, smashing windows, and looting stores. More than 120 cars were overturned and set afire. Stones, steel barricades, garbage bins, and bottles were hurled at the office of the high commissioner, the highest-ranking French official in French Polynesia. Police tried to surround and arrest the demonstrators, many of whom were jailed. Military personnel were brought in from France and New Caledonia to augment those already in Tahiti. Damage was estimated to be around US$40 million. Fortunately, only forty people were injured, none seriously.

A phrase used repeatedly by the local media during this explosive period was that the images of the riots *ont fait le tour du monde* (had gone on a world tour). The words "Fallout in Paradise" graced the cover of the international edition of *Time* magazine (September 18, 1995), and inside were many photographs of the effects of the riot. The Territorial government, ignoring concerns about the events that prompted the demonstrations and riots, chose to blame foreign reporters for the worldwide dissemination of these "ugly" images. Not only was this bottom-up production and distribution of the images out of the government's control but the images themselves were also in complete contrast to what the French and Territorial governments wanted the world to see. The photos that traveled out into the world—and with people's easy access to the Internet, the images were impossible to control—were nothing like the pictures of "paradise" that for so long had been carefully composed and purposefully circulated. Many of these images of the protests had a particular power that resulted from the "ordinariness" of the violence portrayed—a placeless violence that could occur virtually anywhere. Tourists (and others) who wanted to "stay in the postcard" suddenly had a new repertoire of images to consider.

Although the government did not respond to the relatively peaceful protests and blockades prior to the testing, they responded immediately to the production and subsequent dissemination of these images of violence and destruction that followed the testing. With events spinning out of their control, government officials were visibly anxious and attempted to suppress the reporting of them. Erick Monod, the senior reporter for the government-owned television station RFO (Réseau France Outre-Mer), described what he felt were the government's deliberate political tactics when he was attempting to report what he witnessed:

> I was at the airport when it was burning. Others and I were evacuated from the scene and taken back to Pape'ete. When I got there I wanted to take my camera and go into town to film the burning of Pape'ete for television. Instead, RFO forbid me from going. They decided to shut down the office at 8 PM. This was unprecedented. That decision was one hundred percent political. (Erick Monod, personal communication, 1995)

The revolutionary potential of public space, and especially of the street, is enormous. As a passageway between places, the street reflects the potentially opposing forces it links together. Explosive energies are torn from their darkness and thrust into the light of the street, dragged "onto the stage of a spontaneous theatre, where the actors improvise a play, which has no script. The street takes whatever is happening somewhere else, in secret, and makes it public. It changes its shape, and inserts it into the social text" (Lefebvre 2002, 310). What was being dragged out into the street and being inserted into the social text was the battle over place—the clash between, on the one hand, the actions of foreign users and abusers of Tahitian land and, on the other, the feelings of Tahitians for whom *te fenua* embodies their roots, their nurturing mother, and their identity. It was, as Merrifield stated, a battle "between conceiving space through representation and living place through actual sensual experience" (1993, 525).

BATTLING WITH IMAGES

During the months following the resumption of nuclear testing and the resulting public protests, a more cunning battle was escalating over the control of images. Although battles over place can take on a visibly violent character, the struggle can also occur in a more subtle fashion—the form it took now. As I followed the next phase of this confrontation, I became even more deeply aware of the symbolic violence embedded in these idyllic images, and of the government's complicity in their production and distribution. Because the spaces of rebellion that Tahitians produced in the streets were *not* the places the government wanted the world to see, the government fought back—using its top-down control over the production and distribution of imagery as its weapon. As David Harvey has said, "Struggles over representation are as fiercely fought and as fundamental to the activities of place construction as bricks and mortar" (1993, 23).

One week after the "events" of September 6, the government's awareness of this image problem was highlighted in *La dépêche de Tahiti*. On the front page was a picture of a postcard, jaggedly ripped into several pieces, with the headline "La carte postale a été déchirée . . ." (The postcard has been torn; *La dépêche de Tahiti* 1995b, 1). The caption accused the international media of ruining the world's perception of Tahiti. "After the worldwide reporting about the riots, television stations created an image of a shantytown. These images make Tahiti look worse than Rio or Haiti. . . . The foreign media's orchestration of the problems and certain journalists' manipulation of the events have succeeded" (*La dépêche de Tahiti* 1995b, 1).

In reality, a cleverly crafted counter manipulation of the situation by French-controlled or -influenced media, such as RFO and *La dépêche de Tahiti,* had already begun. Although minimal coverage was given to the nuclear test on September 5, exhaustive coverage of the demonstrators' reactions on September 6 soon appeared. On September 9 *La dépêche de Tahiti* included a special twenty-page supplement with the ominous headline "Le mercredi noir de Tahiti" (Tahiti's black Wednesday; fig. 2.7). Each page of the supplement was filled with photographs of charred buildings, shattered glass, dismembered store mannequins lying in the streets, Tahitians hurling rocks, Tahitians lighting fires, and police with weapons. Alongside the photos were captions such as "L'avenir touristique de la Polynésie a également été touché de plein fouet" (The future of tourism in French Polynesia was directly hit) and "Le moral n'y est plus" (Morale is gone). The government now used the same images—which they had previously claimed had been "manipulated" by foreign media to reveal the ugly side of paradise—to threaten Tahitians into submission. They did this by playing up the economic importance of tourism and generating anxiety about the loss of income that would result from these pictures being circulated.

The "Mercredi noir de Tahiti" supplement can be interpreted as the Territorial government's way of fighting back through its media proxy. Using a skillfully orchestrated presentation, the supplement conveyed messages that were subtle but deliberate. The cover image—of a dark building engulfed in

Fig. 2.7 "Le mercredi noir de Tahiti." *La dépêche de Tahiti,* September 9, 1995.

smoke and fire, with silhouettes of two people watching the destruction—was ominous. The text, however, communicated the opposite, namely reassurance about a safe and speedy return to "normality"; for example,

> *Prison ferme pour les pilleurs*
> (The looters are locked in prison)

> *L'aéroport a nouveau ouvert ce matin*
> (The airport reopened this morning)

> *Le filet se resserre autour des responsables des émeutes*
> (The net tightens around those responsible for the riots)

Roland Barthes, a French semiotician, coined the phrase "the photographic paradox" in referring to press photographs in which two different messages exist. One communication (the photograph) is without a code and denotes visible "reality." The other (the text) is with a code and connotes its social significance. The totality of the message is situated at the intersection of these two: the literal and the symbolic. The press photograph is an object that "has been worked on, chosen, composed, constructed, [and] treated according to professional, aesthetic or ideological norms which are so many factors of connotation" (Barthes 1977, 19).

The text of the supplement undoubtedly influenced what people (who had not been present) thought about what happened on September 6, 1995. The supplement was used to transform the images people had in their minds—of darkness, destruction, and social chaos—into the message the government wanted to convey—of safety, security, and normality. "The text loads the image, burdening it with a culture, a moral, an imagination" and thus functions "to integrate man [and] reassure him" (Barthes 1977, 26, 31).

In spite of the attempts by the government to use its media to manipulate people's understanding of the events, Tahitians continued to feel a sense of empowerment rooted in this new capability to project their own images out into the world. Unlike Teva's or Diane's postcards that romanticized Tahiti, the images that angry Tahitians and the international media projected were more in accord with how many Tahitians experienced their world. This contest over the control of the representation of their place was "the essential terrain of struggle" (Shields 1999, 164, referring to Lefebvre's work). Many Tahitians wanted their voices, usually silenced or ignored, to be heard. As a friend told me, "The riots may not be the best way for us to express ourselves, but when we tried peaceful marches, no one listened. The French express themselves powerfully with their bomb. Now we are speaking up and being heard" (Hiti Gooding, personal communication, 1995).

Peaceful protest marches continued over the next few months, as did the testing. Songs, prayers, and silences were used to try and persuade the government to stop. In late September, Jacques Ihorai and Ralph Teinaore, the president and the secretary general of l'Église Évangélique de Polynésie Française, went to France to try to convince President Chirac to end the testing. In pleading with him, Ihorai referred to Tahitian understandings of land, explaining that Tahitians consider the land to be their mother who nourishes them and that the bomb is like a missile of death in "the nourishing womb of the motherland" (*La dépêche de Tahiti* 1995c, 21).[29] Even though Tahitians generally show little interest in the images of Tahiti made for tourists, they react passionately when their own sense of place is violated. When bombs were exploded deep within their land, it was their sense of place that was profoundly disturbed. Because land is seen as nourishing and in need of being nourished—a place to bury the placenta and umbilical cord of one's child—the burying of a bomb in the land is monstrously offensive. When Ihorai compared the nuclear testing to the lodging of a missile in their mother's womb, he spoke about the Tahitian experience of place in a way that postcards could never do.

Tahitians spoke up in other ways as well, such as composing (solely in *reo ma'ohi*) protest songs directed less to the outside world and more to other Tahitians. Angélo Neuffer Ari'itai, one of the leading poets and singers for the younger generation, released a song at this time called *Taero atomi* (Nuclear Poison):

Taero te fenua,	The land is poisoned,
Taero atoa te nuna'a,	The people are poisoned,
Taero atoa te moana,	The sea is poisoned,
Taero atoa te vaha	As are the mouths
O te mau ti'a e ha'avare nei	Of our leaders
Na roto i te fa'aitera'a mai	Who lie
Ia oe e te nuna'a	And tell us
E ere te mea taero roa,	It is not very poisonous,
Te paura atomi.	That bomb.

Taero te reva,	The air is poisoned,
Taero atoa te mau ma'a,	Our food is poisoned,
Taero atoa te mau tamari'i,	The children are poisoned,
Taero atoa te ferurira'a	As is the conscience
O te mau feia e ha'avare	Of those
Na roto i te fa'aitera'a mai	Who lie
Ia oe e te nuna'a	And tell us
E ere te mea ino roa,	It is not very harmful,
Te paura atomi.	That bomb.

Paura atomi,	Atomic bomb,
Aita matou e hina'aro ia oe	We don't want you
I teie fenua.	On our land.

Paura atomi,	Atomic bomb,
Aita matou e hina'aro ia vi'ivi'i	We don't want your pollution
I teie fenua.	On our land.

Paura atomi,	Atomic bomb,
Aita matou e hina'aro te pohe	We don't want death
I teie fenua,	On our land,

Paura atomi,	Atomic bomb,
Haere e atu oe i rapae au	Go away from here
I teie fenua.	From our land.

By his emphatic use of the image of nuclear testing as poison, Angélo accentuated the intertwined nature of the poisoning of the physical world—the land, sea, air, people, and the food from the land—with the poisoning of the representational world—the politicians' deceitful language and misrepresentations.

All these efforts were unsuccessful. Nuclear tests continued on the average of one a month for five months, and the number of tourists visiting, especially from Japan and the United States, declined precipitously. The Japanese, for whom the previous month of September marked the fiftieth anniversary of the bombing of Hiroshima and Nagasaki, were particularly outspoken in their opposition to the nuclear testing. Hotels catering principally to Japanese tourists were almost empty. As the Tahiti portrayed in the media suddenly dimmed from a Technicolor turquoise to a funereal gray, the biweekly flights from Tokyo were cut back to one, and even then carried only a few passengers.

In response, as the testing was drawing to a close, the Territorial government launched a calculated campaign "to replace the image that was shattered, the image of peacefulness, kindness, and island casualness" (*La dépêche de Tahiti* 1995b, 24). As stated in a photo caption, "The myth of French Polynesia is supported by images of women and not by images of broken windows" (*La dépêche de Tahiti* 1995b, 25). Suzanne Lau-Chonfont, who supervised the collection of statistics for the Office of Tourism, told me about plans for new marketing strategies that would communicate that *tout va bien encore* (all is well again) and that *rien ne c'est passé* (nothing happened). President Flosse participated energetically in the campaign. Imagining a Polynesian landscape populated with French personalities, he denounced the protesters as "those who want to fade the colors of Gauguin, extinguish the voice of Jacques Brel, and obliterate the memory of Paul-Émile Victor"[30] (Didier 1995, 21). As part of his long-term plan, President Flosse (as a private citizen) invested in a new 320-passenger cruise ship to tour the Society Islands, and named it the MS *Paul Gauguin,* designated to cater to particularly affluent tourists. Launched in 1998, two years after the nuclear testing had ended, it was advertised as taking tourists to "worlds so breathtaking even the word paradise seems inadequate" (Radisson Seven Seas Cruises magazine advertisement, 1998).

THE BATTLE OVER PLACE WAGES ON

Not far beneath the surface of the postcard image to which tourists are drawn lurks the less picturesque reality of Tahiti's colonial history—and present. This includes nuclear testing, environmental destruction, health problems, and poverty—details Diane Commons was compelled to edit out of her images so that her postcards would sell. When these negative aspects of colonialism surfaced through the cracks in the postcards' veneer, a more disturbing reality came into view, drawing attention to the economic and political power these images support and the symbolic violence lodged within their serenity. *La dépêche de Tahiti* acknowledged this when it stated "the big jolt of September brought to light the fragility of our image and the difficulty in restoring it now" (Frémy 1995, 20).

In general, groups of people whose politics are in opposition to one another generate and inhabit spaces that reveal these contradictions. When Tahitians produce their own spaces, whether peacefully planting a placenta in the earth or violently rioting in the streets, it is a lived space that reflects their cultural identity and experience. In contrast, the state creates spaces that meet its own needs for capital accumulation, military organization, and social order—whether through developing tourism, detonating bombs, or promoting a conspiracy of silence around the nuclear testing program by controlling the production of imagery. When Tahitian-generated space clashed with state-generated space, it destroyed the illusion of paradise and the government's otherwise firm grip on the instruments of its production.

At the heart of this battle over place, where medium and message are merged, creative transformation can take place. Although state management of space necessitates a sense of stability that can be destructive (Lefebvre 1991, 387), the eruption of a bubbling cauldron can be revolutionary. Indeed, in the 2004 elections, the government of French Polynesia was replaced, and Oscar

Temaru, the pro-independence candidate, was elected as the new president of the Territory. Although this new government did not last long (Temaru was ousted and then reelected three more times in the following five years), it managed to disrupt the existing political dynamic (see Gonschor 2009). Once again—indeed, as I write—the battle over place (and the shifting of political power) wages on.

CHAPTER THREE

Keeping the Myth Alive

I n the colonial situation in which the economies of France and French Polynesia are intricately intertwined, the *métropole* benefits greatly by embracing the colony as imagined rather than as experienced. Colonial powers "wrap themselves in representations and myths . . . [which] requires that the state be organized around promoting and supporting these myths" (Shields 1991, 157). In Tahiti, images—whether public spaces, architectural forms, visual symbols, verbal phrases, or branded commodities— play an especially important role. "Images seem to speak to the eye, but they are really addressed to the mind. They are ways of thinking, in the guise of ways of seeing" (Duff 1975, 12). What can the production of these images, as well as their reception in France (and beyond), tell us about the entangled political economies of *métropole* and colony?

Images play a critical role in producing and maintaining a "mythical" world by mediating between myth and reality. An image can be seen as representing something that is real, but, as a representation rather than the reality, it may actually—often in calculated ways—obscure reality. For example, images that present Tahiti as a paradise not only misrepresent the "reality" of Tahiti but can also shield unfavorable truths from view. "This world of images and signs . . . is situated at the edges of what exists, between the shadows and the light, between the conceived (the abstract) and the perceived (the visible). Between the real and the unreal. Always in the interstices, in the cracks." Although this world of images presents itself as transparent and reassuring, uniting the mental and emotional, space and time, and needs and desire, it is in fact fraudulent and deceptive. "When there is talk of art and culture, the real subject is money, the market, exchange, and power" (Lefebvre 1991, 389).

Images of paradise connect Tahiti—the place of desire—to the *métropole*—the place of economic and political power. The intertwined economies of the two places depend on Tahiti being viewed and experienced as a place of blue lagoons, powdery white-sand beaches, exotic men, and seductive women. The task of the tourism industry is to create and disseminate images that maintain this perception. In doing so, they must bring together the Tahiti of tourists' imaginations with what exists on the ground, a task that requires quite some ingenuity. Although tourists expect to see white-sand beaches, these are, in fact, scarce on the main islands and are found most often on the *motus* (small islets on the fringing reef) or on atolls such as those in the Tuamotu Archipelago. Lacking a reef and lagoon, the island of Tahiti—unbeknownst to most visitors before they arrive—has almost no white-sand beaches.[1] Every waterfront hotel in Pape'ete has a swimming pool, some even with sandy bottoms, because guests swimming in the sea would otherwise be pressing their toes into slimy mud and scraping their feet on broken coral. Although tourists may also expect a perfect climate with daily sunshine, such idyllic weather is seasonal. From roughly November to February it is common for humidity to reach lethargy-inducing levels and for storms to rage for days on end, leaving tourists trapped inside hotels with nothing but board games and one another. Travelers may also fantasize about experiencing men covered with tattoos and women like those in paintings by Gauguin. In truth, very few men (often hired by hotels as luggage porters and poolside attendants) might have tattoos, and few women (often employed by hotels as receptionists and wait staff) might look as if they had stepped out of a Gauguin painting.

What Tahiti offers is the myth that creates a place of desire in people's imaginations and fuels Tahiti's tourism industry.[2] As the brochures and Web sites of several travel agencies state, "Close your eyes and imagine an oceanfront Garden of Eden for you and your Adam—or Eve—and you've probably just conjured up Tahiti."[3] The promotional literature of Tahiti Tourisme North America unambiguously states that Tahiti is "a destination so exotic, it exists only in one's dreams."[4] Keeping these dreams alive is a constant challenge that relies on ever more premeditated and mediated—and government orchestrated—manipulations. The former president of French Polynesia,

Gaston Flosse, declared that the perpetuation of the myth was one of the Territorial government's main goals, underscoring its importance in achieving a robust economy. In a letter to the public, which appeared in government publications and on Web sites encouraging foreign investment in the Territory, Flosse stated,

> The names "French Polynesia" and "Tahiti and Her Islands" evoke the myth of New Cytheria and "heaven on earth," whose legend has been told by many writers since the islands were first discovered by the outside world. . . . [Our goal] is to maintain this dream. . . . Tourism will definitely remain the cornerstone of economic development in the twenty-first century.[5]

In 2005, the then president of the Territory, Oscar Temaru, voiced the same sentiment at a Tahiti Invest seminar held to mark the inauguration of the nonstop Air Tahiti Nui service between New York and Pape'ete. He announced, "French Polynesia—Tahiti, her islands, archipelagoes, and population—continues more than ever to evoke a myth, that of New Cytheria of the early explorers. Tahitians are the guardians of this paradise-on-earth image."[6]

Much has been written about the myth of Tahiti, and a number of books and articles have appeared in the past two decades.[7] Most of these highlight the existence of the myth and explore its origin and dimensions. The contemporary perpetuation and manipulation of the myth for economic and political gain has not been explored. What is the complex relationship between Tahiti's deeply entrenched history of mythical images, tourists' expectations and experiences, and the methods and politics of marketing Tahiti as a tourist destination? How has this enduring dynamic intensified in the post-CEP economic and political climate, where the government greatly increased its investment in, and promotion of, tourism?

POST-NUCLEAR-TESTING INVESTMENT IN TOURISM

This post-CEP climate, with its new economic and political agenda, began soon after January 27, 1996. On this day—nearly thirty years after France conducted its first nuclear test in French Polynesia—it conducted its last. President Chirac, yielding to international pressure, announced that France would permanently cease its nuclear weapons testing program in the Pacific. As welcome as the end of testing was for many Tahitians, it also caused some anxiety. The program had been the principal motivation for France to commit substantial funds to the Territory. Now there was the very real possibility that France would no longer consider French Polynesia to be economically or politically useful and would withdraw its financial support. In 1996 France and the Territory entered into the Pact of Progress, which stated that over the next ten years the annual payments to the Territory would gradually be reduced from US$180 million to US$100 million.

The Territorial government directed these remaining funds toward internal "development." Expending funds in this way not only provided an economic base and infrastructure for a more self-sufficient Tahiti but also maintained political support for the Territorial government. The development projects included, among others, constructing airstrips on remote islands, paving roads, upgrading village water and electricity systems, rebuilding houses that had been destroyed by cyclones, and constructing and maintaining new public spaces. Especially conspicuous during this period were the red-shirted *hommes d'action au service des Polynésiens* (men of action in service to Polynesians).[8] Women of action, of whom there were far fewer than men, wore white shirts. Otherwise known as GIP (Groupement d'intervention de la Polynésie), these men and women were jokingly referred to by some as FIP (Flosse's Intervention Service) because they were steadfastly loyal to President Flosse and were seen as his personal militia.[9] They were employed as crew members on government ships, construction workers on road-paving projects, security personnel at public events, and groundskeepers for public spaces. The GIP logo—a double-hulled voyaging canoe accompanied by the phrase "Te Toa Arai" (Intervention Warriors)—was prominently displayed on the workers' shirts, trucks, ships, and equipment, as well as on objects such as public waste bins, all aimed at etching the government's "good work" (through its GIP proxies) in the public's mind.

In the post-CEP economy, with the need for new avenues of economic self-sufficiency, the Territorial government identified tourism as *the* main source of foreign revenue. French Polynesia, like many Pacific island nations, has relatively few options for bringing in foreign exchange. Despite the problems tourism can bring, it can be a significant source of income. The government wanted a substantial increase in the number of tourists, hoping that the income from tourism could replace that lost from the departure of CEP, which caused a major economic shift that was even portrayed in political cartoons (fig. 3.1). As part of this effort, the Territorial government developed a new slogan: *Le tourisme c'est l'avenir* (Tourism is the future). Variations of

Fig. 3.1   Tourists arriving to replace the departing military, 1993. Cartoon courtesy of Gotz.

the slogan—*Le tourisme est l'affaire de tous* (Tourism is everyone's business), *Nous resterons leur meilleur souvenir* (We [Tahitians] are tourists' best memories), and *Développons le tourisme, pour créer les emplois de demain* (Develop tourism to create tomorrow's jobs)—appeared in prominent advertisements in an effort to encourage everyone's participation. *La dépêche de Tahiti* began a section appearing on Fridays that focused on tourism. The government also designated Friday as the day when service-industry employees, whether waiting tables in a restaurant or bagging groceries in a supermarket, should dress *en style local*, meaning they should wear colorful "Tahitian" clothing (coordinated in each workplace) and wear crowns of flowers or leaves on their heads.

One government strategy for increasing tourism was to develop the cruise ship industry. For this, they needed not only the support facilities and services for the ships but also new public spaces on shore that would make Tahiti more attractive to the ships' passengers. In 1998 President Flosse invested in a luxury liner named, fittingly, the MS *Paul Gauguin*. In 1999, the Territorial government also contracted with the Radisson cruise line to have two other ships, the *Renaissance I* and the *Renaissance II,* sail throughout the Society Islands, which resulted in a 25 percent increase in the annual number of tourists. Major alterations, including new piers, shops, and public facilities, were made to places where the cruise ships would dock, as well as to the adjacent areas where tourists might visit.

TRANSFORMING PUBLIC SPACE

My research trip in 2001 was during the post-CEP period with its growing intensity of economic and political activities, thus prompting my desire to explore the escalating promotion of tourism. While living on Huahine, I made a trip to Pape'ete to interview upper-level managers at GIE Tahiti Tourisme,[10] the Territorial government's international tourism marketing organization.

The evening of my arrival in Pape'ete I went to my favorite place to get some dinner—the *roulottes,* or mobile restaurants, on the waterfront—but was startled by what I found. I had eaten at the *roulottes* many times, although not since the nuclear testing had ended, and recalled how the area, which during the day was an unattractive, poorly maintained parking lot, was filled in the evening with *roulottes* and their customers. I remembered the owners parking the restaurants in what appeared to be no particular order, propping open the sides of their vans, setting out menu boards to advertise their specialties, and cooking. As the aromas of sizzling steaks, chow mein, pizzas, and crêpes filled the air, crowds of both locals and tourists gathered to eat. My previous visit to the *roulottes* had been during the rainy season (as was this one now), and I had to be careful to avoid stepping in puddles that collected in the potholes in the parking lot. Now, during this visit, I found the area transformed beyond recognition.

Previously, the parking lot gave no hint during the day at what would be happening in the evening. Now a prominent sign, which rose on pillars from a platform of stones, announced that this was Tahua Vaiete (also called Place Vaiete). The entire area of nearly three acres had been completely redesigned, turning this section of Pape'ete—where the cruise ships docked—into *la porte d'entrée* (the front door) and *le coeur vivant* (the living heart) of Pape'ete (Puputauki 1998, 2). Now each of the thirty or so *roulottes* had a designated spot. There were communal dishwashing facilities for the food handlers, spotless public restrooms with GIP attendants, new coconut palms

Fig. 3.2   Tahua Vaiete, with GIP workers taking care of the grounds, and with the MS *Paul Gauguin* in the background, 2001.

along the waterfront, manicured plantings, low stone walls demarcating the area, an artificial waterfall, fancy street lamps, benches, and a concert area with a Parisian-style 1,000-square-foot pavilion (G.I.P. 2001). The entire area was also paved with granite stones from France. As one young man told me, "Imagine, each of these stones was brought from France and laid in these fancy patterns over the old dirt surface! That was Flosse's decision. He did it so when the tourists take photos they have a nice background. But now it looks like Paris. It's no longer Tahiti" (Tafira Teri'itapunui, personal communication, 2001). During the day GIP workers kept the area immaculately clean by sweeping and hosing down the stones, pruning the bushes, and weeding the flowerbeds (fig. 3.2).

Now, as evening fell each day, Tahua Vaiete changed from a nearly empty, but manicured, space into a well-orchestrated hub of activity. At about 5:00 PM the *roulottes* began arriving. Their owners propped open the sides of their vans and set up for the evening (fig. 3.3). Tahua Vaiete became a sea of people

Fig. 3.3 *Roulottes* setting up for the evening at Tahua Vaiete, with the cruise ship *Renaissance I* in the background, 2001.

strolling around or sitting down to enjoy a meal at one of the *roulottes* parked in neat rows in this newly managed public space, which was greatly appreciated by tourists. I noticed that the *roulottes* had also changed in appearance. They were painted with colorful designs, were much cleaner, and had new accoutrements: a rectangular mat under the outside cooking grills to catch the dripping grease; plastic covers on their menus; more professionally designed menu boards; and more elegant place settings at the counter or at tables nearby. When I asked one of the *roulotte* owners about the changes, he succinctly said, "C'était Flosse qui nous l'a dicté" (Flosse required us to do this).

The orderliness, of course, was strategic. "It turns out on close examination that spaces made to be read are the most deceptive and tricked-up imaginable. The graphic impression of readability is a sort of *trompe-l'oeil* concealing strategic intentions and actions" (Lefebvre 1991, 143). A space such as Tahua Vaiete, which the government planned and executed, served multiple purposes. In this instance, the redesign promoted tourism and demonstrated to the public that the government was serving its people (see Low 2000). It also became part of *l'espace conçu* (now advertised in guidebooks) that tourists would imagine and that, upon disembarking from their cruise ship, they would experience as *l'espace perçu*. On the surface it may look as though spaces are produced for economic reasons, but they are also political and strategic products. "The state and each of its constituent institutions call for spaces—but spaces that they can then organize according to their specific requirement" (Lefebvre 1991, 85). The strategic space of Tahua Vaiete, carefully designed with its choreographed components of elegant paving stones, sanitary facilities, and orderliness, was exactly that—both a prerequisite for, and a result of, government activity.

GLITTERING TRAPS OF DETAIL FOR THE EYE

The following day, with images of Tahua Vaiete's sparkling (and now puddle-free) area fresh in my mind, I headed off to various interviews. Waiting in the reception area of GIE Tahiti Tourisme for my first appointment, I was surrounded by familiar images. One wall was completely covered with a large photo montage showing a blue lagoon with overwater bungalows, an underwater diving scene with colorful fish swimming through the water, a smiling man and woman with flower garlands, and some shimmering black pearls peeking out of the water. Surrounded by these icons, I began to realize the great extent to which the marketing of a specific destination relies on the synthetic arrangement of decontextualized images and signs, carefully organized to convey the sense of place that tourists expect and hope to experience.

Tourism is an industry that—through the use of imagery—has extended the promotion of places both out into the natural world and back into our imaginations (Norris 1994, 3–4). Tourism can be seen as "a collection of projected images that establishes the boundaries of experience. The images define what is beautiful, what should be experienced, and with whom one should interact. Understanding . . . tourism is thus, above all else, an analysis of images" (Dann 1996, 79). As an industry based on the packaging and selling of place, tourism constructs, inhabits, and transforms the geographies of the world in ways that have profound physical, economic, social, political, and psychological repercussions. Tourism can create a whole new range of landscapes, including—as is the case in Tahiti—airports, docks for cruise ships and yachts, roads, hotels, artificial beaches, museums and cultural centers, tourist sites, markets and craft stands, public places such as

Tahua Vaiete, visitor centers, and tourism offices. Tourism also stimulates the growth of particular professions, such as tour operators, travel agents, marketing and advertising agents, guidebook writers, hotel architects, and hotel directors, whose goal it is to organize human desires and leisure time around the idea of temporarily escaping from one place to another.

In French Polynesia tourism is the engine that drives the economy. Not only does it bring necessary foreign exchange into the Territory, but it also allows the upper class to maintain the lifestyle they acquired during the CEP period. Owners, managers, directors, and chief executive officers of the various tourist enterprises are some of the wealthiest individuals in the Territory. This, however, is not the case for everyone involved in tourism. For many Tahitians, especially those on the outer islands, a job in the tourism industry is simply one—and often the only—option as a source of income, and even then the pay is low.[11] Henri Hiro commented on this, saying, "We have the impression that that is our destiny: to become the servants of tourists. That's our image of the future" (Stewart, Mateata-Allain, and Mawyer 2006, 78). Etienne Puaritahi Faaeva, the owner of a small, family-run hotel on Huahine, eloquently expressed this dependence on tourism when he told me, "Tourism is just a source of money. There are different motivations for us in it. Tourism is very, very complicated. It isn't something that is simply good or bad. It's a job. It's a source of income. Our problem is that we live like Americans now but we don't produce anything that gives us money. So we have tourism." This lack of income-producing options creates philosophical challenges for Tahitians. Jean-Marc Tera'ituatini Pambrun, a Tahitian anthropologist, commented on this conundrum, saying, "The problem we have today is no longer a question of claiming our culture, but of knowing how to cope with the commercialization and exploitation of it, and to do so without getting caught in the dream manufacturer's net" (Pambrun 2005).

After a few minutes of sitting in the GIE Tahiti Tourisme office, contemplating these images and tourism's dependence on imagery as I waited for my first appointment, the receptionist called me for my first meeting, which was with Brigitte Vanizette, then the directrice générale of GIE Tahiti Tourisme. What she shared was an eye-opener for me about the research-backed decisions that go into creating such purposefully planned synthetic arrangements of images. She showed me one of their most successful products: a travel planner whose cover displays an excellent example of these pastiches.

The travel planner, distributed to all travel agents and tour operators, is a hefty, glossy publication. Enhanced and redesigned each year, it has increased in size from 150 pages in 2001 to 250 pages in 2009. It contains a detailed section about each of the five island groups, including information about transportation, lodging, eating, shopping, and general activities. In 2001 planners were produced in six languages (English, French, German, Italian, Spanish, and Japanese), although now two more languages have been added (Chinese and Thai). Within each year the editorial content of the planners for each of the language versions is virtually identical, but the covers are different. Even within one language version, such as English, there are different covers for the travel planners intended for the United States, Canada, England, and Australia/New Zealand. The 2001 cover was a montage of juxtaposed images surrounded by a border, whose color (turquoise, green, dark blue, or orange) changed according to the country targeted (figs. 3.4a-d).

As Vanizette showed me the various covers, she explained the cultural typecasting that emerged from her office's marketing research:

Fig. 3.4   Travel planner covers, 2001. (a) England. (b) Australia/New Zealand. (c) USA/Canada. (d) Italy.

(a)   (b)

English people like eco-tourism, so the English cover includes images of people scuba diving and horses grazing on a hillside [fig. 3.4 a]. In Australia and
New Zealand, people like cultural things, so their cover has a man re-enacting
a ritual and two smiling Tahitian girls. They also like water activities, so we
included a sailboat [fig. 3.4 b]. Americans like some of everything. They still
have a fascination with Bora Bora, and many are honeymooners. Their cover,
which is blue, features a man and a woman holding hands and looking out to
sea, with overwater bungalows in the lagoon and a cruise ship in the distance
[fig. 3.4 c]. Italians like lively activities and romantic settings, so their cover is
orange and has a fire-dancer, a colorful sunset, some overwater bungalows,
and a table set with food that is serenaded by a man and woman holding a
guitar and ukulele. [fig. 3.4 d]

As we finished looking at the covers, she explained, "We show everything
there is. There is no discrepancy between the image and the reality. We just
rearrange the pictures according to what we know people want, but these are
real pictures. They show real things."

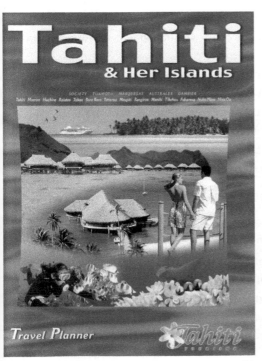 

(c)   (d)

Later that day Christel Bole, the marketing manager for GIE Tahiti Tourisme, explained the details of the marketing research that informs and directs
the design of the different covers. Extensive research is conducted on how
tourists perceive the meaning of specific images. She told me,

> Each image stands for something. Smiling Tahitian children indicate people
> who are friendly and welcoming. Dancers in colorful regalia communicate the
> idea of cultural traditions. A couple standing in front of a sunset will make
> tourists think of romance. A man hiking up a mountain with a backpack
> makes people think of eco-tourism.

Marketers want to meet tourists on the turf of their imaginations, creating a Tahiti tailored to their clientele—for example, "friendly," "cultural,"
"romantic," "ecological," and so on. This strategy can occasionally produce
an image that appears somewhat surreal. The cover of the Italian version has
one image showing a Tahitian man and woman serenading an empty dining
table.

Malek Alloula refers to this type of purposeful synthetic arrangement
when he talks about postcards (which, in many ways, are like the travel planner covers) and the need to saturate the image by accumulating accessories
and setting glittering traps of detail for the eye. He calls it "counterfeit realism" because it requires only a minimum of truthfulness and instead much
painstaking attention to detail (Alloula 1986, 52). This imagery "proves to
be so pliable because the 'art' of the exotic postcard is an art of sign and not
an art of meaning. The few signs distributed here and there over the reflec-
tive surface of the postcard . . . are its true subjects" (Alloula 1986, 64). In
this process the signifier and signified collapse into one another. "Fragments
cohere into apparent wholeness, standing for irreducible truths" (Edwards
1996, 216).

Rearranging images to appeal to different audiences (whether the government's creation of Tahua Vaiete or GIE Tahiti Tourisme's design of travel
planners) is not only at the core of contemporary marketing strategies but
has also been used since the days of first contact between Europeans and
Tahitians. Bougainville, preparing his journal for publication, added references to goddesses, nymphs, and noble savages to make it more appealing to
his eighteenth-century readers. Webber, painting Poedua's portrait, draped
a white cloth from her waist and placed her in front of a pastoral landscape.

Gauguin incorporated elements of Greek, Egyptian, and Japanese art into his Tahitian settings, combining them in ways he thought would appeal to the art market in Paris. Teva Sylvain placed a coconut leaf basket in the hands of a French model to make her look "Tahitian" and, thus, more like what Western male postcard buyers expected. Similarly, Diane Commons composed an image of tropical serenity with her camera by editing out the piles of trash in which she was standing.

Today travel agents and tour operators can even create these pastiches themselves. GIE Tahiti Tourisme has more than 2,000 photographs on a Web site that can be accessed by tourism professionals. Travel agents and tour operators are able to select images from various categories, such as "outrigger canoe," "smiling girl," or "palm tree," and then use these to create their own marketing materials. Karine Villa, manager of promotional material for GEI Tahiti Tourisme, explained, "A lot of work goes into composing each image in the photo bank so that the elements are recognizable to tour operators." GIE Tahiti Tourisme also records who chooses which image, allowing them to anticipate the desires of tourists from different markets.

Lefebvre noted the destructive elements of this type of fragmented imagery, referring to "the world of the image" as "the enemy of the imagination." "Images fragment, they are themselves fragments, cutting things up and rearranging them, découpage and montage, the art of image making. Illusion resides in the artist's eye and gaze, in the photographer's lens, on the writer's blank page" (Lefebvre 1991, 97). The visual world makes a fetish of fragmented imagery and imposes these as the norm.

TINKERING WITH IMAGES

A month later I again visited Papeʻete, this time to attend La Conférence des Représentants de GIE Tahiti Tourisme—the annual conference for their international representatives. I hoped to learn still more about the marketing of Tahiti by following the process of how images were produced and disseminated to places where GIE Tahiti Tourisme has offices. Today this includes Europe (France, Germany, Italy, England, Spain, and Denmark), North America (U.S.A.), South America (Chile), and the Asia-Pacific region (Japan, Australia, New Zealand, Thailand, Singapore, Hong Kong, and Taiwan).[12]

After arriving at the airport, I made my way via *le truck* (the local public transportation) to the site of the conference—the Sheraton Hotel on the outskirts of Pape'ete—during an unusually fierce, but seasonally appropriate, rainstorm. At the hotel, I could see that the rain was affecting everyone's day. Rain was dripping into an open-roofed corridor that led from the lobby to other areas, splashing water onto the wicker furniture and forming puddles on the stone floor. An employee was setting up yellow plastic "*attention*" cones. Small groups of guests were huddled together on the covered outdoor staircase landings, watching the waves beat against the piers. I'm sure nothing—certainly none of the brochures that had lured them to Tahiti—prepared them for a tropical storm of such dramatic magnitude.

I walked through the opulent lobby, descended the circular staircase to the meeting rooms below, and joined some 250 people attending the conference. Nearly half of them worked for GIE Tahiti Tourisme in one of the countries where it had offices. The rest had come from within French Polynesia—directors of large and small hotels, owners of pensions (family guesthouses), travel agents, representatives of the airline companies, and owners and operators of tourism activities (such as four-wheel-drive island tours or scuba diving trips). As the newspaper reported, "The goal of this meeting among the various tourism professionals is to improve our product—Tahiti and Her Islands—because everyone knows that tourism is the means by which French Polynesia will achieve social and economic development" (*La dépêche de Tahiti* 2001c, 32).

Barely three months after September 11, 2001, the atmosphere at this particular conference was one of worry and distress. The tragic events in New York had, among other things, resulted in a severe decline in tourism worldwide. The decline, especially troubling for Tahiti, was an indicator of how fragile an economy based on tourism can be. I sensed a strong desire on the part of the government to establish a tone of confidence and optimism at the meeting. The conference also took place where, nearby, the two relatively new 700-passenger cruise ships, the *Renaissance I* and the *Renaissance II*, sat idly in Pape'ete's harbor. The cruise ships had been very successful, but, after the post–September 11 drop in tourism, had declared bankruptcy. The government had impounded the ships as security for the debts owed to both the government and the private businesses that had furnished supplies and services. This crisis was an opportune moment for me to gain greater insight into Tahiti's tourism industry and its myth-maintaining techniques.

As the conference began, directrice générale of GIE Tahiti Tourisme, Brigitte Vanizette (who had shown me the travel planners the previous month) took her place at the podium. Behind her was a full-sized reproduction of

Gauguin's largest painting, *D'où venons-nous? Que sommes-nous? Où allons-nous?* (Where do we come from? What are we? Where are we going?), painted in 1897 while feeling disappointed and in despair about the "ruined" life he found in Tahiti, in himself, and in mankind in general (Estienne 1953, 91; Shackelford and Frèches-Thory 2004). In the dark wood on the front of the podium was a relief sculpture of a Marquesan tiki. It reminded me of the long history of appropriations of tikis by Europeans, starting when, for example, William Hodges placed one in the foreground of his 1776 painting *Oaitepeha Bay* (fig. 1.1). The tiki on the podium also brought to mind the contemporary proliferation of cheap, mass-produced, souvenir tikis, which were often not made in Tahiti or even in Polynesia.[13] Standing between these two icons, each echoing a different shade of disenchantment and potential deception, Vanizette welcomed the conference participants with warmth and enthusiasm:

> We are fortunate that we have an excellent product. What we offer is some-thing authentic in a natural environment. But we need to do a better job promoting our image. Last year we had over 180,000 tourists and we hope to have more in the future. . . . North America is definitely our top customer. But we must diversify our international clientele. The crisis of September 11th demonstrated that it is dangerous to depend too heavily on one market. Tahiti Tourisme wants to expand into other countries. We need to highlight the fact that Tahiti is a destination that is original, authentic and unique. . . . The gov-ernment will do everything possible to support tourism.

Nicole Bouteau, then minister of tourism, also welcomed the conference participants:

> Since the tragic act of September 11th tourism has suffered. The government wants to attack this problem with the same vigor the terrorists used. . . . We are negotiating with other cruise lines. . . . We have lowered hotel prices for local residents. . . . Many investors are continuing with their investments. . . . Three new hotels will open in the near future. . . . We are a safe destination. We are a "harbor of peace." Tourism is the pillar that supports our autonomy.

These remarks, during a time when the number of tourists had declined precipitously and the morale of tourism professionals was low, reinforced the main message of the conference: Le tourisme c'est l'avenir (Tourism is the future). Indeed, the government representatives present were even more deeply invested in the promotion of tourism and more dependent on its success than were most conference participants.

Once the conference began, I went from session to session, listening to the various presentations, talking with participants during the breaks, and studying the different displays of promotional material. The conference did, indeed, expose me to a more complex world of imagery and marketing than I had been aware of. Several things in particular struck my attention.

First, I noticed rosy optimism everywhere. In contrast to the sobering tone of the opening remarks by the government officials, the tenor of the participants' presentations was consistently positive. I listened to numerous talks about market trends, survey results, competing destinations, key selling features, targets, action plans, and challenges—each pointing toward great accomplishments. At one session, the director of marketing and promotions in North America recounted glowing statistics about their marketing successes. He announced that they had met all their goals for the year: advertising had reached over 300 million people; the office had produced a thirty-eight-page vacation guide and distributed these to 50,000 travel agents and tour operators; workshops had taken place in twenty-four cities; more than 1,500 agents were trained for the Tahiti Tiare program, qualifying agents to specialize in promoting Tahiti; and their Web site received more than a million visits each month.[14]

However optimistic this report was, it teetered precariously on a base of clever image manipulation. For example, the representative from North America talked about the need to market Tahiti as a year-round destination so travelers would visit even during seasons with inclement weather (which appeared as an important concern again in their 2008 marketing plan).[15] To do this, however, Tahiti had to be reinvented. As the representative explained,

> We want to open up the season. It's important to stop talking about Tahiti as having a "wet season" and a "dry season," as we did in the past with counterproductive "wet season" marketing. We've put a lot of effort into quantifying the positive climate aspects that make Tahiti a potential year-round destination. We hired a professor of Atmospheric Science at the University of California to do a ninety-day study to change the image.

As I followed the presentation of his graphs of monthly amounts of sun and rain in Tahiti and how these statistics compared to those for major North

American cities in winter, I thought about the yellow plastic cones next to the puddles in the lobby and realized that nothing on the graphs quite captured the "wet season" storm outside.

The second thing I noticed was a remarkably restricted and redundant repertoire of imagery. This sense of confinement was both historical (more than two hundred years of repetitive imagery, almost all of which could be traced back to Bougainville, Loti, and Gauguin, among others) and circular (as marketing imagery fed tourists' expectations, which in turn influenced marketing). Although the opening remarks had emphasized the need to reach out to a new clientele, diversify the product, and reinvigorate the message—and to pursue tourism more creatively—marketing presentations seemed merely to repeat the same images and ideas.

For example, a number of representatives discussed how they had come up with "new" images to reach different clientele, yet the images they used were the same as before. The British representative said they were going to use the "new" vision of Tahiti as being "the most romantic place on earth" and "a place with friendly and welcoming people." She also described her "new" idea of staging an exhibit of Tahitian art at the Royal Geographical Society in London. The representative from Germany had the "new" idea of bringing Tahitian dancers to Germany. The posters displayed on walls and the brochures and press kits set out on long, skirted tables in each room also looked very familiar. All the promotional material attempted to beckon seductively, presenting well-known images of shimmering turquoise waters, seductive women, smiling children, and overwater bungalows aglow under tropical sunsets (fig. 3.5).[16]

This redundancy of marketing strategies and imagery, in fact, capitalizes on a highly efficient mode of communication. In discussing iconographic redundancy, anthropologist Christopher Steiner has interpreted such highly repetitive messages as semiotic shorthand for establishing credibility. Just as language patterns need to be repetitive for people to understand linguistic meaning, visual patterns that are repetitive establish representational authority and create their own "truth." A person's ability to see images as accurate depends not on their originality but on their adherence to the familiar (Steiner 1999, 92). Tahiti's long history of narratives and images is redundant to the point of having created and maintained Tahiti as its own referent. As a result, people who market Tahiti can be seen as merely engaging in "a self-referential discourse of cultural reality that generates an internal measure of truth-value" (Steiner 1999, 95). This is consistent with marketing strategies,

Fig. 3.5 Promotional images, La Conférence des Représentants de GIE Tahiti Tourisme, Pape'ete, 2001.

which recommend that "refinements may be made . . . but essentials of the brand personality should remain constant" (Morgan, Pritchard, and Pride 2002, 13).

One of the goals emphasized was to encourage tourists to visit different parts of French Polynesia. Some marketing strategies tried to "shift" the image and "move" the tourists. But "tourists' perceptions of places are . . . notoriously difficult to influence" (Morgan, Pritchard, and Pride 2002, 12). The magnetism of the familiar—not of the new and unexpected—was powerful. The representative from Japan talked about trying to change Japanese tourists' desires and to "move" them from Bora Bora to other islands, such as the Marquesas. Regardless of what advertising tricks he tried (for example, subtly inserting images of the Marquesas into montages with images of Bora Bora), nothing worked. At the end of his presentation he lamented, "I try to get people to go elsewhere, but they refuse. Bora Bora is what they want." Not surprisingly, in 2008 the marketing plan for Tahiti Tourisme North

America still listed one of its main objectives as introducing people to places beyond Tahiti, Bora Bora, and Mo'orea. This time the phrase "Tahiti's hidden paradise" was chosen to promote less well-known islands such as Huahine, Raiatea, the Marquesas, and the Tuamotus (Tahiti Tourisme North America 2008, 56).

The third feature I noted at the conference was the importance of "branding" places with memorable phrases and images, thus applying marketing techniques to a specific "product." This is done to make the places appear more familiar and accessible, turning them into packaged, brand name commodities for which people can shop. In capitalist societies, which require that cultures be based on images to stimulate buying, "the freedom to consume a plurality of images and goods is equated with freedom itself" (Sontag 1979, 178–79). This visual branding resonates with what anthropologist Robert Foster has written about "lovemarks," which are brands that are not only respected and trusted but also loved (R. Foster 2007, 708). Because people's attachments to lovemarks go beyond reason, premium prices can be charged.[17]

The North American representative maintained that creating a "brand" for the different islands was essential to attract tourists:

> Americans tend to remember the brand names more than the Tahitian names of islands. The name "Garden of Eden" is easier to remember than the name "Huahine," so we call Huahine by that name. The Marquesas are the "Mysterious Islands," Mo'orea is the "Magical Island," Bora Bora is the "Romantic Island," and so on. The island of Tahiti is being branded as "Queen of the Pacific" to communicate the idea of a center.

Even branded as a "Garden of Eden," Huahine presented a particular challenge. It did not fit in the tried-and-true triad of Tahiti-Mo'orea-Bora Bora, islands whose legendary beauty made them very popular. Nor could it be considered an exotic, "untouched" destination like Rangiroa or the Marquesas. As the GIE Tahiti Tourisme representative from South America explained,

> Huahine is one of the islands in which the South American market is developing an interest, but we have not been able to come up with a concept of what it is. We are trying to show the diversity among the islands and to find something unique about each one, but we are having trouble with Huahine.

The usual package for people who stay one week includes the three islands of Tahiti, Mo'orea, and Bora Bora. If people stay a few more days, as people from South America often do, then we add a fourth island and that's usually Huahine. But we're having problems identifying and selling it. We need to find a concept for Huahine.

Emblematic of Huahine's difficulty to be branded by the tourism industry, and consequently its inability to be "consumed" by most tourists, is the long list of brand names that have been tried. Within recent years Huahine has been labeled as the "Garden of Eden," "Garden Island," "Wild Island," "Savage Island," "Secret Island," "Rebellious Island," and "Authentic Island." And, of course, the "Garden of Eden" epithet is nothing more than a contemporary version of the name New Cytheria that was bestowed upon Tahiti by Bougainville, who, upon arriving on the island, said, "I thought I was transported to the Garden of Eden" (Bougainville 1772, 229).

Reducing a place to a visual or verbal image is, of course, highly problematic. While conjuring up an idea of a place, images in fact substitute an imagined space for the material reality. Substantial differences get reduced to, and replaced by, signs (a coconut palm, a sandy beach, a smiling woman) or phrases ("Garden of Eden," "Magical Island," "Romantic Island"). In the case of Tahiti, these signs are so redundant, predictable, and saturated that they leave little for the imagination. As the Japanese representative bemoaned, even when presented with alluring images of different islands, Japanese tourists still "want Bora Bora." Even savvy marketing experts couldn't move away from familiar icons any more than Japanese tourists could be coaxed away from Bora Bora. The directrice générale of GIE Tahiti Tourisme could only speak about their "original," "authentic," and "unique" product of Tahiti when framed by the Gauguin reproduction behind her and the generic tiki on the podium.

EVERYDAY LIVES

The various depictions of place that GIE Tahiti Tourisme so carefully constructs derive from, and further define, relations of power.[18] Representations are not innocently simplistic or erroneous. They can do violence (often concealed as a "picturesque" violence) to people and environments. Representations of places are enmeshed in global politics, and human lives are ensnared in the politics of representations. One is "never outside representation—or rather outside its politics" (H. Foster 1983, xv). Representations can easily become tools used to conceal, pacify, or control. Pictures of seductively posed smiling *vahine* distract one's attention from nuclear tests that take place alarmingly nearby. The cosmetic makeover at Tahua Vaiete provides an elegant veneer of touristic comforts behind which poverty and unemployment remain out of sight. Images of burning buildings and urban looting, which appear in page after page of a newspaper supplement, may coerce Tahitians into behaving according to government wishes.

This lived space that exists at the intersection of global politics, local beliefs, and marketing imagery is where Tahitians live their everyday lives. The powerful media images portraying Tahiti as a "paradise" have relentless consequences. The confining walls on which the images have been traced and retraced for centuries can create stifling personal enclosures. The imagery prevents outsiders from seeing local residents for who they are. More importantly, it also restricts Tahitians in their ability to "be free" to be themselves. What Chantal Spitz has said about Rarahu, the young Tahitian woman in Pierre Loti's nineteenth-century novel, could have been said about any of the marketing images:

> Oh, Rarahu, my shadow . . . I don't want to be a myth; I just want to be a human being equal to all other human beings. . . . Rarahu sticks to my skin like those labels on bottles that, no matter how much one moistens, rubs, or scratches, stay permanently affixed. Indelible. Rarahu is tattooed on my soul, my identity, and my humanity. . . . This exotic, eternal myth will not die. . . . Oh, Rarahu, if only you had never existed I could be free to be me. (Spitz 2000)

The ways in which different individuals—whether Tahitians such as Chantal Spitz, Westerners such as Pierre Loti, or employees of GIE Tahiti Tourisme—communicate their beliefs about a place usually speak past one another. Dominant Western representations in literature, art, media, and advertising create a meta-language that, though speaking to the Western world, can discourage *ta'ata ma'ohi* from participating in the discourse.[19] It speaks past everyday Tahitians in a language of verbal and visual imagery that objectifies them—which is why they do not necessarily "see" themselves in the "Tahiti" of the West.

In contrast to the way in which Western media portray Tahiti through images of pristine lagoons and topless women, Tahitians communicate their feelings and ideas about their place and themselves primarily in more spiritual, nonvisual ways rooted in *te fenua*. When their sense of place is threatened—not the postcard or marketing poster images of paradise, but the nurturing abilities of land—they speak forcefully and eloquently. They respond with the modern tools of democracy, such as written petitions, canoe protests, peaceful marches, popular songs, and purposeful potholes. When all else fails, they resort to other means, such as setting fire to a hotel, an airport, or even parts of the capital city. All of these acts serve to communicate unmistakably to outsiders, as one woman said, "E fenua ma'ohi teie, e'ere to o'e fenua" (This is our land, not your land). They are attempts, in Chantal Spitz's words, to disentangle themselves from the shadow of Rarahu and be free.

IMAGES ON TOUR

Tahiti's economic dependence on tourism[20] has meant that the government plays the leading role in marketing tourism and orchestrating its various initiatives, each carefully scheduled throughout the year. Every October GIE Tahiti Tourisme produces new travel planners and distributes these to travel agents and tour operators worldwide. Every December GIE Tahiti Tourisme hosts the annual conference in Pape'ete where its various international representatives present their regional marketing plans. And every January the representatives' postconference enthusiasm is used to inspire travel agents and tour operators, as well as potential tourists, when the representatives set up their tropically decorated booths at trade and travel shows around the world. Vanizette summed up the ultimate goal of these coordinated image-dependent efforts when saying, "All these activities are designed to educate and win over travel agents, to sell them on Tahiti, and to increase tourism."

As these images spread globally, they appear in many settings—at tourism trade shows, at travel agencies, and even in department stores that sell "Tahiti" along with their merchandise. I wanted to follow these images to the *métropole* to understand how they reappeared and functioned in different locations, each time further entangling Tahiti and France, as well as their interdependent economies. I was able to do this when, soon after the conference, I went to France to do more research.

In March 2002, at the Salon Mondial du Tourisme (Tourism Trade Show) in Paris, I browsed among the roughly two hundred booths that highlighted destinations around the world. As entertainment during the trade show, cultural performances were staged at one end of the hall. At one point, the loud, characteristic sound of Tahitian drumming began echoing through the area. Many people in the crowd stopped what they were doing and, as if pulled by a magnet, quickly made their way to the performance area. By the time I arrived, all the seats were taken, and the people standing on the margins were pressing into the crowd, straining for a better view. It was clear to me—as Paulette Viénot, Tahiti's "queen of tourism," had predicted half a century earlier—that Westerners found Tahitian drumming and dancing exotic. After the performance I spoke with the elaborately tattooed principal dancer, who told me that he had been hired by GIE Tahiti Tourisme to travel from trade show to trade show, dancing to advertise Tahiti.

The trade show featured some two hundred destinations. It was Tahiti, however, that was highlighted in the six-page center spread in the trade show's official catalogue, *Bon Voyage*, which enticed visitors with such phrases as *un avant-goût du paradis* (an impression of paradise) and *Tahiti et ses îles, vous n'avez pas fini d'en rêver* (Tahiti and her islands: your dreams have only just begun), and then invited them to come discover Tahiti and her islands at Booth A109 in Hall 6 at the Salon Mondial du Tourisme. The article included the usual icons—a full-page photo of women dancing in shredded leaf skirts and coconut cup bras, a picture of a tattooed man, and a caption next to a photo of colorful *pareus* that referred to "the warm colors of Gauguin." The article concluded with the travel writer's description of how the Gauguin myth had turned into reality right in front of his eyes: "Two young women, each with a hibiscus flower in her hair, let their *pareus* drop as they walked towards the sea. I now understand more, watching Gauguin's canvas come to life in front of my eyes, why some men have permanently set their anchor in Tahiti" (Mahé 2002, 25).

What I observed at the Salon Mondial du Tourisme reminded me of the carefully juxtaposed images discussed at the conference in Pape'ete. The trade show booth with its tropical decor, the wild rhythmic drumming resonating through the hall, the tattooed dancer on the stage, the trade show catalogue with its images of dancers and tattooed men and its descriptions of Tahitian women gracefully undressing as they walked into the sea—everything was deliberately packaged for the (mainly French) audience at the trade show. Each detail or nuance worked in concordance with the others to give the audience "an impression of paradise" and a vision of Tahiti coming to life in front of their eyes as they strained to see—to almost experience—Tahiti in Paris. The next step, of course, would be to purchase an airline ticket and *really* see and experience the Tahiti of their dreams.

A few months later I went to La Maison de Tahiti, the Parisian head-quarters of GIE Tahiti Tourisme on Boulevard Saint-Germain, where I had arranged an interview with Mme Christine Sauvagnac, the assistant man-ager. From the street, La Maison de Tahiti looked like a typical travel agency, although one that obviously specialized in Tahiti. Its windows were filled with Tahitian travel posters, Tahitian flags, potted Tahitian gardenias, tikis, and shells. La Maison de Tahiti has several employees of GIE Tahiti Tourisme who educate the public (mainly people who walk in off the street) and train travel agents and tour operators on how best to promote Tahiti. Indeed, the manager had been at the same conference in Pape'ete that I had just attended.

Christine Sauvagnac was friendly and forthcoming, telling me she had spent most of her life living with her family in various French colonies. "I grew up in Tahiti and fell in love with the islands, and now I think of my work as selling my heart and selling the soul of Tahiti," she explained. "To me, the islands present themselves as images. I see atolls as gentle and feminine, pro-tected by lagoons. I see high islands (especially the Marquesas) as masculine, volatile, and violent." She elaborated on the importance of mental images:

> When most people think about Tahiti, they think of Bora Bora; it's the myth of the Pacific. So if you add Bora Bora to any tourist package, people will go. But if they want something more authentic, then I recommend Huahine. It's an island that's authentic, warm, like a woman, like a spa, like a retreat, almost shy. No matter where people want to go, when planning their trip, we try to save the best for last so they go home with a postcard image in their mind.

Like most travel agents and tour operators, she relies heavily on photo-graphic images to respond to people's dreams and to help sell her product. She showed me a book (Bacchet 1999), which consists of only photos, no text, and explained that all she had to do was open the book and turn the pages in front of customers without saying a word. "The photos do all the work. I tell people, 'There's no filter here, what you see in the photos is what you get.' People look at the photos and want to go." Looking at the book and listening to her comments, I thought of Diane Commons and the efforts she made to create her photographs, so similar to what I was seeing in the book in front of me.

Using images to trigger insatiable desire resonates with Sontag's observation about capitalist societies relying on images to stimulate the buying of commodities. Photos, in particular, can elicit imaginative flights of fancy. "A photograph is both a pseudo-presence and a token of absence. Like a wood fire in a room, photographs—especially those of people, of distant landscapes and faraway cities, of the vanished past—are incitements to reverie . . . attempts to contact or lay claim to another reality" (Sontag 1979, 16).

Photographs constantly hold a promise, albeit an ambiguous one, of something more. This can be seen with the 1936 launching of *Life* magazine, the first American mass-media magazine. Two things were prophetic about it. First, advertising financed the magazine (a third of its images were devoted to product promotion), rather than subscriptions or newsstand sales. "The second prophecy lay in its title. This is ambiguous. It may mean that the pictures inside are about life. Yet it seems to promise more: that these pictures *are* life" (Berger 1991, 53–54).

Sauvagnac's reliance on photography—rather than on words—is a reminder that images, like money, can be used as a form of currency, as a way of unifying subjects within a global network of valuation and desire.

> In teaching us a new visual code, photographs alter and enlarge our notions of what is worth looking at and what we have a right to observe. They are a grammar and, even more importantly, an ethics of seeing. Finally, the most grandiose result of the photographic enterprise is to give us the sense that we can hold the whole world in our heads as an anthology of images. (Sontag 1979, 3)

Although Sauvagnac showed me the book to explain how she used the photographic images to trigger desire, the trick with photography is that—like the photographs in *Life* that "seem to promise more"—it never satisfies the desire.[21] One needs to continually tinker with the reality to make it match the photographs, getting caught up in a never-ending spiral.

I continued with my search for traces of Tahiti in France and went to La Samaritaine, the fashionable department store near the Seine (now closed), which was having a display of Tahitian goods. As I approached the store, I saw a sign in one of its windows—*Exposition Tahiti, Escale à Bora Bora, 3ème Étage* (Tahiti Exhibit, Port of Call Bora Bora, 3rd Floor)—and went in. When I reached the third floor, I followed the turquoise, Tahitian gardenia-shaped markers on the ground, whose signs and arrows directed me to the

Fig. 3.6   Display of Tahitian merchandise at La Samaritaine, Paris, 2002.

Exposition Bain de Mer (Ocean Bathing Exhibit). There, GIE Tahiti Tourisme had set up a 3,500-square-foot exhibit of Tahitian goods and crafts (fig. 3.6). Brightly hued *pareus,* sandals with tropical designs, pandanus placemats, black-pearl jewelry, flowers, *monoï* (scented coconut oil), and coconut soaps perfumed with vanilla or gardenia filled the area with color and fragrance. Arranged on shelves and tables to attract customers' attention, merchandise and place mingled in a dazzling display of "elsewhere," where shoppers could choose an item and purchase "Tahiti." Walking among the displays of merchandise, I suddenly discovered a makeshift travel agency, its walls covered with posters, maps, hotel advertisements, airline banners, and a reproduction of a Gauguin painting. There, customers could effortlessly become future tourists, literally getting to their destination through strategically placed portals of consumption in Paris.

Walter Benjamin, who in 1933 fled to Paris after the Nazis seized power in Germany, focused his intellectual energy on a vast compilation of information about Paris. Calling Paris "the capital of the nineteenth century," he wanted to understand the social history of the explosive capitalist relations of commodity and spectacle that from a small beginning had come to smother the globe (Benjamin 1999). For the last thirteen years of his life, Benjamin focused on Paris' shopping arcades—iron and glass-roofed passages that cut through buildings and "housed chaotic juxtapositions of shop signs, lighting, and attractive window displays of commodities and mannequins" (Leslie 2006). Benjamin saw the arcades as a microcosm of capitalism. Much like the display in La Samaritaine, they represented both an invigorating promise of abundance and a shattering disappointment of that promise when broken. Turning other places (and their inhabitants) into commodities to be depicted, advertised, and purchased is a strategy that works well—indeed, that goes hand in hand—with the capitalist entanglements between the colonizer and the colonized. "Capitalism is the first mode of economy . . . which is unable to exist by itself, which needs other economic systems as a medium and a soil" (Luxembourg 1963, 368).

In all my wandering in Paris during those months, the only place where I expected to encounter Tahiti but couldn't find it was in the most obvious capitalist site and the epicenter of the entangled economies of *métropole* and colony—as I went one afternoon from one prominent bank to another on the Champs-Elysées, trying to exchange some Tahitian bank notes for euros. The tellers squinted at the bills, frowned, shook their heads, and insisted that they had no idea where the money was from. "I've never heard of French Polynesia," one teller said, "I think it's in Africa."[22] No matter how much I tried to explain, no one would exchange the currency. Even in Paris (perhaps precisely in Paris, the nucleus of the colonial *métropole*), the myth of Tahiti was more real than the reality; here *l'espace conçu* overshadowed *l'espace perçu*. Many would-be tourists had rushed to watch the exotic, tattooed dancer at the Salon Mondial du Tourisme. People visiting La Maison de Tahiti had looked at images in a book and "wanted to go." And shoppers at La Samaritaine had wandered effortlessly from a display of *pareus* and scented coconut oil into a travel agency where they could purchase an airline ticket. None of the bank employees, however, had any idea about where the real place was or even that it was "part" of France. Ironically, it is the exchange of capital that connects the two places *and* that necessitates keeping Tahiti as an imagined place of desire, rather than a place that is honestly experienced.

THE MYTH IN THE AGE OF THE INTERNET

The first years of the twenty-first century—with the inconveniences of air travel after September 11, 2001, economic dislocations, widespread outbreaks of violence, and, most recently, a near global economic recession resulting

in massive unemployment and the loss of personal savings—have been difficult for the tourism industry. The effects of these events have been especially severe for French Polynesia, where the majority of tourists come from
North America. The number of tourists in French Polynesia dropped 30 percent from 2008 to 2009, hitting a thirteen-year low—the fewest number of
tourists since 1996, following the protests and riots after the nuclear testing
program was resumed. As a result of these low numbers, recent marketing
efforts have increased dramatically, especially those aimed at a North American clientele.

As stated in Tahiti Tourisme North America's marketing plan for 2008,
the primary target customer for French Polynesia is educated, affluent, a
seeker of exotic destinations, and an Internet user. For them, Tahiti offers
specific "brand attributes"—luxury resorts with their overwater bungalows,
romantic settings, and seclusion—that appeal to this segment of the population. The plan stated that one of the main goals was to have "more website promotion" and especially "dynamic packaging on the Internet" (Tahiti
Tourisme North America 2008, 3).[23]

> As Internet penetration is closely aligned with a household's relative
> education attainment and to a lesser extent, affluence, the Internet has
> become the most cost-effective tool for an up-market brand to keep in
> touch with its customers. For Tahiti Tourisme North America the website
> www.Tahiti-Tourisme.com is central to nearly all market activities and
> focus is continuously placed on maintaining site visitor-growth from the
> North American region. (Tahiti Tourisme North America 2008, 16)

One example of "more website promotion" was an Internet contest
called "Invest in Your Love," held in 2009–10. It made creative use of the
global financial crisis by juxtaposing the dire consequences of financial investment against "investing in your love" and, perhaps, winning a
"love stimulus package," a free trip to Tahiti. As stated on the site, "stocks, bonds,
401ks . . . oh my! Looking for a better return on investment? It's time to
invest in something real . . . your love. Known as the most romantic destination in the world, a trip to Tahiti is an investment that will pay dividends
for a lifetime."[24] To enter the contest, one needed only to follow "four easy
steps": (1) make a video about how a trip to Tahiti can help you invest
in your love, (2) upload your video to YouTube, (3) fill out the entry
form on the Web site so you can be notified when voting begins, and

(4) tell all your friends to watch the video and vote for you. The videos by and large featured overworked, stressed-out couples, often living in cramped quarters with small children, needing to rekindle their love by vacationing in "paradise." Several of the videos showed the couples trying (unsuccessfully) to replicate a Tahiti vacation at home by doing such things as floating tents in swimming pools, sprinkling sand around their feet, or wearing snorkeling gear while splashing in their children's wading pools. The contest cleverly turned these hopeful participants into marketing ambassadors by providing incentives for them to get the greatest possible audience for their videos.

Along with increasing use of the Internet for promoting a destination comes the democratization provided by the Internet through the postvacation distribution of photos on blogs and Flickr, and videos on YouTube. Not surprisingly—because the majority of tourists to Tahiti stay in the tourist "cocoon"—the personal images and narratives they post tend to replicate marketing imagery and validate their experiences. These include "postcard" visions of blue lagoons and empty beaches, the isolated beach chairs under coconut palms, honeymoon couples dining on private verandas, rainbows above overwater bungalows, and fiery tropical sunsets. These are accompanied by verbal descriptions of breakfasts arriving by canoe at one's bungalow and luxurious spa treatments that include massages with scented coconut oil and body wraps with volcanic sand and black pearls. One blog described a picnic that the hotel organized to a sandy *motu* where food was served on "plates" of woven palm leaves and eaten with "spoons" of seashells. The blog's author, after talking to the ukulele-playing tour guide on the *motu*, wrote that he thought the experience gave him a glimpse of what "real life is like in French Polynesia beyond the deluxe resorts."[25] The blogs and photo galleries include practically no images of Tahitian people, other than those within the hotel cocoon. One tourist, upon discovering the local transportation in town, commented, *"le truck* is the cheapest way to get around . . . as long as you don't mind riding with the locals" (clearly distinguishing between the category of hotel employee and that of "local").

THE ENDLESS HALL OF MIRRORS

Undeniably, the marketing of a dream, a myth, a fantasized place, is a calculated and (hopefully, for marketers) effective mechanism to lure visitors (and their money) to a destination. Far more important, by manipulating images and impressions—whether by using paving stones brought from France, decorations on the *roulottes,* smiling children on the cover of the travel planner, brand names of "mysterious island" or "magical island," photos in a book that make tourists "want to go," or on-line video contests—marketing professionals and others attempt to bring different (and potentially conflicting) views of a place into alignment with one another. As if appearing in an endless hall of mirrors, these various perspectives of a place all reflect, refract, and recast images of one another. The calculated process of marketing validates consumers' choices. It reassures tourists that the destination they have chosen is indeed the one they've imagined, and that their vacation will be well worth the time and expense invested.[26] This is why, as Christine Sauvagnac told me, "Tahiti is not a destination to which you can just go on your own; you need a travel agent to arrange the details of the trip for you." In other words, you need a travel agent to arrange (in Alloula's words) "the glittering traps of detail for the eye."

Because this ephemeral world of marketed images fails to fully reflect the physical reality it attempts to sell, it is in constant need of being reworked in the endless hall of mirrors (such as at GIE Tahiti Tourisme, the conference, or La Maison de Tahiti). Not surprisingly, the marketing of Tahiti takes its inspiration from the more-than-two-hundred-year-long entrenched history of narratives and images. The expectations of tourists also have been influenced by this same history of relatively predictable images that has, especially in the Western world, established Tahiti as its own referent.

Like many such images and narratives that represent a stereotype, "cultural production has been driven back inside the mind . . . it can no longer look directly out of its eyes at the real world for the referent but must . . . trace its mental images of the world on its confining walls" (Jameson 1983, 118). "It is a world that flees, a world with a perpetual, indeed a dizzying, need for rejuvenation. It even seems at times that this world is about to disappear" (Lefebvre 1991, 390). Unable to be supported by an outer reality, it turns inward within its own unimaginative and confining walls and feeds upon itself. Victor Segalen had bemoaned the fact that once Tahiti was "discovered," there would be nowhere left to dream about. How wrong he was! Had he lived a century later, he would have seen that once Tahiti was "discovered," the dream was shaped, and reshaped, through redundant images, into a reality of its own.

CHAPTER FOUR

In the Cocoon

When tourists decide to travel somewhere, their choice is usually influenced by sights they expect to see and experiences they hope to have. They make their choices "because there is an anticipation, especially through day-dreaming and fantasy, of intense pleasures . . . involving different senses from those customarily encountered" (Urry 1995, 132). If Tahiti is their destination, their decision has probably been based on specific images they have seen in brochures, on videos and Web sites, or at tourism trade shows, and then imagined in their mind's eye. Research conducted by GIE Tahiti Tourisme has found that tourists see the islands of Tahiti as being pristine, beautiful, unique, untouched, authentic, and romantic (Tahiti Tourisme North America 2008). Given that these perceptions do not always accord with what one might actually see or experience in Tahiti, the tourism industry has to create touristic experiences that are consistent with what most visitors expect. Thus, the myth of Tahiti is given physical definition in the landscapes that tourists visit, revealing a particular "Tahiti" that although intentionally constructed, appears to be completely natural. Most tourists, of course, know that their experiences are not necessarily "authentic" but give this fact little critical thought. "Whether these are natural or simulated matters little. . . . What is wanted is materiality and naturalness as such, rediscovered in their (apparent or real) immediacy" (Lefebvre 1991, 353).[1]

A conversation I had in a hotel lobby with an American couple supported these ideas. Noticing the strands of shells around their necks and the suitcases by their side, I asked if they were waiting for the van to the airport, and they told me about their vacation while they waited.

The husband said, "We came to Tahiti because my wife just celebrated her fiftieth birthday and we were looking for a vacation where we could celebrate in style. We've already been to Hawai'i, so we decided to come here. Hey, I've had Tahiti on my mind for many, many years. In fact, when we first got married, I used to tell my wife, 'If you ever give me any trouble, I'll go to Tahiti and never come back.' We're very glad we came. The hotel was everything. It was excellent. The oceanfront setting was spectacular. And the service was amazing. After the first day, all the people who worked at the hotel could already read our minds. Tahitians are naturally so friendly. Oh, and the dance show was out of this world. Everything was exactly as we had imagined it would be."

His wife added, "I cried this morning because our vacation is over. It was so wonderful. It has been amazing. Really, it was perfect."

"Yes, a perfect experience is what you pay for," the husband said. "That's what you want. When you go on vacation, that's why you go. If I wanted to have problems and headaches, I could stay at home. When I go on vacation, I want everything to be perfect—I want it to be like a dream."[2]

Having been a guest at several resort hotels in French Polynesia (as a tourist in 1976, while doing research for a Tahiti guide book in 1994, and as a guest of an employee in 1996 and 2001), I knew just what he meant. People writing about tourism over the years have used different terms for these dreamlike spaces. Daniel Boorstin (1964) coined the term "pseudo-event" to describe the ersatz experience that he felt American tourists prefer to a real experience. Later Louis Turner and John Ash (1975) discussed how tourists are placed at the center of strictly circumscribed worlds, which restrict them to visiting only designated areas and seeing only chosen attractions. They concluded that this leads to the construction of unimaginative hotels and the selection of predictable tourist sites, which make up "a small monotonous world that everywhere shows us our own image . . . the pursuit of the exotic and diverse ends in uniformity" (Turner and Ash 1975, 292). Dean MacCannell's (1976) idea of "staged authenticity," which creates room for various levels of manipulation, has become one of the most popular (and also contested)[3] concepts in tourism studies. Umberto Eco (1986) and Jean Baudrillard (1988), discussing hyperreality and simulacra, singled out tourism as the prime example of these fake "realities." Dennis Judd described how "standardized venues of the tourist bubble seem mass-produced, almost as if they were made in a tourism infrastructure factory" (Judd 1999, 39). These spaces—whether called pseudo-events, staged authenticities, hyper-realities, simulacra, managed spaces, or bubbles—are especially popular with tourists in French Polynesia, even when other forms of accommodations and activities are available.

In pondering these many terms, I have decided to use a different word—"cocoon"—to refer to this type of intentionally constructed space. In choosing the term "cocoon," I hope to convey the sense of a space whose construction is a meditated activity and ongoing process the aim of which is to create a space that is intricate, comforting, and relatively opaque. The word "bubble," while also evoking an image of an artificial space, seems less apt because it conveys the idea of a space that is sealed off and intact, even able to expand, burst, or disappear. Cocoons, however, are always in the process of being spun.

About 90 percent of all tourists to Tahiti stay in these self-contained and carefully managed accommodations, which are defined as resort hotels with luxury accommodations and a full range of amenities (Institut de la statistique de la Polynésie française 2008).[4] In 2006, there were about fifty such hotels in French Polynesia (with a total number of about 3,200 rooms), more than one-third of which were on the island of Tahiti (with most of the rest located on Bora Bora and Moʻorea). For most tourists, this is what is firmly entrenched in their image of Tahiti. Claude Robineau, an anthropologist who worked on Moʻorea from the 1960s to the 1980s, has commented on these hotel complexes, describing them as "geographic blocks or aggregates composed of large scale tourist units . . . [that] operate as closed systems" (Robineau 1975, 67). Tourists, even when traveling away from the hotels, move within an enclosed space—such as the hotel van—cut off from contact with the local population. "The tourist goes from hotel to tourist site by way of tourist cars; he moves side by side with other tourists; with the services they offer, the big hotel units make it unnecessary for the tourist to make use of the facilities used by the people of the country" (Robineau 1975, 67).

Luxury hotels also tend to be isolated. On the mainland of Bora Bora there are only two miles of white-sand beach, most of which is not suitable for a large resort development. As a result, most new resort hotels have been built on the *motus*, or islets, on the barrier reef forming the lagoon. Only accessible by boat, these hotels isolate guests even further. Typically, when

hotels are located on main islands, rather than on a *motu,* they are in locations far removed from local services. Hotels then provide transportation
to and from the airport and to hotel-sponsored activities. Convenient local
transportation is mostly unavailable to tourists.[5] Once tourists arrive at the
hotel, it is difficult for them to leave, or even to get information about how to
do so. I once overheard a guest inquire at a reception desk, "How do I get out
of here?" The receptionist's response, offered without so much as a smile, was
unambiguous: "You don't."

This degree of isolation, privacy, and exclusivity, of course, is often the
main attraction for people vacationing in Tahiti. An escape to a dream world
of exoticism and luxury is exactly what is offered in many advertisements
(with the newest hotels being given names that include "resort and spa"),
often exploiting the idea of fulfilling simple "savage" pleasures on a remote
island—ideas Rousseau and Gauguin helped instill in the minds of Westerners. One hotel, which opened in 2002 on a *motu* off the island of Taha'a, was
highly praised as "the most exclusive resort in French Polynesia."[6] *Travel and
Leisure* magazine described the experience one would have there:

> If you've always thought Gauguin had it right when he swapped Paris for
> Tahiti, then this 60-room resort is bound to light your *tiki* torch. Each bun-
> galow is airy, with bark cloth paintings, dried-leaf light fixtures, and a private
> plunge pool. There's plenty to keep active guests busy, but quality time is best
> spent lying on your backs, side by side, during banana-leaf wraps and vanilla-
> oil massages. Or reenact Gauguin's *Two Nudes on a Tahitian Beach* with a pic-
> nic of champagne on a deserted atoll [which costs $404 extra per couple, on
> top of the room price of $900–$1,250 per night]. (*Travel and Leisure* 2003, 91)

The creation of spaces that are physically and socially segregated is, of
course, not necessarily typical of all tourist destinations in Tahiti. A range of
accommodations exists, each with a different level of exclusivity. For example,
pensions, typically owned and operated by Tahitian families, cater mainly to
a French clientele who already live in French Polynesia and are looking for
a weekend getaway, and for whom there is no language barrier. Hotels in or
near Pape'ete also offer a different experience because there a guest can walk
outside, get on a bus, take a taxi, or rent a car. However, the managed hotel
spaces in French Polynesia (and especially those with overwater bungalows,
a type of accommodation designed exclusively for tourists and, until recently,
found only in French Polynesia) are especially emblematic of a vacation in

Tahiti. Not only do 90 percent of tourists choose to stay in them but tourism advertising also focuses on them. Everyone involved in tourism—marketing specialists, travel agents, architects, hotel directors, hotel employees, and, of course, tourists themselves—plays a part in creating and maintaining these carefully constructed simulacra.

COCOONS

Cocoons serve several important purposes. Ideally, they are spaces of total control that are physically managed to replicate an imagined place. A cocoon is an excellent example of how the Tahiti of the imagination—*l'espace conçu*—influences the physical experience of Tahiti—*l'espace perçu*. Control, of course, is a key element for these spaces, which allows hotel designers to screen out the "mess" of reality and present only the dream, hopefully keeping the tourists content. It is a highly effective strategy for coping with the disjuncture between the larger reality of a place—with its mosquitoes, ordinary buildings, and everyday Tahitians—and those expectations that have been created by advertising.

Keeping tourists in a cocoon is critical because left on their own to wander freely outside these controlled spaces, they might be disquieted—perhaps thinking that their vacation was not living up to what they had imagined. For example, on Huahine, tourists being driven to their hotel from the airport would come to a fork in the road. The road to the right is paved and leads to the hotel. The road to the left leads to the market gardens and a few houses. Although more heavily used than the road to the hotel, it is unpaved and rutted (and, ironically, is a more direct route to and from the airport). Or if tourists were to leave their hotel-approved "island tour" and find themselves at the edge of the main town, they might notice lots of people waiting on benches outside the government-run clinic for an appointment with a health care provider (not the private French doctor that French residents or tourists would see if they needed care). Or tourists staying at the hotel on Sunday morning enjoying the sumptuous buffet would not see the colorful local market, where they might stumble upon empty beer bottles on the ground next to a bench, the remnants of Saturday night. Or at the hotel, swimming in the crystal clear, chlorinated water of the swimming pool, they would not see Tahitians gathered around a spigot at the side of the road, filling plastic bottles with water and loading these into large laundry baskets in the backs of their pickup trucks. Ideally, most tourists would not see the deeply rutted dirt roads, the long lines at the clinic, the discarded beer bottles, or the lack of potable water in homes. Cocoons serve to shield them from these and other aspects of daily life that are not described or pictured in their guidebooks. Within a cocoon, however, all manner of fantasies can be crafted, providing the illusion of a picturesque, "authentic" Tahiti.

Needs and desires can be seamlessly united in a cocoon, and tourism advertising plays on this harmony. "Specific needs have specific objects. Desire, on the other hand, has no particular object, except for a space where it has full play: a beach, a place of festivity, the space of the dream" (Lefebvre 1991, 353). A popular phrase in Tahitian tourism advertising is *une rencontre de la tradition et de la modernité, de la culture polynésienne et des conforts modernes* (a meeting of tradition and modernity, of Polynesian culture and modern comforts). One hotel on Bora Bora, which has eighty overwater bungalows and the "first-ever, one-of-a-kind, overwater wedding chapel in French Polynesia," advertises itself as having "a very New York meets South Pacific feel to it. . . . Its modern architecture and technology flourish side by side with traditional authentic local arts and crafts," and the spa "combines the soothing powers of the islands and the European therapeutic regimen of deep seawater's curative benefits."[7] Other advertisements are similar: "A French kiss is a passionate version of an ordinary one. . . . Hotels are no different! Le Méridien Hôtels de Polynésie . . . traditionally French, decid-edly Polynesian." And "Would you fly that extra mile for the most recklessly romantic islands on the face of the earth? Tahiti invites such impetuosity. This is where vibrant, easy-going, open-armed Polynesia marries the sophis-ticated, energizing *joie de vivre* of France" (Tahiti Tourisme North America Travel Planner 2001). For a hotel to offer French food and wine is always seen as a plus: "Anywhere the French have been, you can count on the food being delectable. . . . Enjoy Cordon Bleu classics, flaming crêpes, croissants and mousses." Or you can drink champagne in Tahiti that is "fine enough to be imbibed on the Champs Élysées" (Ariyoshi 2001, 873).

The utility of a cocoon disappears when it is not controlled. This is the case with pensions, or family guesthouses, mainly owned by Tahitians. There are about 200 of these, able to accommodate about 1,000 guests. At a pension there is little focus on maintaining the myth. The client of a pension is either someone from the local French population or, much less frequently, a budget traveler seeking less expensive accommodations. There is no air conditioned van to bring them from the airport (although there might be a pickup truck). There is no young woman wearing a flower crown at a reception desk when they arrive, and no tattooed man to take their bags. There are no overwater bungalows. In fact, there is probably no lagoon. The guests won't see an evening dance performance or a demonstration of how to wrap and wear a *pareu,* or be given a shell necklace when they leave.

The Tahitian owner of one such pension (where a bungalow cost about US$45 a night at the time) described what tourists receive at her guesthouse and why, from her perspective, the economics of running such a business keep her family focused intently on the basics:

> Here everything is natural. It is not *chichi,* not all done up, like at the hotel. Some people want things to be fancy. But others prefer things simple, natural, and local. If they want things to be local, people come here. Running a pension is a good job, but you need at least two people because it's hard work. I clean all the rooms and wash all the laundry. And my husband cuts the grass and cleans up the yard. And it costs a lot of money too. You need to have many things. You need a car or truck to get the people from the airport. You need insurance. You need a license. Now there's tax too. And you have to pay for water, gas, and electricity. All these things cost a lot. You have to be thrifty. You have to really think about all the expenses and be careful to make ends meet. Each month I have to figure out how many guests will be in the pension, how much money we'll earn, and how much we can spend. It's good work, but you don't earn a lot. Many pensions have gone out of business. They went bankrupt because of how much it costs to run them. (Henriette Colombani, personal communication, 2001)

Tahiti's tourism infrastructure only minimally accommodates pensions. Most advertising is aimed at the *haut de gamme,* or top-of-the-range, tourist. The government, which stands to gain the most from tourism, strongly encourages and promotes this high-end tourism, a clear indication of how the Tahiti of the imagination is valued much more than the Tahiti of a pension. Only recently has the government begun to support or advertise these accommodations. The owner of a pension, who was also the representative for Huahine's association of pensions, explained the government's shift in attitude:

> For a long time the government has ignored the existence of family pensions. In fact, it has boycotted them. That's because the government doesn't earn any money from them. Family guesthouses have existed since the 1960s, but the

government only started paying attention to them in the early 1990s. Things changed because, with the introduction of the Internet, we could take things into our own hands. We were able to outsmart the government and advertise on our own. (Etienne Puaritahi Faaeva, personal communication, 2001)

Even with the availability of Internet advertising, most tourists who visit Tahiti still choose the luxury resort rather than the basic accommodations of a family pension.

THE UNVEILING OF A NEW COCOON

Given the importance of resort hotels for Tahitian tourism, it is understandable that the Territorial government is deeply invested in them. In addition to buttressing economic development, these hotels are also visible symbols of the government's political success. In 2001, a new hotel opened on Tikehau, an atoll in the Tuamotu Archipelago, an hour's flight from Pape'ete. In French Polynesia many differences exist among the islands, which range from precipitous, lagoonless islands (the Marquesas Islands or Tahiti) to atolls enclosing lagoons rimmed with powdery, white-sand beaches (like most of the islands in the Tuamotu Archipelago). Some islands, such as Bora Bora or Mo'orea, have mountainous cores surrounded by a lagoon. Ironically, tourists need to leave the island of Tahiti to find the "Tahiti" of their dreams with a white-sand beach. With its remote location, powdery white-sand beaches, small population (roughly 400 people), and reliable airstrip, Tikehau seemed an ideal site for such development.

Due to several financial difficulties, the construction of the Tikehau hotel took more than ten years. An Italian investor originally launched the project in the late 1980s, but then went bankrupt, leaving cement pilings and bare platforms standing in the lagoon. In 1995, a Japanese-American investor stepped in, but pulled out a week later when, from his home in Los Angeles, he watched CNN coverage of Tahiti's airport bursting into flames during the rioting against nuclear testing. Because of the pivotal role that tourism needed to play in the post-CEP Territorial economy, the government established and funded the FHP, or Financière Hôtelière Polynésienne (which can be glossed as the Polynesian Hotel Financing Agency), the goal of which was to bring resort hotels to the outer islands to "diversify the tourism product." FHP capital, and thus hotel ownership, has always come from the same combination of commercial and government sources.[8] In 2000 the FHP provided new investors, South Pacific Management, with about US$10 million, and the Tikehau Pearl Beach Resort was quickly completed.

In 2001, the Pearl Beach Resort hotel chain was the largest chain of resort hotels in French Polynesia. It is an excellent example of vertical integration — where companies are connected to one another hierarchically and share a common owner, with each controlling a different segment of the total product. Those in charge of building and managing these hotels are a small, elite segment of the population. At the time, all Pearl Beach Resort hotels were financed by the FHP and were managed by South Pacific Management, the president and CEO of which was also the president of Tahiti Nui Travel, the largest travel agency in French Polynesia (originally founded by Paulette Viénot). The role of the FHP in transforming the image of "paradise" into a "reality" was acknowledged by a caption under the photo of the interior of a Tikehau bungalow: "Maeva au paradis. . . . Robinson Crusoë en aurait sans doute rêvé . . . la FHP l'a fait" (Welcome to paradise. . . . Robinson Crusoe would have doubtless dreamed of it . . . the FHP accomplished it; *Les nouvelles de Tahiti* 2001, 25).

Although I could not be present at the opening of the hotel, I felt inundated with news about almost every facet of the event. Broadcast and print media covered its opening in thorough and vivid detail. Television viewers could see the entire hotel in its splendor. One newspaper published articles about the hotel on three separate days, even giving it front-page status on one day (*La dépêche de Tahiti* 2001a). The other published a two-page color spread about the hotel's inauguration (*Les nouvelles de Tahiti* 2001). The opening of the four-star Tikehau Pearl Beach Resort in French Polynesia — at the time, the seventh in a growing chain of Pearl Beach Resorts — took place on October 20, 2001. It had thirty-eight bungalows, most of which were on pilings over the water (fig. 4.1).

The opening of the Tikehau Pearl Beach Resort was accompanied by great fanfare. The morning of its inauguration, the rain cleared auspiciously as numerous flights arrived with public figures and politicians. Among these were the high commissioner of the Republic of France, the president and vice president of French Polynesia, the minister of tourism, the chief executive officer of FHP, the president and CEO of South Pacific Management, the mayor of Rangiroa, the Tahitian man who sold his land for the construction of the hotel, and inhabitants of Tikehau atoll.

Luxury hotels in French Polynesia, such as the one on Tikehau, are sites for both the management of physical space for tourists and the flaunting of

Fig. 4.1   Aerial view of Tikehau Pearl Beach Resort. Courtesy of Tim McKenna.

success by politicians. Like the turn-of-the-century Expositions Universelles, new luxury hotels are used as symbols of the accomplishments of those in power. In the ceremony celebrating the Tikehau Pearl Beach Resort's opening, several politicians gave speeches thanking the government and those individuals who provided financing for the hotel. As the president of FHP said in his list of acknowledgments, "Thanks to the Loi Pons and the Loi Paul that allowed the patrons to bring their investment to fruition. . . . Thanks to the President of French Polynesia and his tax-exempt laws, thanks to his passion and perseverance"[9] (*La dépêche de Tahiti* 2001a, 36).

Other speeches focused on the symbolic significance of the hotel, suggesting that its opulence was a promise of economic well-being and political security for French Polynesia. Predicting a rosy future for everyone, President Flosse found many opportunities to refer to the new government-owned airline, Air Tahiti Nui, which was being launched at the same time, and to the direct Paris-Pape'ete flights that were to start soon. Indeed, much like the Eiffel Tower at the 1889 Exposition Universelle, which glorified French progress and modernity, the Tikehau Pearl Beach Resort was described as a monument to the glory and success of the Territory. Both the president of French Polynesia and the high commissioner of the Republic of France used the same phrase: "La réalisation de cet hôtel est un acte de foi et de confiance en l'avenir" (The opening of this hotel is an act of faith and confidence in the future).

Away from the blue lagoon of Tikehau, however, much of the rest of the world was still in shock from the events of September 11 in New York. As a contrast to other tourist destinations, Tikehau (which, coincidentally, means "peace belt"), and French Polynesia in general, were now being promoted as havens of peace and security. Stark images of the fear that raged elsewhere in the world were used in the speeches to remind people of the tranquility of Tikehau. For anyone coming to Tikehau, "terrorist threats, attacks in Afghanistan, and letters suspected of carrying anthrax all seem so far away" (*Les nouvelles de Tahiti* 2001, 24). The CEO of FHP described the new hotel as "a peaceful refuge" (*un havre de paix,* a phrase soon widely adopted by many others). He told those present that with astute marketing, which would capitalize on the fear that pervaded the rest of the world, tourism in French Polynesia would recover:

> No one can predict the future of global tourism. . . . But one point is certain. Today we are experiencing the most serious crisis in international tourism in fifty years. . . . But, Polynesia can benefit from a new international outlook on tourism, one that focuses on the safety of the destination. This is the card that, from now on, we must play. (*Les nouvelles de Tahiti* 2001, 24)

While the politicians' speeches focused on the symbolic resonance of the hotel with the government's agenda, the newspaper articles concentrated on the visually alluring details of the hotel. They described the ways in which the hotel "married" the conveniences and comforts of the modern world with the natural charm of Polynesia, once again emphasizing how needs and desires are united within the cocoon. One journalist wrote that the hotel "has combined tradition and modernity so that today's Robinson Crusoes can take hot showers and put ice cubes in their cocktails" (*Les nouvelles de Tahiti* 2001, 24).

Just as tourism marketing draws on Tahiti's long history of imagery, so did the publicity for the new hotel. One journalist waxed poetic about the hotel's beauty, repeatedly referring to eighteenth-century imagery of paradise, with

its timeless visions of pristine nature, Arcadian beauty, and childlike inno-
cence. Another reporter described the hotel as "an architectural pearl that,
covered in woven coconut fronds, blends with the surrounding palm trees
and rises from the white sand like a child's castle on the beach" (*Les nouvelles
de Tahiti* 2001, 24). Several articles stressed the idea that the hotel possessed
a "natural harmony." The key to the positive reception of the hotel seemed
to have less to do with any present-day reality it embraced and more with its
role as an embodiment of past imagery and the myth of Tahiti:

> "Beauty is the promise of happiness," wrote Stendhal. This promise is held by
> these thirty-eight bungalows, which are in perfect harmony with a nature that
> is resplendent in its simplicity. . . . Here everything is tranquility and beauty,
> luxury and voluptuousness. . . . This is the Polynesia of New Cytheria, the
> myth transformed into reality. This is nothing like Disneyland or some other
> American-style dream machine. Here, it is nature that directs the show. . . .
> [This is a] Polynesian attraction, where time stands still, where the environ-
> ment itself is a form of art, and where Polynesian culture is the producer of
> this legendary Rousseau-like harmony. It is far from an industrialized tourist
> trap. (*Les nouvelles de Tahiti* 2001, 24)

The creation of these "picture-perfect" tourist experiences, of course,
necessitates far more manipulation of the environment than simply relying
on what nature provides. The staging of experiences—such as sitting on the
veranda of one's overwater bungalow in the evening while enjoying a tropical sunset over the lagoon—becomes the main goal. Behind this mirage of
tranquility and simplicity lies complex modern technology, misleading the
guests into believing that "nature directs the show."

At the Tikehau Pearl Beach Resort, for example, two solar panels, each
twenty-seven square meters, guarantee abundant hot water for guests' showers. Two oil-fueled generators hum in a remote part of the complex to assure,
among other things, that the ice cubes will freeze. A desalinization station
provides 1,700 liters of clean water an hour so that, when turning on the
faucets in their bungalows, guests will have potable water. An incinerator is
used for waste treatment in which garbage is cooled before being burned to
facilitate combustion and to avoid a proliferation of flies. And regular fumi-
gation of the area reduces the number of normally ubiquitous mosquitoes to
almost zero (*La dépêche de Tahiti* 2001b, 54).

ORDER FROM DISORDER

Although the Tikehau Pearl Beach Resort provides an example of a new luxury hotel, all such hotels in French Polynesia serve as examples of how the many players—architects, hotel directors, hotel employees, and even the tourists themselves—take part in creating and maintaining these cocoons. The experiences of tourists, from the moment they arrive at the airport (where they are greeted by women handing them Tahitian gardenias and by men playing lively Polynesian string band music) to the moment they depart, are managed to give them a unique, dreamed-of experience. Through the manipulation of the natural, architectural, and social environments, these spaces serve very specific purposes. The hotel's white-sand beach, the fish that swim under its overwater bungalows, the thatched roofs of its buildings, the décor in the lobby, the Tahitians who serve drinks at the bar or rent out snorkeling equipment, the after-dinner floor show, the flowers, the trumpeting sound of the conch shell, and even the scented, chilled, moist towels the tourists receive upon arrival are all elements designed to keep tourists in their cocoon.

The resort hotel is an excellent example of Foucault's idea of a heterotopia. He first used the term (originally a medical term denoting the displacement of a human organ from its normal position) to indicate incongruity and disorder in language (Foucault 1966). In a lecture a year later, he gave new meaning to the term by applying it to spatial forms.[10] Heterotopias are "spaces of alternate ordering" (Hetherington 1997) that are engineered through the artificial displacement and recombination of elements. In these spaces, "difference, alterity, and 'the other' might flourish or (as with architects) actually be constructed" (D. Harvey 2000, 184).

Unlike a utopia, which comforts and consoles because it is entirely imaginary, a heterotopia bewilders because it combines the imagined and the tangible. It does this by mixing elements from different places and times to appear as if they belong together. In a heterotopia, "the relationship of material space to representational space becomes ephemeral and in some cases completely detached" (Low and Lawrence-Zúñiga 2003, 30).[11] Heterotopias are spaces "with a multitude of localities containing things so different that it is impossible to find a common logic for them . . . [they are spaces] in which everything is somehow out of place" (Relph 1991, 104). They are a "disorder in which fragments of a large number of possible orders glitter separately . . . without law or geometry" (Foucault 1966, xvii). As a result of these artificial juxtapositions, heterotopias can be jumbled and jarring. As examples of heterotopias, Foucault cites formal gardens,[12] cemeteries, prisons, libraries, museums, and colonial settings (see also Kahn 1995). To this list Edward Relph has added Las Vegas, megamalls, theme parks, gated communities, and the cultural hodgepodge of inner cities (2001, 154).[13]

Ironically, although disordered, a heterotopia is a calculated attempt to impose a sense of order, coherence, and truth. It creates meaning by establishing an intentional design and internal logic. Everything is arranged for the observer into a system of signification, declaring it to be a signifier of something further. As such, a heterotopia creates a kind of magic. It becomes a management tool, a means of taming details that would otherwise remain resistant to immediate comprehension. Because of their design, such places orient the visitor, even if to a false reality. This kind of space "takes us by the hand, it guides our eyes, it tells us a story—a story we can understand. It confers order and coherence" (Kramer 1982, 62).

In Tahitian resort hotels, "nature" is a substantial element of the hotel complex and is creatively manipulated. Nature, on its own, "presents itself as it is, now cruel, now generous. It does not seek to deceive . . . it never lies" (Lefebvre 1991, 81). When nature is brought into the cocoon, however, it is shaped, molded, transformed, and commodified. "Natural" features are embellished to create settings where the replica appears more "real" than reality. In places where there is no white-sand beach, hotels will dredge thousands of cubic meters of sand from the lagoon. The white sand is then deposited on the shore and in the water below the overwater bungalows. The abuse of the natural environment—to create a picture-perfect "nature"—can be considerable and is opposed by many Tahitians who engage in numerous, and often successful, attempts to block hotel developments using petitions, protests, and boycotts.

Fish, naturally plentiful, soon move to calmer areas when hotels dredge lagoons for beach sand, and when pipes, pumps, filters, and tourists invade their natural habitats (fig. 4.2). One of the most prominently advertised features of an overwater bungalow is a glass panel in the floor for viewing colorful fish. On Bora Bora it was necessary to have marine biologists advise hotels on the best means of luring the fish back so that guests wouldn't be disappointed when they looked through their glass panel. The solution recommended was to reintroduce coral into the lagoon. At Bora Bora's Pearl Beach Resort, a marine biologist "began rescuing stressed coral and intro-

Fig. 4.2 Pylons and pipes under Moana Beach Hotel, Bora Bora, 1994.

ducing healthy coral by cementing mini-reefs under the bungalow walkway"
(Chiang 2005, 21). The irony in these "natural" recreations, of course, is that
the environment has been denaturalized to present nature *in situ.* "However,
in the process, life-sustaining resources are removed, making the wild organ-
isms domestic, totally dependent on the human apparatus for their continued survival" (Desmond 1999, 178).

The "natural" setting of the buildings is carefully planned to make tourists' fantasies and expectations—such as enjoying evening cocktails over
water rather than over land—become realities. Richard Shamel, who over-
saw the planning and construction of a resort hotel on Huahine, described
the process of constantly trying to imagine, and then accommodate, tourists'
dreams:

Just when the hotel's main building was almost finished, the plans were
changed. Originally the main building was to be half over land and half over

water. The wharf and walkway were already completed when the President and CEO of South Pacific Management came to visit. We walked around, and he said to me, "If you had a choice, would you prefer to have your evening cocktail here over the land or there over the water?" I said, "Over the water." Without even a pause, he said, "Yes, the building needs to be changed." So we had to rebuild everything, including the wharf and walkway. (Richard Shamel, personal communication, 2001)

Architecture, of course, is a key medium through which a hotel communicates a sense of place to tourists. As a system of signs, architecture is forced to articulate a language that expresses something external to the building itself (Eco 1980, 57). Imagined places that get transformed into built form are incapable of vanishing into the purely imaginary. Foucault highlighted the relationship between power and architecture, seeing architecture as a political act working out the concerns of the government (1979). President Flosse, discussing the important link between economic growth in the Territory and the revival of Polynesian architecture, said, "A good supply of hotels is already showing the way."[14] The architecture of Tahitian resort hotels consciously responds to the myth by providing visitors with the visual cues that define "Tahiti." Because these elements have become such iconic markers of "Tahiti," hotels use them frequently. French Polynesia is famous for its accommodations that consist of thatched-roof bungalows perched on pilings over the lagoon, a neo-Polynesian style of hotel architecture that originated in the late 1950s when American architects introduced it for a hotel on Mo'orea, deliberately imitating traditional Polynesian house styles (Robineau 1975, 71). Resort hotels tend to have many standard elements: a large central reception building open to the outdoors, with a lobby with a soaring roof of thatched pandanus; interior walls often covered in split bamboo or woven pandanus leaves; a fanned arrangement of overwater bungalows perched over the lagoon (as well as other "beach" and "garden" thatched-roof bungalows); a swimming pool; and a white-sand beach (which, unless the hotel is on a *motu*, is often artificial) bordered by coconut palms.

The lobby of a Tahitian resort hotel can be seen as a heterotopia par excellence. It is carefully but disjointedly assembled, with each detail literally being out of place. Lobbies typically combine some, and sometimes all, of the following: outrigger canoes suspended from the ceiling; chandeliers made from hundreds of shells; light fixtures covered with bamboo fish traps; walls decorated with *pareus,* fishnets, bark cloth, and Gauguin reproductions; pot-

Fig. 4.3   Phone booth in lobby of Te Tiare Hotel, Huahine, 2001.

ted tropical plants; and wooden cutouts of "Polynesian" motifs (breadfruit leaves, canoe paddles, fish, and so on) decorating furniture. Necessary items, such as life vests, are often stored in boxes that are camouflaged with local materials so they blend in with the "natural" setting.

The phone booth in the lobby of one hotel was made to look like a Tahitian *fare,* or house, with a roof thatched with pandanus leaves and walls covered with panels of woven pandanus. Flat wooden cutouts of tropical flowers and fish adorned its walls and swinging doors (fig. 4.3). Not surprisingly, guests respond to this type of heterotopic environment in positive ways. I once overheard a woman say to her husband, "Look at that phone booth, it's so cute! Oh, you've got to take a picture of it for me." He dutifully took the photo, which is probably not something he would have done, or something she would have asked him to do, if they had seen the public phone booth in town (fig. 4.4). The photo of the "cute" phone booth in the hotel lobby not only validated the woman's vacation but will also perpetuate these constructed images of Tahiti when shown to her friends back home.

In addition to the architects (of both "nature" and buildings), hotel direc-

Fig. 4.4   Phone booth in town of Fare, Huahine, 2001.

tors and staff also have roles in creating managed hotel space. Making decisions about their hotel, directors try to see things from their guests' point of
view. As one hotel director told me,

> We definitely use images of the sun, the blue lagoon, coconut palms, and
> overwater bungalows to promote our hotel. Tourists don't have these things at
> home. They've been dreaming about these for a long time, so that's what we
> use to attract them to come here. The main goal is always to think about the
> clients and make them happy. (Etienne Ragivaru, personal communication,
> 2001)

Hotel directors can also believe in the artifice that their hotels create. As
another director told me,

> The image that my hotel conveys is one of paradise, sensuality, *vahine*
> [women], and authenticity. It indicates that Tahiti is simply the best. And I
> agree that this is the reality. Yes, when tourists arrive here, this is what they

get. Maybe they don't get it in Pape'ete, but they certainly get this on Huahine and on other outer islands. They get all this and more. (Jean-Merry Delarue, personal communication, 2001)

A hotel director tries to make sure guests' experiences meet their expectations. When their experiences do not accord with their images, guests can feel cheated and will often complain. They may even leave. Brochures, of course, never depict a hotel in the rain. Also not shown are mosquitoes buzzing in the room or geckos clinging to the wall. Hotel directors have a repertoire of entertaining stories about unhappy clients:

In general, people aren't prepared for the way things are here. Sometimes people complain a lot, especially when it's raining. They also complain that there are mosquitoes and other things. One time a man came to the lobby and said he was leaving on the spot because there was a crocodile in his room. I couldn't imagine what he was talking about, so I went to see. It was a harmless four-inch gecko on the wall. People say that they haven't been warned about the reality here. Advertising needs to be more accurate. (Etienne Ragivaru, personal communication, 2001)

Tourists have their own stories that confirm their desire for a leak-proof cocoon. One American tourist told me,

We met some people who were staying at a very fancy hotel on Mo'orea, but they said there were mosquitoes in the room. When the man went to complain at the front desk, all he was told was, "Oh, mosquitoes are part of the ambiance here." The man told the staff member, "Ambiance is okay if it's outside my room, but not inside the room. I didn't pay for this kind of ambiance." So they immediately checked out and went to a different hotel. (Bob McFarlane, personal communication, 2001)

Hotel staff members also participate in the creation of place. The clothing they wear, the crowns of leaves they place on their heads, the flowers they tuck behind their ears, even their smiles, are all recognizable place markers of "Tahiti." When guests arrive at a hotel, an attractive Tahitian woman usually greets them. After they check in, a porter, wearing a *pareu* wrapped tightly around his waist, and often with traditional tattoos on his body, takes their luggage to their room.

For a Tahitian man to have tattoos can be a definite advantage if he is seeking a job in tourism. In the 1980s, Tahiti experienced a revival of several forms of cultural expression—including tattooing, which was abandoned after missionaries suppressed it in the nineteenth century. This form of personal adornment also fit well with the "exotic" images that hotels wanted to project. Some of the first Tahitian men to go to Samoa and get tattooed in the 1980s came back and soon found work as porters at the hotels on Tahiti, where they gained instant notoriety. As a photographer and longtime visitor to Tahiti told me, "Can you imagine getting out of the van at the hotel and having a gorgeous god, fully tattooed, step out to carry your bags!" (Claire Leimbach, personal communication, 2001).[15] The effect has been so successful that some of these same men, as well as others who followed in their footsteps, have easily moved into various hotel positions—porters, nautical specialists, or members of dance groups—where the display of attractive bodies responds to what tourists anticipate. These tattooed, muscular, brown bodies represent and authenticate the fantasy of Tahitian beauty (a "gorgeous god") and do so through explicit use of tattooed designs, which, inscribed on bodies, can become vehicles of commercialism. For example, the extensively tattooed man I met at the Salon Mondial du Tourisme in Paris travels to tourist trade shows around the world, where he appears as the lead singer and dancer, demonstrating in person what a tourist can expect to see when visiting Tahiti.

It is common knowledge among hotel directors that, in making hiring decisions, they look for attractive individuals—whom they lightheartedly refer to as "hotel Tahitians." As one director explained, "Tahitians often leave school early and look for work. A few can work in hotels and get trained on the job, especially girls who are pretty and friendly. We train them after they've been hired." Part of the training consists of learning how to look and act like the image tourists expect. "While we were in training, we were told to wear a crown of flowers on our head every day and to smile all the time," said a friend who worked in a hotel. This commodification of the smile is a by-product of tourism, especially in places "where in the absence of a common language, coded gestures and expressions become an important part of the hospitality industry" (Guth 2004, 83).

Once guests have been welcomed by a beautiful woman with a warm smile and their luggage has been carried off to their bungalow by a "gorgeous god" with tattoos, the hotel staff must also respond to tourists' desires for "authentic" experiences. This is done by offering entertainment within the hotel or by recommending tours and activities that show tourists carefully chosen sites. As the director of a mid-sized hotel on Huahine told me, "You can't just give people their room key and say, 'Have a nice day.' You need to offer a variety of things for them to do." These things, of course, will differ according to the setting of the hotel. Guests at a hotel on a *motu* may be content to do very little, while guests on the island of Tahiti may want an island tour. Entertainment offered at the hotel, which brings tourists in contact with Tahitian staff, also needs to meet their guests' expectations. There is generally a limited repertoire of typical "Tahitian" activities to engage tourists, such as preparing an earth-oven feast with local foods, demonstrating the many ways to wear a *pareu*, showing how to weave a hat from coconut fronds, offering Tahitian dance lessons, and providing floor shows. Of these, the most popular (as well as the most photographed and video-recorded) is the floor show or dance performance, an event that each major hotel hosts at least once a week and can involve ten to twenty dancers and musicians.[16]

DANCING THE IMAGES TO LIFE

Dance, an important aspect of Tahitian life, is also a cultural expression that meshes well with tourists' anticipations. Although not every Tahitian dances, most do. "We like to dance; it's our passion, our culture," one dancer explained. On most islands, major festivities or events, such as the arrival of dignitaries, school functions, or Christmas celebrations, usually include dance performances that can last late into the night. In Pape'ete, where residents come from many different islands throughout French Polynesia, large dance contests are common. Dance groups from the different islands, each with their own dances and costumes, compete for prizes awarded for various "bests." The most prestigious of these competitions is the Heiva festival in Pape'ete every July. While also enjoyed by tourists, Heiva is still first and foremost a festival for the local population.

When dancers perform for tourists in a hotel, it can be more than simply an additional avenue for them to do what they otherwise enjoy. It's a way for dancers to earn money (dancers say this is the main reason they dance for tourists),[17] exploit travel opportunities, express themselves creatively, and have fun as well. To be a member of a successful dance group involves hard work, some business acumen, and collegial commitment. Dancers often practice several times a week to ensure that their performances are of high quality. Costume designers spend many hours searching for prized materials and creating beautiful costumes.

Tourism, however, has encouraged a particular type of dance to develop for performances at resort hotels. Marietta Tefaataumarama, the former leader of a Huahine dance group, described these changes:

> Hotels sprang up and needed dance groups to entertain tourists. Because hotel dancers get paid, money entered the picture. When dance became a hotel show, everything changed. The songs and dances began to lose their meaning. Normally music, words, and special hand gestures go with every song. Tahitians know these details because they live inside the dance. It's their culture. But in a hotel performance, these details no longer communicate any real meaning because dancers combine different elements to create a spectacle. They borrow elements from everywhere, especially from other shows they've seen. Today dancers chase after spectacles to create shows that appeal to tourists. The girls hike up their *pareus*. They smile and show their teeth. They do some hand gestures. Tourists like that because it's an attractive show to watch. It's pleasing to the eye. It makes a good video. But the meaning is gone. Plus, the hotel tells you to dance for thirty minutes and that's all. After half an hour, you're finished. You can't dance about your culture and your history in half an hour. But there are some things, like the *otea mau*[18] for which there is great respect, which will never appear in a hotel show. (Marietta Tefaataumarama, personal communication, 2001)

Dance was first used to promote tourism in the early 1960s, and it still plays a dominant role in the global marketing of Tahitian tourism. Paulette Viénot started the tradition with only a handful of dancers; now the government sponsors several large groups that travel overseas to provide publicity for GIE Tahiti Tourisme. As Marietta explained,

> You see Les Grands Ballets, which has about sixty dancers, and realize how dance has really become a business. It's very popular but it's all imitation. Imagine! They dance with an Air Tahiti Nui airline banner behind them on the stage!

Tahitian dance—once suppressed by missionaries because of its sensual character—is now the main feature of Tahitian culture presented outside

Tahiti to encourage people to visit the islands. As Marietta described, dance has changed from a meaningful cultural expression to a staged commercial enterprise—exhibiting its own synthetic arrangement. Like the covers of the travel planners that offer a montage of photographic images chosen to appeal to different clienteles, or the hotel lobby where decontextualized details of décor are assembled to communicate "Tahiti" to visitors, performers now combine dance elements in nontraditional ways to keep the performances dazzling and the tourists happy. Although dance is an important cultural expression for Tahitians, in the tourist setting it becomes primarily only spectacle. For tourists, it has become *the* anticipated and unrivaled *visual* experience—a "must-see" for every visitor (see Kahn 2011).

Spaces exhibit an "increasingly pronounced visual character. They are made with the visible in mind. . . . The predominance of visualization . . . serves to conceal repetitiveness. People look, and take sight, take seeing, for life itself" (Lefebvre 1991, 75–76). Dance, an activity that is colorful, animated, and completely "other," is one of Tahiti's primary visual icons. It brings tourists in contact with Tahitians in a clearly defined, acceptable, and picturesque setting. The visual dominates. Tourists' main experiences are reduced to the decoding of messages by the eye, which relegates people and objects to a safe distance and turns them into spectacle. The visual takes on special meaning when language is a barrier (Guth 2004, xiv).

For members of a dance group, the transition from living their daily lives to performing in a hotel appears seamless. The dancers go to the hotel, put on their dance costumes, perform, change back into their regular clothing, collect their pay, and leave. I observed this transition several times while attending performances of a dance group from Huahine, Tamari'i Mata'ire'a Nui. I once arrived about thirty minutes before a dozen or so dancers and musicians were to perform, and was able to visit with them while they got ready. They were spread out, some sitting on the wooden floor in the main lounge area and some in the adjoining corridor. Surrounded by their dance costumes, as well as by plastic bags containing fresh leaves and flowers, they diligently added finishing touches to their costumes before the show began.

The musicians, with their drums, guitars, and ukuleles, were already seated on their stools at the far end of the dining room, playing music for the guests as they finished their meals. When the dance show was about to begin, the drummers began to beat more forcefully to announce the dancers' arrival. The performers appeared, flowing gracefully through the dining room and onto the stage to the rhythm of the thundering drums. They began

Fig. 4.5   Floor show with tourist dancing, Intercontinental Moʻorea, 2007. Courtesy of Justin Fulkerson.

dancing—the women with stately headdresses slightly bobbing, shredded-leaf skirts swaying, torsos steady, and hips gyrating, and the men with arms powerfully gesturing and legs pulsating. Songs alternated, as always, between the wild, rhythmic ʻoteʻa (drum dances), which were accompanied by the vigorous sounds of the drums, and gentler, graceful ʻaparima (storytelling dances with words and hand gestures), which were accompanied by more melodic music that included guitars and ukuleles.

The audience was mesmerized. The men in particular watched intently, many abandoning their dinners as they gazed with rapt attention. In fact, many watched much of the performance through video cameras. Near the end of the performance, as is the custom, the dancers went into the audience, inviting individuals—whether eager or reluctant—to be their partners (fig. 4.5). Dancers want to create memorable experiences and photographic moments for the tourists, and take care to invite as many guests as possible. Images of place are made up of more than just visual representations. Also included are experiences that one consumes—such as snorkeling, having a massage, hiring a local guide, or being invited to dance. The consumption of these experiences is interdependent with the consumption of place (Urry 1995, 28). "Ultimately, having an experience becomes identical with taking a photograph of it, and participating in a public event comes more and more to be equivalent to looking at it in photographed form. . . . Today everything exists to end in a photograph" (Sontag 1979, 24). As one dancer elaborated, "Usually tourists like to get invited to dance. They can try out their dancing. And their spouse can take a picture of them. The photograph becomes a nice souvenir" (Jean Yves Teri'itapunui, personal communication, 2001).

When the floor show came to a close after thirty minutes of animated performance, the lead female dancer announced that there would be a fire dance out on the dock (safely close to water), and several guests moved outside to watch. While the fire dancer was rapidly twirling his burning baton, and handling and swallowing fire, a skill he had perfected over many years (a crowd-pleaser that features male bravado, which Tahitians originally imported from Samoa), the rest of the dancers quickly retired to the lounge area to change back into their regular clothing and gather up their belongings. It was obvious that the details of this finale were carefully planned. As soon as the fire dance was finished, the operator of the hotel transfer boat started the engine to take the performers back to town.

Loaded down with various bags and bundles, musical instruments, and musicians' stools, the dancers and I all climbed into the boat and off we went. As the boat cruised through the dark night, the dancers talked about their performance, expressing general satisfaction with how they had danced but saying that they could have performed still better if they hadn't been so exhausted. Most were tired, even before performing, because it was a Friday—a workday and the end of the workweek for most of them. The lead male dancer had spent the day waiting on customers at the fabric store in town. The lead female dancer had spent the morning doing custodial work at the bank. The fire dancer had been hanging onto the back of a garbage truck, jumping off at each house to unload the contents of heavy garbage cans. The lead musician had been performing his duties as a policeman, and another musician had been driving a van for one of the hotels, shuttling guests to and from the airport. Many of the others had worked as well. Yet, tired as they were, they now relaxed. They picked up their guitars and ukuleles and continued to play and sing—for themselves—for the fifteen minutes that it took for the boat to race across the water and arrive back in town. Listening to them play and sing, I thought, as I often did in such spontaneous, post-performance, musical moments, about the differences between performing for others (inside the cocoon) and making music for themselves (outside the cocoon), and about what, for them, appears to be a seamless transition between the two realities.

At a hotel, dance plays an extremely critical role—perhaps the most crucial—by providing tourists with the most picturesque, and most widely advertised, cultural encounter they may hope to have. Dance is such a prominent and repeated feature of the tourist experience that, as tourists move from island to island, they may see dance performances at each of their hotels. There are always a few tourists who, perhaps at their third or fourth hotel, only glance up occasionally as they eat their dinner. After all, they probably captured the performance on video at the first hotel.

Dance is also emblematic of the distortions that occur in how Tahitians are involved and represented within a managed tourism space. For a hotel to highlight Tahitians only as they appear on stage dancing in their exotic costumes is misleading. It is akin to a tourist in France only being shown French people eating snails or drinking wine in a château, or a tourist in the Netherlands only being shown Dutch people walking in wooden shoes along windmill-lined canals. Within the context of the hotel, guests only see Tahitians in limited ways—either as they dance on stage or as they unobtrusively provide the services that are essential to the hotel's operation: registering guests, carrying suitcases, making beds, serving food, raking the grounds, or weeding the flower beds. For tourists to be able to watch Tahitians dance in colorful costumes serves to validate marketing images and tourists' senses of place. An encounter with a Tahitian, weeding a flowerbed in his shorts and T-shirt, does not. Tourists have not been prepared by the marketing brochures to encounter the gardener anymore than they expect to find mosquitoes or geckos in their rooms. Housekeepers, dishwashers, and gardeners are absent from the images in brochures and on postcards, and do not usually appear in tourists' snapshots or videos (at least not in their shorts and T-shirts, although sometimes these individuals are members of a dance group). Yet when the drums beat loudly and dancers appear, tourists grab their cameras and are ecstatic, realizing that they are witnessing—in front of their own dinner table—the scene they had hoped, and have been prepared, to experience. Indeed, their video cameras are already poised by their dinner plates as they wait for the performance to begin. Through this visual experience, the images in the brochure are brought to life. Through photography, the images are reproduced and circulated. At that moment images of *l'espace conçu* and *l'espace perçu* are united. Expectation and experience, myth and reality, are immediately and vividly joined. I once overheard a tourist tell her husband as the dancing began, "Oh, my gosh, can you believe what we're seeing! It's just like those pictures in the brochure. This is incredible!" Click.

WORKING THE MAGIC

All vacations do come to an end. In French Polynesia, according to government statistics (for 2008), it happens after an average of 13.8 days. To capitalize on the moment of departure and bring symbolic closure to the vacation, many hotels choreograph another Polynesian experience: the placing of a *hei,* or shell necklace, around each tourist's neck to bid them farewell. In the same way that a *tiare tahiti,* or fragrant gardenia, is given to tourists at the airport when they arrive, a *hei* is given to them upon their departure from a resort hotel. These customs about flowers and shells have a clear Tahitian logic. Tahitians make (or buy) flower garlands and present these to family and friends whenever they arrive in French Polynesia. The flowers wilt within hours, but by then the person who received the garland will be surrounded by the natural scents and beauty of Tahiti. Upon departure, Tahitians present family and friends with shell necklaces because shells last forever. The shell necklaces become tangible reminders of the person who bid them farewell. Hotels have adopted these (and other) symbolic Tahitian gestures for their own use. The French director of one hotel insisted on staging an event to bring a photogenic closure to the guests' experience — an event that, however, was not in accord with Tahitian custom. He wanted the departure to include a staff member blowing into a conch shell.[19] "Once guests have paid their bill," he said, "the staff members often forget to pay attention to the guests. So I wanted to do something that would continue to give them a memorable experience." He described his idea:

> The arrival and the farewell are the guests' most important moments. For the arrival we have a strong, muscular Tahitian man who blows into a conch shell to announce the guest's arrival as the boat pulls up. And a beautiful Tahitian woman places a garland of flowers around each guest's neck. And another one gives each guest a chilled moist towel scented with gardenia oil. But, at their arrival, the guests are overwhelmed and unprepared, and they don't think of taking any pictures. So I wanted to have the same thing happen when they leave because then they would have their cameras ready. When guests leave, they're sad because it's a transition back to their everyday life and work. The

vacation is over. The departure is the most important moment. I asked the staff to also blow the conch shell for the farewell. They were adamant that they couldn't do that because the conch is blown only to announce an arrival or a special event, but never a departure. But I insisted that they do it anyway, and now they do.[20] It's these little touches, like blowing into the conch and giving out a scented towel when guests arrive, that make a big difference for the tourists. (Jean-Merry Delarue, personal communication, 2001)

As he had predicted, the magic worked. Soon after the director told me how he crafted these details to create memorable moments, the boat arrived with four guests. As if on cue, a handsome Tahitian man went down to the dock, picked up the large conch shell that permanently sat there, and blew into it, producing a long, deep, sonorous sound. As the guests climbed from the boat onto the dock, an attractive Tahitian woman handed each one a chilled scented towel while another put a garland of flowers around each guest's neck. As one woman took her moist towel, she said, "Oh, this is so wonderful!" And, as predicted, the visitors were too overwhelmed by the magic of the moment to think of taking any photos. I knew, however, that because of the director's foresight and the employees' acquiescence, the guests would have the opportunity again when they would leave a few days later—to the sound (culturally inappropriate as it was) of the trumpeting conch.

John Urry has said that "tourist entrepreneurs and the indigenous populations are induced to produce ever-more extravagant displays. . . . Over time, via advertising and the media, the images generated of different tourist gazes come to constitute a closed self-perpetuating system of illusions" (Urry 1990, 7). These managed spaces, or cocoons, however, are not merely "illusions," pseudo-simulacra, or ersatz realities. They truly constitute an important part of the material reality, albeit fashioned to accord with the myth. The artificial white-sand beach, the phone booth made to look like a "cute" house, and the thirty-minute dance show—and the tourists' photos, blogs, and videos of all of these—provide future tourists with the information they want for selecting places to visit, sights to see, and "realities" to experience. Indeed, it is inside such cocoons that the tourists' dreams and realities, desires and needs, are brought together, reinforced, and kept under control.

CHAPTER FIVE

From Our Place to Their Place

T ourists wanting to venture beyond the cocoon in Tahiti usually go (guidebook in hand) to a sight or an activity recommended by their hotel or cruise ship. Where they go, what they see, and how they make sense of things all provide them with a sense of place. Although these spaces may appear to be relatively fixed, they are, in fact, extremely dynamic and are continually redefined.

On Huahine the principal tourist attractions are a number of dramatic archaeological features along the shore of Lac Fauna Nui in the village of Maeva: the remains of the *marae* of the eight chiefly families who ruled the island before the arrival of Europeans. Today tourism brochures, guidebooks, Web sites, and postcards depict these *marae* in their picturesque setting. Until recently, Huahine's *marae,* although visited by tourists, were not part of a tourist cocoon. They were sites imbued with senses of local identity and ancestral pride. With tourism and its economic benefits becoming ever more important, a small group of Maeva's residents wanted to make the *marae* more accessible and attractive to visitors. In 1995, they created a cultural center at the site, with the goal of serving both the local population and tourists. Because these efforts were successful, the Territorial government soon realized that the *marae* and the cultural center had great potential. Thus the government decided to make the area even more appealing to tourists, who in the late 1990s were arriving in large numbers as passengers on the new cruise ships. An understanding of this transformation—as the area changed from the villagers' "place" to the government's "place"—offers insights into how local and territorial politics play critical roles in these transformations. This particular site was also one with which I was very familiar because of my participation in some of these transformative activities. My involvement was due, in part, to my friendships with people who worked at the site. More importantly, villagers saw my past professional experiences—of having worked in several anthropological museums—as helpful to them.

HEADING OUT TO LEARN ABOUT CULTURE

To learn about how these archaeological attractions were portrayed for tourists, I joined a small group of sightseers on a half-day tour of the island on a delightfully breezy and sunny afternoon in 2001. Firmin Reea Faaeva, the guide, was an acquaintance of mine and, knowing about my research interests, generously invited me to join the tour with three couples (two American and one French). I sat with them in the open back of the vehicle, surrounded by their backpacks bulging with guidebooks, cameras, sunscreen, and snacks. All three couples told me that they were looking forward to visiting the "archaeological sites" after having read about them in their guidebooks and having seen the tour company's brochure, which promised "magical surroundings in a comfortable four-wheel-drive vehicle, warmly guided by a local expert" and "postcard images, unforgettable landscapes, breath-taking views, and archaeological sites."

Before we left Fare, Firmin pulled out his well-worn map of Huahine from behind the sun visor and pointed out various landmarks we would see. He also pushed a small box from the front of the vehicle onto the floor in the back, telling us to help ourselves to water, sunscreen, and mosquito repellent. Leaving town on the road that circles the island, he turned to us and said (switching easily between English and French to make sure everyone understood), "Our first stop will be near the village of Maeva, about eight kilometers away, to visit the archaeological sites and the museum. Later we'll see a vanilla plantation, the sacred eels in Faie, beautiful views, and interesting off-road areas" (map 4).

As we left Fare and headed toward Maeva, we passed the handicraft stand at the edge of town, with its colorful *pareus,* somewhat faded from too many days of hanging in the sun and fluttering in the breeze; the Collège de Fare (the equivalent of a junior high school) made up of low cinderblock buildings connected by covered walkways; the white neocolonial post office with

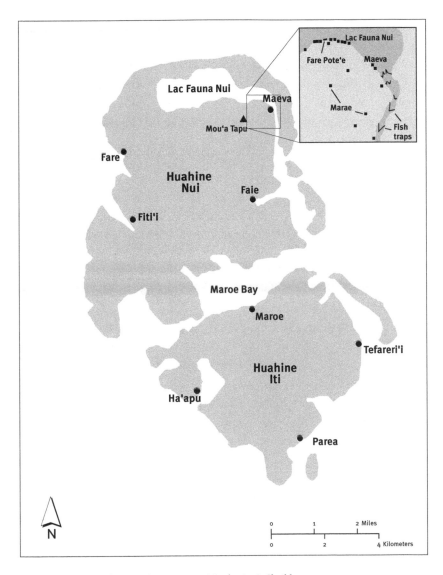

Map 4 Huahine, with inset of Maeva area. Map by Amir Sheikh.

Victorian gingerbread decorations on the façade; and the French-owned car rental business. Behind the buildings, the landscape was a mix of verdant tropical vegetation in the hillsides to our right and flat ground that stretched to the sea about half a mile away, to our left. We drove past family dwellings, most of them modest, built in a variety of styles. Some were older, elongated structures with corrugated iron roofs and louvered windows. Others were new, square, pre-fabricated dwellings raised on cement blocks, which the government had provided for families whose houses were destroyed in the 1998 cyclone. We passed one house that was little more than a plywood shack. We also passed one with a locked gate, behind which lay well-maintained gardens and—what none of the passengers could see or know—the only private swimming pool on the island. We saw people outdoors busy with various activities: hanging up laundry, repairing a motorcycle, and chatting with friends. As the passengers looked left and right, they commented to one another about things they saw, wanting to absorb and make sense of every detail. And once they learned that I was an anthropologist, they turned to me with their questions, seeking explanations for everything.

About halfway to Maeva, Firmin pointed out an expansive body of water called Lac Fauna Nui (meaning a lake with a "large head").

"This inlet, which we call a lake, was created long ago," he explained, "when sand from the ocean was built up to connect the reef to the island. The inlet is full of fish."

As we got closer to Maeva, we could see a distinctive building, which I knew intimately. Perched on pilings over the water at the edge of the lake, it was large and oval in shape. Its roof was made of thatched pandanus leaves, and its walls of thin bamboo poles.

"That's the Fare Poteʻe," Firmin said. "That name means 'oval house.' It's oval so people can sit inside against the wall and talk to one another, facing one another, the way the elders did in the past."

The Fare Poteʻe is at the western edge of Maeva, nestled between Lac Fauna Nui and the slopes of Mataʻireʻa Hill (literally "yellow wind," but glossed as "playful breeze"). Maeva is a typical Tahitian village. Houses hug both sides of the road, which threads its way along the narrow stretch of level land between the water and the hill. In the middle of the road there are usually a few dogs, which move lethargically aside whenever cars come through. By the side of the road, in the shade of some mango trees, men usually play *pétanque* (also called *boules*). The Protestant church, with its imposing steeple, dominates the center of the village, next to the *école primaire* (elementary school). At the end of the village, the road divides, one fork leading to the bridge that connects Huahine's mainland to the *motu*,[1] and from which one has an excellent view of Maeva's church, the fish traps made of stones, and the small shelters for the fishermen and women who use the fish traps (fig. 5.1).[2]

Arriving at the Fare Poteʻe, Firmin parked along the side of the road. The

Fig. 5.1   View from the bridge to Maeva's church and fish traps, 2001.

three couples, guidebooks and cameras in hand, climbed out. Before any of us could wander away, he gathered us together to tell us about the site (fig. 5.2). He pointed out three other smaller buildings, also with bamboo walls and thatched roofs. He then turned to the *marae* that have attracted visitors from all over the world. I listened as he briefly explained the history and meaning of these particular *marae*.

Marae are prominent features in the Tahitian landscape, physical remnants of ancient, sacred sites that today still provide Polynesians with an emotional and spiritual sense of identity and historical continuity (fig. 2.3). When the missionaries William Ellis and Daniel Tyerman arrived on Huahine in the early 1800s, they made note of the active use of these "temples":

> Every object around the lake, and every monument of art or labour, in
> the district of Maeva, bore marks of its connection with their ancient
> religion. . . . Temples to the gods of the water were erected on every point
> of land, and family *maraes* were in almost every grove, while the national
> temple of Tane [god of the forest] stood near the northern extremity of the
> lake. (Ellis 1969, 6)

Fig. 5.2   Firmin talking to the group of tourists in front of the Fare Pote'e, 2001.

Today, the remnants of Huahine's principal *marae* that represent the original ruling families—flat rectangular areas covered with paving stones and
their large altars—are more than silent features in the landscape. Although
they have not been used regularly for religious rituals since the missionaries suppressed non-Christian beliefs in the early nineteenth century, they
continue to be deeply respected as places that mark the presence of deities
and ancestors. They are prominent reminders of the important connections
between people, their ancestors, and the land. Precisely because of this powerful ancestral presence at a *marae*, residents still respect these sites—and
occasionally fear them—and discourage inappropriate behavior on or near
them that might displease the ancestors. Certain activities, such as re-enacting ancient rituals on the *marae* for tourists,[3] or removing any of the stones,
are unthinkable.

In addition to being deeply respected reminders of the past, *marae* are
also part of the contemporary, living landscape. Many *marae* are in locations where residents go about their daily activities, such as setting crab pots,
launching canoes, draping fishnets to dry, or pulling up boats to unload their
catch of fish. There are several families living on land with *marae* who simply
go about their lives on, near, and around the *marae*.

When Maeva was first settled around 800 A.D., the location was desirable because it possessed all the essential elements for survival (Carroll 2005): a saltwater inlet with a constant supply of fish; ample sources of fresh drinking water from springs on the hillside; an easily defended location that provided protection against outsiders; and the majestic Mou'a Tapu ("sacred mountain") as a backdrop. Today these same features and their transformations—Lac Fauna Nui with its picturesque fish traps, the dramatic setting, the many *marae*, and now the Fare Pote'e, with a museum that explains the area's history—provide interest for tourists. Guidebooks always highlight these sites. For example,

> In ancient times, Huahine was a center of Polynesian culture and ruled by a centralized government. . . . Huahine is laden with archaeological artifacts and is sometimes referred to as an open-air museum. Most of the important archaeological sites on the island are . . . in the Maeva area. In that community alone there are sixteen *marae*. . . . The stone slabs of these ancient temples jut out on the landscape, and are eerily reminiscent of the Druid ruins of Stonehenge. (Kay 1997, 244)

This same guidebook even mentioned the project that was underway on the day of our visit; namely, the restoration of the Fare Pote'e and the surrounding *marae:*

> While in Maeva, be sure and stop at the Fare Pote'e, an old-style meeting-house. . . . The 100-year-old, oval-shaped structure, which had fallen into disrepair until it was rebuilt in 1972, is being restored. It will be a small museum and cultural center. Craft demonstrations and tours by local guides to archaeological sites are also planned. A new organization, Opu Nui, has been formed specifically to protect this structure and other ancient monuments from disturbance. (Kay 1997, 244)

INSIDE THE FARE POTE'E

After hearing Firmin's description of the history and meaning of the *marae*, everyone was eager to go into the new museum. We walked across a grassy area dotted with gravel, coral, and crab holes. What I noticed was how carefully composed everything looked. If the tourists had come months, or even weeks, earlier, the area would have looked somewhat neglected. But recently, a crew of young men, hired by the mayor of Huahine (at the direction of the minister of culture), had been hard at work, trimming the grass, pulling weeds from among the stones of the *marae*, picking up litter, and doing whatever was necessary to make the site look presentable. Not immediately apparent to visitors was the fact that the Fare Poteʻe was in a state of transition.

To enter the building we crossed a short bridge. The shoes and sandals of the visitors who were already inside were scattered on the walkway. Noticing this, we all removed our own footwear. As people gingerly stepped inside the building, I heard gasps and exclamations as one by one they noticed the beauty of the interior. Inside were other visitors, some of whom had their heads bent studiously over exhibit cases; others were looking up at the high ceiling, admiring the details of its construction. A young woman was filming with a video camera. At the reception desk I saw a sign that I had helped to write a few days earlier, explaining (in French, English, and Tahitian) that the exhibits were still works in progress.

Marietta Tefaataumarama, who had been hired by the minister of culture to work in the Fare Poteʻe (fig. 5.3), greeted our group warmly. Very adept at guessing tourists' countries of origin,[4] she spoke first in French to the French couple and then in English to the others. "Welcome to the Fare Poteʻe. There are panels for you to read that explain everything. And please ask us if you have any questions." The visitors smiled and nodded in response. One woman marveled at how peaceful and magical the interior felt. She admired its construction—a vaulted ceiling with no central pole for support—and asked how it was built.

The windowless interior (intentionally so, to keep the building cool) was somewhat dark, the sunlight filtering through the narrow spaces between the bamboo slats, casting stripes of light on the displays. I listened to one of my favorite Fare Poteʻe sounds—the gentle creak of the woven, split bamboo floor as it bent slightly with each step a visitor took. I walked past a small outrigger canoe to one of the displays I enjoyed the most, a large topographical map of Huahine under a glass box that students from the Collège de Fare had made from papier mâché in 1996.

At one end of the Fare Poteʻe were display cases of artifacts, each organized according to various themes: fishing techniques and implements; tools made of stone, bone, and shell; bark cloth; and the art of tattoo. At the other end were several tall, flat, wooden posts incised with geometric designs. The sign explained that these were replicas of *unu*, which were originally placed

Fig. 5.3 Marietta talking to a group of school children inside the Fare Pote'e (photo taken during the transition, with the old exhibits still in place), 2001.

in the ground at a *marae* to represent the families who were affiliated with the *marae*. The carved designs on the *unu* were thought to symbolize birds and messengers of the gods. There were several large, professionally prepared panels, each filled with information (in French and English): detailed text, diagrams, color illustrations, maps, aerial views of the site, and sketches of its recent restoration.

While our group was busy looking around, Firmin visited with Marietta, chatting about a favorite topic—local politics. As I listened to the visitors' enthusiastic comments about the Fare Pote'e and also to Marietta's and Firmin's intense conversation, I thought about how these two things were connected in ways not obvious to a casual observer. Indeed, local politics infused every detail of this tourist attraction. This particular group of tourists, like so many others, had signed up for a guided tour of the island, featuring an activity highlighted in every brochure and recommended by every guidebook—a visit to the Fare Pote'e and its museum to learn about Huahine and its culture. What were they *really* looking at? To what place had they come? Long ago the *marae* had been of great cultural importance to the ancestors of Maeva, and now this was the principal place for tourists to visit if they wanted to learn about "culture." One travel writer observed that Huahine is "definitely not a tourist scene—it's the real Tahiti" (Ariyoshi 2001, 882). This newly re-envisioned space on the shore of Lac Fauna Nui—in mirroring the politics of government and community—did represent "the real Tahiti" more than any of the tourists could possibly know.

CODING SPACE

The story of the Fare Poteʻe, like that of many places, is one of dynamic transformation. These changes occur in tandem with shifting interpretive codes, continually assigning, dissolving, and reassigning meaning. It is also a story about individuals with different vested interests, for whom the Fare Poteʻe was a place to realize their personal visions and express their values. Originally, the building was the communal meetinghouse for the village. Then it was dismissed by missionaries and abandoned by the villagers in favor of a new church, relocated and rebuilt by an archaeologist, and eventually developed into a cultural center. Destroyed by a cyclone in 1998, it was rebuilt again and has become a "scientific information center" that French Polynesia's minister of culture, among others, wanted as a tourist destination to further the government's goal of developing tourism in the Territory.

Lefebvre discussed how economic and political changes in a community could generate new spaces planned and organized according to new codes. Space, always simultaneously a locus and a medium (a thing and a process), can become both a site and a symbol of political struggle when circumstances change. For example, Lefebvre discussed the birth of European urban spaces during the Renaissance, a time of major economic and political shifts that occurred as the feudal system gave way to merchant capitalism. In response, cities sprang up and became centers of knowledge and power. New codes fixed every detail of this new language of space. Streets, canals, and public squares were often arranged in accordance with public buildings, palaces, and institutions. Building façades were harmonized to create a sense of perspective, communicating new knowledge and power. Space was rearranged at every level, from family dwellings to monumental edifices, and from private areas to the state as a whole (Lefebvre 1991, 46–47). The city of Venice, for example, which "more than any other place, bears witness to the existence, from the sixteenth century on, of a unitary code or common language of the city . . . [is coded in a way that] combines the city's reality with its ideality, embracing the practical, the symbolic and the imaginary" (Lefebvre 1991, 73–74). The Venice we see today, in which the Grand Canal is lined with elaborate *palazzi,* was deeply linked to merchant capitalism and the dominance of the political power of a merchant oligarchy. Beginning with the first piles driven into the lagoon, every site in Venice had to be planned and brought to fruition by a host of people—political elites, their supporters, and the laborers who carried out the work. Once construction was complete, the city was celebrated with public gatherings, festivals, and elaborate ceremonies. "Here we can see the relationship between a place built by collective will and collective thought on the one hand, and the productive forces of the period on the other" (Lefebvre 1991, 76).

A contemporary example of how spatial codes change along with politics is evident at the site of the World Trade Center in New York City. When the twin towers were built in the 1960s, they symbolized the economic power of lower Manhattan, of New York City, and of the entire United States. On September 11, 2001, the buildings were targeted and destroyed precisely because they were a symbol of American might and power. Now christened Ground Zero, this space overflows with transformative symbols, requiring new codes to help interpret its physical emptiness and symbolic fullness. Since September 11, spontaneous shrines, photographic representations, beams of light, bulldozers, and a visitor center have become moments and mechanisms defining a new sense of place. This new place exists (at the time of my writing) less in concrete form on the ground than it does in various imaginable, tangible, and consumable forms (see Lisle 2004), such as architectural visions, postcards, snow globes, and even bracelets, which allow people to imagine, send, shake, and even carry on their bodies a "place" that is too big, too full, to be easily defined. Places are always in flux. The retaining wall in the basement of the World Trade Center is a place that passes in and out of being, refusing fixed interpretation:

> As that wall has become a place, it has become both a focal point for human anguish and heroism, along with all the other noble and not-so-noble stories we might tell. It has given voice to a host of identities (New York, American, victim, hero, marginalized, etc.). There are many who would want to control the story by making it into a single narrative strand, to make it primarily or even solely a story about heroism or victimization, the triumph of the American spirit or the treachery of the other. . . . The difficulties of constructing

this place as a memorial point to other dynamics here. This is a memorial in a world in which symbolism is exhausted. The World Trade Center is faced with this problem, and it is significant that the call for memorial designs produced more entries [more than 5,000] than any other call of its kind. (Janz 2005, 93)

The spatial recoding of the Fare Pote'e is a far more modest example than the re-design of a Venetian plaza or of Ground Zero. Nonetheless, it is a space that can provide insight into the powerful links among changes in economics, politics, and physical structures.

Through processes of coding, decoding, and recoding, places that appear chaotic and perplexing become intelligible and meaningful. Without a code, a place remains a confusing jumble, much like a sign written in a language one does not understand, or a pile of rocks along the shores of Lac Fauna Nui that visitors see but cannot comprehend. A code lets people know how to relate to, behave in, talk about, and generate a space. "A spatial code is not simply a means of reading or interpreting space: rather it is a means of living in that space, of understanding it, and of producing it" (Lefebvre 1991, 47–48). Codes can be seen "as part of a practical relationship, as part of an interaction between subjects and their space and surroundings" (Lefebvre 1991, 18). Understanding the code is what allows people to gain access to spaces.

A code—whether conveyed through architectural structures, visual images, maps, sounds, or written texts—is a symbolic system with no fixed relation between the code and its object. The symbols of a code can be easily manipulated and altered, as changes occur in people's economic motives, social relations, and political agendas. The individuals who do the coding, decoding, and recoding, as well as the coding systems themselves, are continually changing. This is how places change in response to internal and external forces. The Fare Pote'e and the nearby *marae* are no exception.

The people who first built the *marae* knew the codes (how to arrange the stones and how to behave appropriately at the sites). Since then, and especially since contact with missionaries and other outsiders, the links between these original codes and their meanings, while still present, are more tenuous. The residents of Maeva, while no longer possessing the same degree of intimate knowledge about the *marae*, do understand their significance. Many Tahitians, especially elders, still gain a strong sense of identity from the *marae*.

In contrast to the local residents, the tourists who visit Maeva may look at the *marae*, see only "scattered" piles of rocks or a fiberglass rowboat "disturbing" the scene, and look for a means to interpret what they see. Archaeologists, cultural revivalists, anthropologists, tourism developers, government bureaucrats, and others have all worked to provide ways of interpretation through scholarly texts, brochures, maps, guidebooks, guided tours, and even conversations in the back of a four-wheel-drive vehicle, the details of each interpretation being motivated or influenced by different personal or political ideas. What can the recent history of the Fare Pote'e reveal about this relationship between political power, the dynamics of spatial coding, and the transformations of place?

TRANSFORMATIONS OF PLACE

The first systematic attempt to interpret the *marae* on Huahine and the then existing Fare Pote'e was undertaken in 1925 by Dr. Kenneth Emory, an ethnologist and archaeologist at the Bishop Museum in Honolulu. Following standard archaeological practices of the time, he tried to rectify what he found in the ground with early accounts of Tahitian customs. His investigation of the *marae* used mainly noninvasive techniques, such as measuring the dimensions and photographing the sites. Stressing continuity rather than change, he wrote, "It is obvious to anyone who reads the accounts of [missionaries] Ellis or Tyerman, and has visited Maeva village, that it has changed little since their time [1818]. The fish traps and ruins of *maraes* have remained practically unaltered, and about the same number of native houses line the shore." Other than being told that one *marae* was dedicated to canoe makers and another to the sacrifice of turtles, Emory found that "the villagers could tell him little about the history of the temples" (Krauss 1988, 149).

Several decades later, in 1967–68, Dr. Yoshi Sinoto, a student of Emory's and an archaeologist at the Bishop Museum, began a series of archaeological investigations on Huahine that were to become his lifelong passion and professional mark of distinction. He located some two hundred archaeological sites on the island, more than forty of which were on Mata'ire'a Hill behind Maeva. In addition to being motivated by the scholarly pursuit of knowledge, he wanted to share his findings with the people of Maeva. Sinoto's archaeological methods, like Emory's, have always been conservative. Trained in a Western scientific tradition of conservation and restoration, he believes that the archaeological record is an irreplaceable resource of important scientific knowledge that, once altered, is gone forever. Thus, his approach to restoring the *marae* has been to work only with what remains in the landscape, gathering the stones that had fallen and restacking and stabilizing them, but never adding new material.

Many of the villagers of Maeva credit Sinoto with helping them to overcome their fear of going near the *marae* and encouraging them to take a more active interest in their history and share it with the public. Several of the villagers working with Sinoto became enthusiastic participants in helping him decode the sites. As Marietta explained, "It was Sinoto who revived our history for us, who got us involved in it, and who taught us not to be afraid of it." She shared her memories, saying,

> From the time I was a young child, I always followed Sinoto around when he came to Huahine to do his archaeology. All the children did this. Because of the *marae's* ancestral powers, the old people were afraid of the *marae* and stayed away from them. It was Sinoto who slowly rid the people of their fear. When he worked on the *marae*, he said that the workers had to come along. At first they refused because they were afraid. But he insisted, saying that they were the workers. When he went up the hill, some of the workers followed, and some turned back. Those who followed said that when they reached the *marae*, they heard a special bird sing out to them, which indicated to them that it was okay to be there. This was how, little by little, Sinoto got people to lessen their fear and take an interest in their history. And what he discovered on Huahine was unique. Now we know more about our history. It is important for us to know because these are our ancestors. This is our past, our identity. (Marietta Tefaataumarama, personal communication, 2001)

Dr. Sinoto was also responsible for the first restoration of the Fare Pote'e. In the late 1960s the residents of Maeva planned to build a new church on the site of the Fare Pote'e and wanted to dismantle it to make room for the church. With the villagers' permission, Sinoto moved the Fare Pote'e to its current site at the western edge of Maeva. The relocation and restoration of the Fare Pote'e were completed in 1972. Sinoto and the villagers once again used the restored Fare Pote'e, this time as a cultural center and exhibition gallery of archaeological materials and the history of Huahine. The authentically restored Fare Pote'e was itself a living exhibit (Yoshi Sinoto, personal communication, 2009).

The Fare Pote'e soon became a magnet for cultural revivalism. In 1976, a young artist and musician from Hawai'i, Bobby Holcomb, came to Huahine.

Intrigued by his own mixed cultural heritage (Native American, African American, Portuguese, and Native Hawaiian), he took an interest in understanding, connecting to, and promoting Tahitian culture. His art, inspired by Polynesian legends, and his songs (available on audio tapes and CDs), with Tahitian lyrics and melodies that appealed to Huahine's youth, made "Bobby" a popular cultural revivalist and a beloved local hero. One of his dreams was to use the restored Fare Pote'e as a community center. He wanted to encourage greater access to Tahitian culture by bringing it to life through the use of Tahitian language, the production of art, and the performance of song and dance. Inspired by Bobby, elders came to the Fare Pote'e to teach children about their culture—and in Tahitian, not in French. Older women came to weave baskets, sew *tifaifai* quilts, and visit with one another. In 1991 Bobby died, just when the Fare Pote'e was beginning to show signs of deterioration. Dorothy Levy told me, "On his deathbed, Bobby pleaded, 'Don't let the Fare Pote'e fall into the water.'"

By 1993, after more than twenty years of active use and minimal maintenance, the Fare Pote'e was in dire need of restoration. Some villagers had become interested in it also being used as a small, locally operated museum. They envisioned it as the main interpretive center for the archaeological sites, as well as a place for craft demonstrations and dance performances. This, they hoped, would generate income from tourists who were coming to the island in greater numbers. Two residents in particular, Chantal Spitz (a Tahitian poet, writer, educator, and political activist) and Dorothy Levy (a Tahitian-American who had married into a family from Maeva and had been living in Maeva since the late 1970s), led the efforts.

To achieve their goal, Chantal and Dorothy established an organization, the mission of which was to restore sites of cultural heritage and develop tourism at the grassroots level. Several individuals from Maeva joined them to become the founding group, which they named Opu Nui (literally "big stomach," that is, the seat of wisdom).[5] Opu Nui's goal was to have the people of Maeva take control of the preservation of their heritage. They also wanted to influence how tourists would see and experience Maeva and the Fare Pote'e. As Dorothy was fond of saying, Opu Nui would allow them to "paddle their own canoe." Their plans, however, were easier to envision than they were to accomplish. The first step in what would be an ongoing struggle for Opu Nui was to seek funds from the government in order to pay people from Maeva to rebuild the Fare Pote'e, a request supported by a thirty-eight-page document written by Chantal (Association Opu Nui 1995). Not long after receiving the request, the president, Gaston Flosse, accompanied by several ministers, came to Huahine to discuss the project with the members of Opu Nui.[6]

While giving President Flosse a tour of the site, Dorothy told him, "We want to rebuild the Fare Pote'e and turn it into an eco-museum. This could help Huahine develop tourism. Tourists come to this island because it has important archaeological sites. They come to see things and learn. But when they arrive at the Fare Pote'e, they're disappointed because there isn't any information to explain things to them. So we want to build a museum where visitors can learn about Maeva and Huahine. We want to hire people from Maeva to work in the museum and to be guides and take visitors up to the archaeological sites in the hills."

Looking around, President Flosse commented, "But there's no beauty here. You need to restore the *marae*. You need to plant some grass. You need to make it look more attractive."

She responded, "There is beauty here. It doesn't need to be manicured. All we want to do is explain the area so people who visit will understand what they're looking at."

This brief exchange embodied the core of the ongoing debate between Opu Nui and the Territorial government. Opu Nui wanted the site to be a living, organic community center—similar to Bobby's dream—that was primarily for the people of Maeva, but where tourists would also be welcome. President Flosse, however, wanted a manicured, photogenic destination that, first and foremost, would help promote tourism and thereby benefit the government. Eventually, reluctantly, and only after continued debate, did the government award Opu Nui a grant, administered by the Ministry of Tourism, for the restoration of the Fare Pote'e and the creation of a museum.

With the money in hand, Dorothy organized meetings for Opu Nui and the residents of Maeva to discuss the rebuilding of the Fare Pote'e and to solicit local input. Villagers overwhelmingly supported the plan and expressed their desire for the museum to display original artifacts. Many people were willing to donate items, such as drums, canoe paddles, and fishing gear.

They soon learned that the government wanted to purchase the land on which the Fare Pote'e and the adjacent *marae* were located, but the family that owned the land refused to sell it.

"I will not sell or rent my land," the landowner said. "See those boats at the edge of the water? See that inlet? My family needs those boats and access to the water in order to get fish."[7]

During the following months, people from Maeva helped rebuild the Fare Pote'e. Each day, young men arrived to do the work, erecting the support poles, thatching the roof, building the bamboo walls, and eventually weaving the floor from split bamboo. Government representatives visited periodically to make sure the funds were being used appropriately and that work was proceeding in a timely manner.

In May 1995, President Flosse visited the nearly complete Fare Pote'e. His party included the high commissioner of the Republic of France, the administrator for the Leeward Group of the Society Islands, the director of GIE Animation,[8] and the mayor of Huahine with his assistant. The high commissioner noticed that next to the Fare Pote'e were some outrigger canoes, as well as a motorboat pulled up onto the shore.

Not pleased with this, he said, "I'd like only outrigger canoes here, no boats with motors on them."

Dorothy responded, "The land is privately owned, and the boats belong to the owners."

With a Gallic shrug he replied, "But at Taputapuatea[9] on Raiatea, the government purchased the land and can make all these decisions."

As the group of officials continued walking around, inspecting the setting, the conversation turned to the plans for the official opening of the museum, scheduled for the following year.

Dorothy announced, "People are planning to revive Tahitian kite flying as the main event."

The director of GIE Animation responded, "You need something more spectacular, something that tourists would want. You need to have re-enactments of religious ceremonies on the *marae*."

Dorothy responded forcefully, "The residents refuse to have re-enactments on the *marae* because they are superstitious about disturbing the ancestors. If you do anything against the landowners' wishes, then next time you arrive you'll find barbed wire in front of your faces."

Eventually the family that owned the land on which the Fare Pote'e was located traded that piece of land (but not the one adjacent to it, with the boats and access to the water) to the government in return for another parcel of land and a promise of employment at the cultural center for their children.

The day of the grand opening—September 21, 1996—the Fare Pote'e was filled with villagers, personal objects, and memories. Photographs of the Fare Pote'e, the *marae*, and various villagers, taken by Emory in the 1920s and by Sinoto in the 1960s, were taped onto large pieces of bright red material and placed on the wall at one end of the building. People gathered around them, pointing out photos of their parents and grandparents. Those who had donated family heirlooms came to see them on display. Students from the Collège de Fare were showing friends and family their topographical map, illustrating their artwork as well as a new perspective on their island.

The opening festivities began with prayers and then speeches by various dignitaries. Dances and music were performed at the open area in front of the Fare Pote'e. This was followed by two kite-flying contests, one specifically for children (who, for the occasion, had made kites in school). Later, there would be a second contest for adults on the beach on the far side of Maeva, where more than thirty villagers would participate. The already lively competitive spirit was enhanced by hopes of winning the first prize—two round-trip tickets to Honolulu donated by Hawaiian Airlines.[10]

Once the museum opened, local residents embraced it, and tourists appreciated it. Tourists communicated their reactions in conversations with museum workers, as well as in written comments in a guestbook: "I'm so glad we found you. This all shows how much you care"; "This place has a soul"; "This museum lets us get close to the soul of Huahine"; and "Thank you to the people of Maeva for their kindness, their warmth, and for their desire to share their culture."[11]

In March 1998, only eighteen months after the museum opened, a cyclone hit Huahine. Although no people were hurt, the cyclone ruined many of the houses and totally destroyed the Fare Pote'e, sending its roof and walls flying into Lac Fauna Nui. Fortunately, most of the objects, as well as the photos taped to the red cloth, had been quickly removed before the cyclone arrived.

NEW OARSMEN AT THE HELM

The villagers were greatly saddened by the destruction of the Fare Pote'e. While coping with the many effects of the cyclone, they looked forward to rebuilding it once again. Little could they anticipate, however, that the cyclone had also created new opportunities for the Territorial government. The Fare Pote'e's next transformation—from a local cultural center to a tourist destination designed and directed by the Territorial government—was now set in motion. The destruction of the Fare Pote'e allowed the Territorial government to develop new codes—for the *marae*, the Fare Pote'e, and the objects and narratives within it—using different pedagogical approaches and political visions. Tourist sites tend to "lie at the intersection of diverse and competing social, economic, and political influences" (Low and Lawrence-Zúñiga 2003, 23). The Fare Poteʻe was no exception.[12]

In this post-CEP era, the Territorial government looked upon the *marae* and the Fare Poteʻe in a new light because of the need to redirect the economy toward projects—especially tourism—that would produce foreign exchange. This was also when GIE Tahiti Tourisme began promoting the different islands as having unique identities. Huahine was labeled as the "authentic island" because it offered "culture." As Etienne Ragivaru, a director of one of Huahine's hotels, said, "Tourists who come to Huahine want to learn about the archaeological sites and culture. Sure, they come for the beach and sun. But they also want culture and history. That's what Huahine is known for." His observation was supported by a comment made by one of the American tourists in our group at the Fare Poteʻe.

> We have a package deal that allows us to spend several days on each of the main islands, so we've seen a lot and can compare. We definitely like Huahine best. It's a lot more interesting. The people seem to have more pride in their history. We especially like this area right here because of the museum and the *marae* and all the culture. You don't get that on the other islands.

Thus, in the post-CEP climate—with the economy focused on development projects, with tourism viewed as "the future," and with Huahine flagged as the "authentic island"—the government now took a much more active interest in what only a few years earlier President Flosse had dismissively called *le petit musée dans la boue* (the little museum in the mud). The Territorial government wanted the archaeological sites and the museum to be the showcase for the island that they had advertised as the place where one could see "culture." Although the government had reluctantly supported Opu Nui and the villagers in the restoration of the Fare Poteʻe and the development of the museum, it now moved quickly and with a major financial commitment. This political shift, however, meant the loss of local control of the project. Previously the Office of Tourism had funded the museum's revival. Now the minister of culture took charge. As Dorothy explained, the goal of Opu Nui had been for the people of Maeva to "paddle their own canoe." Now Maeva's residents were commenting that, as happens in life, "the canoe had flipped over and new oarsmen were at the helm."

LOOKING LIKE A GUIDEBOOK

The Fare Pote'e I visited with the tourists on that breezy day in 2001, although still a work in progress, was already a clear demonstration of what the "new oarsmen" wanted, and it was dramatically different from what I knew so well from my 1996 visit to Huahine for the museum's inauguration ceremonies. I immediately noticed that the floor had been rebuilt in a much sturdier manner. Wooden planks were placed beneath the woven split bamboo (to accommodate large tour groups without fear of the floor breaking). Marietta (who had political connections to the minister of culture and who had not been a member of Opu Nui) was hired to manage the museum. New exhibits were in the process of being installed. The transformation from a local cultural center to a managed tourist attraction was striking. As Dorothy told me,

> The Fare Pote'e has changed. Opu Nui's idea was to make it an eco-museum or cultural center that would be primarily for the people of Maeva. There was to be on-going archaeology, and the building was to be filled with objects that belonged to the residents. It was to be a living monument to the people and culture of the village. Now the government has turned it into a tourist attraction. They say there is no such word as 'eco-museum.' They say it's a scientific information center. It's still a beautiful environment, but it's no longer by or for the people of Maeva. The *marae* have been restored by French archaeologists, who turned them into something that looks manicured and pretty, something photogenic for tourists' cameras. The Fare Pote'e is full of panels with lots of writing. Before, a guide from Maeva was a personal interpreter, answering visitors' questions and explaining things to them. Now, with groups of ten or twenty coming from the cruise ships, the crowds are whisked through and shown the panels to read. The Fare Pote'e, which was originally meant to be something emotional for the soul to enjoy, has been turned into something intellectual for tourists to digest. (Dorothy Levy, personal communication, 2001)

To transform the Fare Pote'e into a tourist destination, government officials had recoded it in a way that allowed it to fit more comfortably within the tourism "cocoon." Once a place is managed in this way—described in guidebooks, portrayed on postcards, and promoted in brochures and on Web sites—it must be constructed, named, and arranged according to specific spatial codes. Once it has been labeled as a destination, it needs to look like what tourists expect. As Dorothy so aptly said, "They're trying to make us look like a guidebook." And as James Clifford has noted, "People prefer order to disorder; they grasp at formulas rather than actuality; they prefer the guidebook to the confusion before them" (Clifford 1988, 264).

The arrangement of the site for greater visual appeal transgressed even the sacred space of the *marae*. Much to the shock of local residents, the three *marae* closest to the Fare Pote'e were completely rebuilt. Because the *marae* are sacred, any disturbance of them is thought to agitate the ancestors. One of my friends, Édouard Piha, even as a devout Seventh Day Adventist still understood the respect that must be shown toward the *marae*. As he explained, "It's okay to clean up the *marae*, to pull out the weeds and pick up trash. But it's wrong to disturb them this much. They are living *marae*. These are our ancestors." Yet, without consulting local residents, and in spite of local opposition to what was happening, government officials brought in outsiders to execute the government's plans. The reconstruction included a reorientation of the *marae* and a major rearrangement of the stones, including the addition of large amounts of coral. As I later learned from Maurice Hardy, one of the French archaeologists involved in the work (and whose less invasive plans had been ignored), the level areas of the *marae* were raised to make it easier for tourists to walk over the stones without getting their feet wet, especially where the *marae* extended out into Lac Fauna Nui. The result was that the *marae* appeared tidy and rigid. What before had looked like a jumble of rocks was now so smooth that, as one resident said, "One can now play tennis on the *marae*." Tourists generally considered the effects successful. One tourist, upon walking up to the *marae*, said, "Oh, I'm sure this area has been restored because it looks so beautiful." And because tourists like to purchase postcards of beautiful things they've seen, Teva Sylvain produced a postcard of these particular renovated *marae* (fig. 5.4).

Once the restoration of the *marae* was complete, government officials developed the area around the *marae* into a tourist "complex." In addition to the Fare Pote'e, three other structures were built. A sign was placed in front of the Fare Pote'e that, using an unusual mixture of Tahitian, English, and French, gave it a specific name: Fare Pote'e House, Site Archéologique, Lac Fauna Nui, Maeva, Huahine. The three new buildings were also labeled: Fare Va'a (canoe shed); Fare Ia Manaha (caretaker's quarters, which originally would have housed sacred treasures and images of the gods); and Fare Hau Pape (cookhouse). These buildings, although photogenic, were left empty, with attention directed toward the Fare Pote'e as the interpretive center of the site.

Huahine
Marae de Maeva

Fig. 5.4 Huahine: *Marae* de Maeva. Photo by Teva Sylvain, Pacific Promotion, Tahiti. Photo courtesy of Pacific Promotion, 2001.

The interior of the Fare Poteʻe was arranged according to what the Ministry of Culture thought was appropriate for a "scientific information center." Instead of artifacts and objects donated by local families, there were items that were newly made but fashioned to look as though they were old. *Unu,* which in precontact times were placed outdoors to represent the families affiliated with the *marae,* were propped up inside the building against the wall. Because missionaries, as well as their Tahitian converts, had destroyed all original *unu,* there were no contemporary models to show how to make them. A French artisan, hired to make reproductions of the *unu,* had to use illustrations by the artists who accompanied Captain Cook. The villagers of Maeva resented these modern *unu,* commenting on how "wrong" they looked. They felt the *unu* should be outdoors, not indoors,[13] and should be made from Tahitian, not Hawaiian, wood. They said the *unu* looked "too straight, too perfect, and as though they were made with a machine." Like the newly "restored" *marae*, these *unu* caught the eye of many tourists, who, reaching for their cameras, often headed straight for the *unu*.

The relief map of Huahine made by the students was no longer there. The minister of culture (originally from Huahine) thought that it was unattractive and unprofessional. She had requested that it be removed.

As decisions were being made about what to include in the exhibits, the most contentious disagreements arose around whether, and how, to portray Huahine's cultural hero, Henri Hiro. Residents were adamant that there should be an exhibit about him that showcased his life, philosophy, and poetry. The government, having no desire to highlight an anticolonial spokesperson, vetoed the idea.[14]

Because the site was now a "scientific information center," containing scholarly research for tourists to digest, signage became imperative. In the past, information had been presented primarily through personal exchanges between the young woman working in the Fare Pote'e and the visitors. Now an official narrative was printed for visitors to read, complete with a list of the scholars and authorities (and their credentials) that had provided the information. In addition to the signposts in front of each building, large panels with detailed text were placed inside the museum to explain the exhibits.

This change in how to transmit information—from an oral style to an official written text—parallels a shift from a Tahitian to a European mode of communication. When I asked for her opinion about the explanatory panels, one local resident said, "Farani tera" (Tahitian for "that's French"), in a tone that communicated, "What do you expect?" Her response conveyed the close relationship between choice of language, mode of communication, and politics. Although Tahitians might want to know how a hafted axe was made or how holes were drilled in stone net sinkers, the code that would give them access to this information would be presented orally, not in writing, and would be in Tahitian, not French.

These new codes—aggressively reconstructing the site, straightening and tidying the *marae*, rebuilding and naming structures, making new artifacts fabricated to look old, removing "unprofessional-looking" exhibits, silencing a local hero and his poetry, writing official narratives—are all attempts to make the site intelligible for tourists, to communicate a sense of authority and authenticity, and to render the "site" more of a "sight." The Fare Pote'e and *marae* had become photogenic "images" rather than the homegrown place the villagers had known.[15]

Because Huahine was promoted as the island that offered culture, much thought went into how "culture" should be portrayed. The minister of culture was ultimately responsible for what was to be included as "culture" and how it was to be presented. At a meeting to discuss plans for the museum, she talked about culture as a concrete, circumscribed thing, something that one could safeguard and pass on to others. She said, "We need to develop the museum to protect our culture so we can give it to our children in the future. Bora Bora is fine with all its hotels. But Huahine is an island with culture. It's the 'authentic island.' We need to protect that and make use of it" (Louise Peltzer, comments at public meeting, 2001).

Jamaica Kincaid, the Caribbean author, has commented on the irony that exists when a country appoints a minister of culture and yet has people who are living their culture within the country on a daily basis:

> Have you ever heard of any culture springing up under the umbrella of a Minister of Culture? . . . In countries that have no culture or are afraid they may have no culture, there is a Minister of Culture. And what is culture, anyway? In some places, it's the way they play drums; in other places, it's the way you behave out in public; and in still other places, it's just the way a person cooks food. And so what is there to preserve about these things? For is it not . . . that people make them up as they go along, make them up as they need them? (Kincaid 1988, 49–50)

As Kincaid indicates, culture is flexible, fluid, and alive, and is generated and utilized as needed. Culture is not simply a *marae* leveled for easier access and picked clean of weeds for photogenic appeal. Nor is it best embodied by replacing a modern motorboat with an outrigger canoe. Nor is it reducible to a set of preserved objects and visual fragments that are arranged to create an illusion of "authenticity." Culture is, as Kincaid said, what people construct and use as the need arises. In the words of the owner of the land on which the Fare Pote'e and *marae* were located, culture is "those boats at the edge of the water . . . that inlet," all of which were essential for him to feed his family. As one of the tour guides on Huahine told me, "If you have to put 'culture' in a museum and preserve it, then it's too late."

People who "live inside a culture," who understand it and behave appropriately within it, know its codes. Having internalized the codes, they do not need to read about culture on a written panel. They have been taught how to act near a *marae* and how to fish from canoes as well as from motorboats. They also know how to respond to inappropriate codes. They know when the *unu* look wrong. People outside a culture — such as tourists — who want to peek in and gain even a shred of understanding need to rely on others to decode what they encounter so that they might comprehend what they see, know how to behave within a space, and perhaps talk about this "cultural" experience with others. The difference between living inside a culture and understanding it intellectually from without lies in one's ability to access the appropriate codes. Living inside a culture amounts to nothing more than knowing and maintaining the codes. The ongoing struggles about how to define and use the Fare Pote'e were battles about which codes would be used. The new codes spoke to the villagers through the power dynamics of the Territorial government. These codes transformed the Fare Pote'e, which had been part of their life for so long, into something foreign and impersonal.

THE BOOBY BIRD'S NEW HOME

Looking back, I wonder about what kind of place the tourists — who respectfully removed their shoes, stepped into the Fare Pote'e with me, read the panels, admired the exhibits, and clicked their cameras — had visited and experienced. Over the past century or more, the Fare Pote'e has changed from one type of place to another. Those who originally produced the space (in this case, villagers, fishermen, dancers, artisans, kite makers, and others) were no longer the same individuals who moved in and directed its 2001 development (local politicians, government presidents, ministers of culture, high commissioners, and directors of tourism development). Those who moved in and took over operated in ways that left little room for others to intervene.

Although transformations of a place are always political, the post-CEP change of the Fare Pote'e involved politics on a level that was more Territorially oriented than ever before. Now national political forces began to take over what others on a local level had once produced. As Lefebvre said, states establish their power on the ruins they have created, displaying their authority in the form of knowledge, text, technology, money, objects, works of art, and other symbols (Lefebvre 1991, 49). Or, as Dorothy more picturesquely observed, "It's as though a booby bird has moved into the hummingbird's nest and taken it over as its own." Yet, occupied and animated as this new space appeared, it embodies an ongoing tension between full and empty. The Fare Pote'e became the perfect embodiment of the "invisible fullness of political space" (Lefebvre 1991, 49).

Residents of Maeva reacted in different ways to the booby bird's new home. Some bought into the plan in exchange for promises of economic gain, like the family that traded its land to the government in exchange for work at the site for its children. Others tried their hand at entrepreneurial ventures, like setting up small stands with fruit, green coconuts, or handicrafts across the road from the Fare Pote'e, patiently waiting for tourists to arrive. Chantal Spitz, one of Opu Nui's founders, responded passionately in a letter to the newspaper, saying, "The Fare Pote'e has now received its official stamp of exploitation like a vulgar construction without history, without soul—further proof, if proof is still needed, of the complete numbing of our spirits" (Spitz 1999). Some individuals were less vocal but equally effective in their expression of resistance. For example, a few days after a visit by the minister of culture, during which she had made disparaging comments about the presence of motorboats near the Fare Pote'e, I was at the site talking to Marietta, who is also a friend and confidant of the minister of culture. Our conversation was interrupted by a thunderous noise. Startled, we looked up and watched the son of the owner of the land on which the *marae* and motorboats were located as he loudly revved up his pickup truck, drove it across the newly restored *marae*, and parked next to his boat. He moved a few supplies from his truck to his boat and then sped off again, his vehicle rattling as it lurched across the site, while from the corner of his eye he watched us watching him, making sure Marietta saw everything. The message was crystal clear, and he knew it would reach the minister of culture soon: this was his land, not hers.[16] What spoke most poignantly about how Maeva's residents felt, however, was that they visited the Fare Pote'e much less after the restoration.

Tourists, of course, keep coming to the Fare Pote'e and seem to enjoy what they see, commenting, as one did in the guest book, that "this museum lets us get close to the soul of Polynesia and puts us under its spell . . . don't change anything." The past, however, has already slipped away, as the government has tried to recreate and preserve its idea of the past at this tourist site, which has been transformed as all places constantly are.

This—namely, this photogenic, choreographed, and manicured space of "authentic" culture, coded for tourists, highlighted in guidebooks, and now also available on a postcard, invisibly full of political agendas and relatively empty of local residents, transformed and always still transforming (indeed, it has already changed again since I wrote this)[17]—is the place in which the tourists and I found ourselves on that sunny, breezy day on our tour of the island to learn about its "culture."

CHAPTER SIX

Everyday Spaces of Resistance

The exercise of power over others—the essence of the relationship between colonizer and colonized—is often expressed through the establishment and control of boundaries. Spaces are claimed, named, mapped, and regulated. The power relationship also defines what behaviors are acceptable within these spaces. By transgressing or ignoring these boundaries and behaviors, people can create spaces of resistance. They might do this through heroic struggles and grand gestures carried out in full view of the powerful. To protest the resumption of nuclear testing in 1995, Tahitians drove bulldozers through Faaʻa International Airport. To call attention to environmental destruction caused by tourism development, Tahitians in canoes have surrounded the dredges that pump white sand from the lagoon onto the otherwise muddy shore. As Hiro remarked, "A symbolic gesture expresses a break, a shock, and it's understood as a provocation. Thus, it is necessary to choose significant gestures" (Hiro 2004, 85).[1] For him, one particular gesture was the wearing of a *pareu* instead of Western clothing. He said,

> That's a story in itself! I was a joke! Everyone's joke! The poet! The dreamer! The intellectual! The bumpkin! Because of the *pareu*, I lived through a period of ridicule. Some people confronted me directly, but since I wore it on all occasions and everywhere, it shocked people and then became ordinary. And then, more and more people started to wear it. The *pareu* reconciled Polyne-

sians with what was always profoundly a part of them. It reconciled them with themselves. (Stewart, Mateata-Allain, and Mawyer 2006, 80)[2]

As seen with Hiro's *pareu,* challenges to conventional behavior do have the ability to effect profound change.

Whereas spaces of domination are those of exclusion, spaces of resistance are multiple and dynamic. They are usually dislocated from spaces of domination because "the powerful are continually vigilant of the borders" (Pile and Keith 1997, 16). These spaces of resistance can occur in myriad ways, both brazenly provocative and quietly subtle:

> Potentially, the list of acts of resistance is endless — everything from foot-dragging to walking, from sit-ins to outings, from chaining oneself up in treetops to dancing the night away, from parody to passing, from bombs to hoaxes, from graffiti tags on New York trains to stealing pens from employers . . . and the reason for this seems to be that definitions of resistance have become bound up with the ways that people are understood to have capacities to change things through giving their own meanings to things, through finding their own tactics for avoiding, taunting, attacking, undermining, enduring, hindering, mocking the everyday exercise of power. (Pile and Keith 1997, 14)

EMBODIED ACTS OF PLEASURE

Everyday acts of resistance tend to be those that are more subtle, habitual, and ambiguous. As de Certeau has observed,

> Innumerable ways of playing and foiling the other's game, that is, the space instituted by others, characterize the subtle, stubborn, resistant activity of groups which, since they lack their own space, have to get along in a network of already established forces and representations. . . . Like the skill of a driver in the streets of Rome or Naples, there is a skill that has its connoisseurs and its aesthetics exercised in any labyrinth of powers, a skill ceaselessly recreating opacities and ambiguities — spaces of darkness and trickery — in the universe of technocratic transparency, a skill that disappears into them and reappears again, taking no responsibility for the administration of a totality. (de Certeau 1984, 18)

These less obvious spaces of resistance are opaque and ambiguous, quietly disappearing and reappearing. Emerging from everyday acts of empowerment, people, almost unconsciously, behave in ways that are meaningful to them and that express their identities. Rather than deliberate acts of aggression, these behaviors are usually embodied acts of pleasure. Rather than expressing anger, frustration, and fear, they are about desire, joy, and playfulness as people seek places that are familiar and comfortable within a space otherwise bounded, administered, or denied. These spaces weave themselves seamlessly and subversively through geographies of power, creating spaces outside the dominant realm. They are low-risk, yet highly effective, means of resistance (see Scott 1985).

Tahitians often create such ephemeral counter-spaces in ways that are visible and audible only to one another. Their foods, music, dance, language, and humor are particularly productive channels for doing this. In fun-loving ways they claim power "through the appropriation of space and the exercise of the ability to invent new forms of space—for example a space of enjoyment" (L. Stewart 1995, 615). Within dominant spaces of global or state power they can, and do, find ways, both as individuals and in groups, to define more comfortable spaces for themselves. Through their behavior they create counter-discourses that have not been grasped by apparatuses of power. For them, these occasions are all the more fun and entertaining—and successful—precisely because they operate under the radar of the state.

Lefebvre has emphasized the critical role the human body plays in producing spaces—and counter-spaces—through everyday practices and experiences. This occurs most creatively when human beings spontaneously act, react, and interact within space, thus assuming power and agency in their everyday lives. He underscored people's ability to resist organized authority and reclaim power in their "quest for a counter-space" (Lefebvre 1991, 383). He examines the history of human bodies to understand the nature of resistance, treating space as produced by the body and not simply as the physical imposition of space upon the body. "Resistance, he thinks, has to start with the human body, with its corporeal ability to produce space. This ability to *produce* space, rather than just to *conceive* space, is the means by which people can take back power in their everyday lives" (L. Stewart 1995, 609–10).[3]

Through bodily practices—eating, singing, dancing, joking, laughing, talking, remaining silent, sitting down, or getting up and walking away—people appropriate space in ways that are difficult for others to disrupt or control. Colonizers might raise flags, draw new maps, design street grids, or erect fences, but they cannot as easily control other people's bodies (see Rhodes 2004). As Merleau-Ponty noted, embodiment is a reflexive, expressive, practical dialogue that occurs between subject and object "in the flesh" (1945, 1968). He recognized that one's body is simultaneously physical and experiential, "outer" and "inner," biological and phenomenological, thus underscoring the corporeality of human consciousness. Place, when known through the body, is not a collection of objects but is "the horizon latent in all our experience and itself ever-present and anterior to every determining thought" (Merleau-Ponty 1945, 92). Because human beings are always located within a web of social connections, they are active agents, moving in places that are simultaneously in the land and in people's bodies.[4] As Hiro has said, "A life that is Polynesian in its totality includes everything: home, nutrition, clothes, economy, conduct, chants, dances, music . . . the whole thing" (Hiro 2004, 83).[5]

A CRUISE SHIP

I gained insight into how Tahitians produce embodied counter-spaces by participating in two trips. The first, to an anchored cruise ship with a dozen villagers, was between home and ship, Tahitian and tourist, basic subsistence and extravagant abundance. The second, a trip to a neighboring island with one hundred elders, was between home and elsewhere, Tahitian traditions and French impositions, group cooperation and colonial opposition. Both journeys involved ships, and on both occasions Tahitians within dominant spaces created counter-spaces of resistance through spontaneous, fun-loving behavior.

The first journey occurred on September 3, 2001, when the American-owned and -operated luxury liner *Renaissance II*, with 700 passengers and 300 crew members, was anchored in Huahine's Maroe Bay during its seven-day cruise through the Society Islands. At the time, there were two *Renaissance* sister ships in French Polynesia. They offered excellent value for their clients, who were primarily middle-class Americans.[6] A Web site that reviews cruise lines noted,

> *Renaissance* ships are quite elegant—not sleek and contemporary . . . but old-world elegant, like an English country manor, with lots of dark woods and brass and wrought iron. The libraries are like none you've ever seen—with ceilings painted à la Sistine Chapel, fireplaces, overstuffed sofas and armchairs and an unbelievable selection of books. The staterooms are larger than those on ships whose cruises are priced at two and three times what the *Renaissance* rates are. A very large percentage of the cabins are outside—that is, with

Fig. 6.1 On board the *Renaissance II*: *Pareu*-wearing demonstration with handicraft tables in the background, 2001.

doors, picture windows, or portholes. . . . The A suites are not to be believed—with living room, dining room, bedroom, two bathrooms—one with a Jacuzzi—and a wrap-around deck.[7]

When the *Renaissance* came to Huahine (about two or three times a month during the cruise season), a group of twelve to fifteen Tahitians (the composition of the group always changed) went on board to sell their handicrafts and to entertain the tourists with Tahitian dancing and demonstrations of the many creative ways to wear a *pareu* (fig. 6.1).

The two *Renaissance* ships began coming to Huahine in (post-CEP) 1999, one of the successes of the government's investment in the cruise ship industry. The president of French Polynesia, Gaston Flosse, who had invested in these ships, put great effort into creating interest in them. Although previous efforts to invest in cruise ships for French Polynesia had not always been successful, the *Renaissance* ships seemed to promise the vision of expanded horizons and new perspectives that their name evoked. Dorothy Levy, wanting to make sure that the local residents would also benefit from this venture, entered into discussions with the vice president of the *Renaissance* line. After consulting various residents, she proposed that each time the ship would come to Huahine, a group of up to fifteen Tahitians could go on board to sell their handicrafts, which would give them an opportunity to earn some money. The vice president agreed, and a contract was drawn up, stating that the Tahitians would be compensated for their visit only with food; that is, they would be fed while on the ship. As one woman told me, "It's a good idea. I would rather be paid in food than in money. If they pay us in money, how much would they pay? Not much! But to pay with food is good because we can eat all we want."

Each time the ship came to Huahine, which was always early in the morning, Dorothy drove around the island to pick up anyone who wanted to go on board for the day, never knowing who would show up. As time went on, more and more people wanted to go and even planned ahead for the visits by making more craft items to sell.

As Dorothy told me, "The Tahitians love going to the ship because it gives them something different and fun to do. They get to earn some money selling their crafts, they get to check out the tourists and their fashions, and they can take home lots of food for their families. It takes them out of their daily life for a few hours. They get to be 'queen for the day,' just like the tourists on the ship."

In an essay about his Caribbean cruise on the MV *Nadir*, David Wallace describes how a sense of luxury is created on board through a display of abundance and perfection (1996). He draws a link between a cruise ship's perfectly arranged "other" space, passengers' desires, and global capitalism. Everything on the MV *Nadir* was carefully planned to give passengers a sense of being continually indulged and pampered. Yet, all of this was buttressed by a capitalist system that rested on the backs of hard-working "Third World guys":

> This grim determination to indulge the passenger in ways that go far beyond any halfway-sane passenger's own expectations is everywhere on the *Nadir*. Some wholly random examples: My cabin bathroom has plenty of thick fluffy towels, but when I go up to lie in the sun I don't have to take any of my cabin's towels, because the two upper decks' sun areas have big carts loaded with even thicker and fluffier towels. . . . And each of the sun decks is manned by a special squad of full-time Towel Guys . . . a Towel Guy materializes the minute your fanny leaves the chair and removes your towel for you and deposits it in the slot. . . . Down in the Five-Star Caravelle Restaurant, the waiter will

not only bring you a lobster—as well as a second and even a third lobster—with methamphetaminic speed but will also incline over you with gleaming claw-cracker and surgical fork and dismantle it for you. . . . Every public surface on the *m.v. Nadir* that isn't stainless steel or glass or varnished parquet or dense and good-smelling sauna-type wood is plush blue carpet that never has a chance to accumulate even one flecklet of lint because jumpsuited Third World guys are always at it with Siemens A. G. vacuums. (D. Wallace 1996, 44–45)

Cruise ships, of course, are notorious for their abundance of food. Whenever Tahitians told me about their visits to the *Renaissance,* their conversations inevitably turned to the sumptuous amounts of food. They tended to describe their visits and the day's schedule in terms of food and eating. One woman told me, "I've only missed three visits to the ship the entire time. I like to go because the time slot (10:30–4:30) is a good time to eat. Last week was good because we ate Mo'orea food."[8] As another woman told me when I asked about the day's schedule, "We set up our craft tables at 10:30, eat lunch, do a dance show at 1:00, eat pizza, do the *pareu* demonstration and offer dance lessons at 3:00, eat cookies, cake, and ice cream, and then go home." Tahitians who visited the ship always told me playfully about how, when they left the ship, they took large amounts of food with them—stashed in plastic bags that they tucked into the various baskets that (with foresight) they brought along.

On one occasion when the *Renaissance II* was anchored at Huahine, Dorothy invited me to go along. The two of us went on board about noon, the Tahitians having arrived earlier to set up the tables with their crafts. When Dorothy and I took the launch to the ship there were about fifty *Renaissance* passengers with us. Judging by the grains of sand that stuck to their slightly sunburned, suntan-oiled skin, and their tote bags of snorkel equipment, I guessed they were returning from a much touted "land-and-water tour." As the launch raced across the bay to the ship, I couldn't help but hear the conversations closest to me. One woman, strategically making her way to the exit area, said, "Fran, let's get off first so we can get to the dining room quickly—I'm starving." Someone else within earshot said, "Good idea, boy am I hungry, yeah, let's get to the lunch line before the crowd arrives." When the launch pulled up at the ship, with many of the passengers pushing to get off, we encountered another large group of passengers waiting to leave for the afternoon "land-and-water tour."

Once on board, Dorothy and I spotted the Tahitians eating lunch in the dining room. As we approached them, I could already sense their intense focus on the food. One woman was returning from the buffet line with her plate piled high with pizza, and those at the table were busy organizing their food. After we greeted everyone and sat down, one woman asked me how many plastic bags I had brought with me and whether I could give her some. Others chimed in with various playful requests.

"Miriama, could you take some pizza for me? My bag is already full."

"Hey, Dorotéa, can we use your hat as well? If we turn it upside down it will make a nice plate for carrying our food."

One woman told me that in the past she had brought large bottles to fill with soda. When I noticed someone else arranging her food into separate piles, she smiled and, pointing to each in turn, told me which family member would receive it after she arrived home that evening.

For Tahitians, as for Pacific Islanders in general, food is a powerful form of social communication. Food is meant to be shared, something noted by many anthropologists who have worked in the Pacific.[9] As one woman told me when I did fieldwork in Papua New Guinea, "We are not like white people; we share our food. If we are eating and someone sees us, we have to offer the food to that person." Food is an important mode of symbolic expression that is used to convey a variety of beliefs and feelings about people and relationships. It is the main vehicle through which people express their concern and care for one another. To withhold food is the worst of social sins; it sends a message of disrespect and willful neglect.

For those who went on board, food was doubly meaningful. It was their "paycheck" and the tangible item that they took home to share with family and friends. In addition—and perhaps of even greater significance—food became the main medium through which they created their own counter-spaces while on the ship. As much as the visit to the ship was an adventure for them, the experience was also tinged with feelings of dislocation and disappointment. There were almost no social, and very few economic, exchanges between the Tahitians and the tourists. The passengers knew very little French, and no Tahitian, so verbal communication between the two groups was almost nonexistent. Also, the Tahitians occasionally complained about how the tourists inspected their handicrafts—shell necklaces, flower crowns, hats of woven coconut or pandanus leaves, and hand-made *pareus*—but purchased little.

What made them feel at ease, however, was the food. They turned their access to the food into the highlight of their day, figuring out how much they could eat and take home with them. I saw this as their way to turn an uncomfortable, boundary-laden experience into a setting in which they could—through their own behavior—feel comfortable. They transformed the abundance of food for the passengers into something that meshed with their own cultural values about sharing food. With constant joking and laughter, they piled up as much as possible on their plates, wrapping food in paper napkins and stuffing these soggy packages into their baskets and plastic bags.

As the visits by the Tahitians continued, problems arose. The Tahitians' desire to take as much food as they could became a source of tension between them and the ship's staff. On one visit to the ship, a steward pulled Dorothy aside and told her that the "stealing" of food was getting out of hand. He complained, "I notice that when the Tahitians walk past a bowl full of fruit the bowl suddenly becomes empty. We don't mind feeding them, but we can't feed the whole island!" The Tahitians, having noticed the large amounts of food consumed by the ship's passengers (some of whom, as I had just seen, moved to a new spot on the launch for the sole purpose of being first in the lunch line), took offense. It appeared that the battle about the amount they took was less about food and more about establishing and challenging boundaries. Indeed, the more Dorothy told them that the staff was upset, the more food the Tahitians took and the more fun they had doing this.

Many boundaries existed between the ship and the shore, marked by such things as gates, tinted windows, and walkie-talkies, each defining spaces of inclusion and exclusion. I once experienced how elaborate these gate-keeping tactics could be when I had an appointment to meet with the program director on a cruise ship—the "floating resort" *Club Med II*, with its mainly French clientele. Like the *Renaissance* ships, it was too large to come directly to the shore and was anchored in Maroe Bay, using a launch to take passengers back and forth. My reason for visiting was that Alain, the program director, had expressed a desire to meet with me because he was looking for someone who could provide onboard lectures about Tahitian culture (in French). Even though he had been informed about my visit, I encountered impenetrable boundaries, both real and symbolic, as soon as I arrived at the dock. With walkie-talkies in their hands, the white-uniformed attendants deliberately walked out of earshot to communicate to Alain (who was on the boat) that I was at the dock. As I waited I had ample opportunity to

observe the many barriers that were created between ship and shore: iden-
tification checks by attendants on the dock, tinted windows on the ship that
made it impossible to see inside, and, ultimately, the dock attendant's denial
of my going on board. Earlier that day I remember telling Dorothy (who
knew Alain), "You would think they'd have an easy time here in Tahiti finding someone to talk about Tahitian culture." "No," she responded, "it's difficult for them because they have no connections with anyone on shore."
After my frustrating trip to the dock, I could understand why. What I could
not understand was the irony of the *Club Med II* (with its many impenetrable
ways to set itself off from Tahitian reality) wanting to hire someone—but not
a Tahitian—to come on board and talk about local culture.

As noted, the Territorial government had purchased the cruise ships when
forces of capital defined them as desirable and profitable. In the same way
that one economic climate can make cruise ships fashionable, a sudden turn
can make a once cost-effective enterprise become unprofitable and obsolete.
This happened with the *Renaissance* ships. Within two years of the Territorial government's investment in the ships, the company went bankrupt.
Within eight days of my visit to the ship, the world of tourism was turned
upside down with the September 11 attacks on the World Trade Center. The
severe post-September 11 drop in tourism ultimately resulted in the bankruptcy of the cruise line. The Territorial government impounded the ships to
ensure payment of port fees and debts owed to local merchants, docking the
two ships in Pape'ete at the quay at Tahua Vaiete for several months—visible
remains of the temporary failure of the government's investment.[10]

VOYAGE TO TAHA'A WITH THE *MATAHIAPO*

The second journey I went on was to the island of Taha'a in the company of
about one hundred elders (known as *matahiapo,* meaning "those who can
see the darkness") from Huahine. They were to attend, along with elders
from the other Leeward Islands (Raiatea, Taha'a, Bora Bora, Maupiti, and
Tupai), the Rencontre des Personnes Agées des Îles-sous-le-Vent, or meeting
of elders from the Leeward Islands in the Society Island archipelago (map 5).
This meeting was sponsored and funded (as were the previous ones, in 1999
and 2000) by two social service agencies of the Territorial government.[11]

Transporting the elders was a major logistical challenge, as more than 250
people had to be brought to Taha'a. Interisland travel can be expensive (by
air) and inconvenient (by boat). This major problem was solved by the use

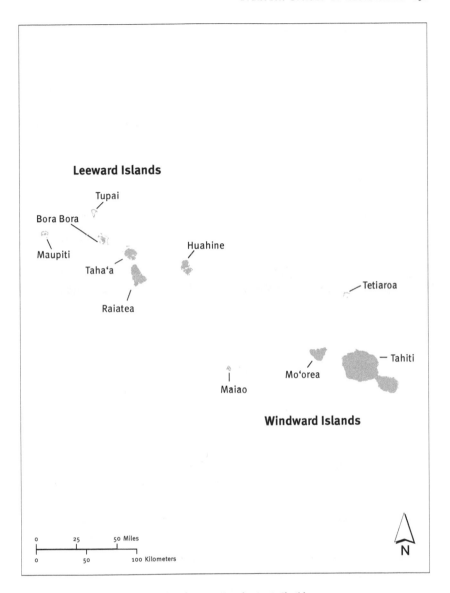

Leeward Islands

Tupai

Bora Bora

Maupiti

Taha'a

Huahine

Raiatea

Tetiaroa

Tahiti

Mo'orea

Maiao

Windward Islands

0   25   50 Miles

0   50   100 Kilometers

N

Map 5   The Society Islands, French Polynesia. Map by Amir Sheikh.

of the *Tahiti Nui*, a ship purchased by the Territorial government with funds from the post-CEP program. Regarded by some as the private motor yacht of President Flosse, it was used to take him and other government officials to those parts of the Territory without air access (such as many islands in the Tuamotu Archipelago) or with inadequate on-shore accommodations and services. It is equipped with a salon that can seat about 150 people comfortably and, at the time, had a crew drawn from the Groupement d'Intervention de la Polynésie (GIP).

My friend Marietta Tefaataumarama was responsible for overseeing the *matahiapo* activities and invited my husband, Richard, and me to attend the meeting on Tahaʻa. Marietta told me that these gatherings were always a mixture of politics and entertainment and that it would be "interesting" for me. "Even though politics is at the core of these meetings," she said, "only about 20 percent of the people go for political reasons. The other 80 percent go to have a good time. The government organizes the trips to make sure they keep the support of that 20 percent."

I soon realized that this would not simply be a casual "weekend" in Tahaʻa. Gathering this number of people together required the government to arrange transportation to Tahaʻa and to see that everyone was housed and fed once there. Each group of elders also had to attend to a number of things in preparation for the trip. It is typical in French Polynesia for different groups to have their own "outfit" of matching clothing. Each island group received bolts of cloth from which each person was given enough to make the clothes needed—dresses for the women and shirts for the men. Each group chose its own pattern; Huahine's material had white hibiscus blossoms on a bright red background. For nearly two weeks before the departure to Tahaʻa, women who were talented seamstresses were in high demand as many elders came to them to make their clothing. Each elder was also asked to bring personal items (sheets, a towel, a bowl, and a spoon) along with the various coordinated outfits.

While sewing machines were humming away, dance practices took place almost every day. I soon learned that not only would Huahine have the largest delegation attending the meeting but also that they were known for winning the dance contests. Much to my surprise, Marietta insisted that Richard and I participate as members of the Huahine dance group to ensure that we would have as much fun as possible. As the day of departure grew nearer, the rehearsals became more elaborate, with each dance being performed numerous times and select spokespeople rehearsing their speeches. At times Richard and I were asked to stand in for the president of French Polynesia and the minister of culture so that members of the group could practice the necessary ritual of presenting food to the dignitaries. Soon everyone was ready for the trip: their clothing made and packed, the dances practiced to perfection, and the speeches flawless.

On the morning of our departure, the wharf in Fare was abuzz with excitement as the elders arrived for the three-hour voyage. The group (of which there were many more women than men) also included some younger family members as a support network (care for the elderly is a family—and a community—affair). While the bags were lowered into the ship's hold, many people went to the store to buy snacks and drinks. Soon family and friends were saying their good-byes and the elders boarded the ship, assisted at the top of the ramp by two GIP workers. Outfitted in their new matching clothing and donning *hei* (crowns) made with hibiscus leaves and gardenia flowers, the *matahiapo* appeared eager for the adventure that lay ahead (fig. 6.2).

The passengers were soon settled in their seats in the large salon. Remembering from the previous year's trip that the cabin had been uncomfortably cold because of the air-conditioning, the *matahiapo* had come prepared with socks, jackets, and shawls. One of the trip's many ironies occurred when a crew member came into the cabin and put a video into the television. The film was *Universal Soldier,* a violent, R-rated American action film (dubbed into French, with English subtitles) about an army's secret project to reanimate dead men and turn them into a near-perfect, nation-worshipping militia. As Richard and I half-watched the movie, with its loud fights and explosions, and as we scanned the subtitles enough to see phrases like "fucking God," "you bitch," and "Oh, Jesus Christ," we couldn't control our guffaws. "Good thing the elders don't understand French—this is a bad choice for a video," said Marietta when she asked—and we explained—why we were laughing. Upon further reflection, however, I thought that the film might indeed be the perfect (ironic) choice for a boat full of what the government hoped would be compliant citizens—dignified elders participating in the government's efforts to make them more docile servants, transported in a teeth-chatteringly chilly boat with incomprehensible American violence on the television (in French). The *matahiapo* for the most part, however, ignored the video and concentrated on trying to stay warm and, for some, fighting off seasickness.

We arrived at Tapuamu, the main port on Tahaʻa, around noon, just as a heavy downpour had ended. A group of *matahiapo* from Tahaʻa warmly welcomed each of us with a flower garland and directed us to the three buses (*les trucks*) that were waiting to take us to Patio, Tahaʻa's main town, with its two small stores, bank, police station, and elementary school. The school, which consisted of several low buildings around a large open courtyard, with

Fig. 6.2 Huahine: *Matahiapo* boarding the *Tahiti Nui* for their trip to Taha'a, 2001.

a kitchen and dining area at one end, and bathroom facilities at the other, was where we were to stay for the weekend. As soon as we arrived at the school, people began to claim spaces in the various classrooms, which was done according to extended family units.[12]

The *matahiapo* from Taha'a had set up two main spaces for the meeting. One was where all the events (speeches, dance contests, story sharing, and so on) would be held. It was a flexible space near the sea, defined by a large red-and-white-striped tarp that covered the area and under which they had arranged some three hundred chairs in neat rows. The other was an area with another tarp, under which were rows of long tables where people could eat.

The first event on the evening of our arrival was a welcome procession with all the *matahiapo* from each island (for this occasion dressed in white clothing). The *matahiapo* filed in, each island group in turn, in a double line behind its leader, who was carrying a homemade banner on a tall pole with the name of the island. Huahine alone brought a flag. When I commented on how its pattern of three broad horizontal stripes in white/red/white was the opposite of French Polynesia's flag of red/white/red, Marietta responded with a twinkle in her eye, "Of course, Huahine is always contrary."[13]

Once everyone was seated the program began. Sitting under the tarp with everyone, I sensed a feeling of mutual sharing and respect among the island groups. Welcome speeches by people from Taha'a were followed by singing and dancing, with each group in turn later sharing something that was unique to its island—a story, a song, a plant, and so on. The *matahiapo* from Huahine had brought a fern that was found only on that island, and they passed it around for everyone to see, touch, and smell. These sharing activities continued for over an hour, in spite of several distractions, which somehow rallied people to pull together even more. First a sudden downpour caused rain to come into the open sides of the covered area, making everyone push their chairs toward the center and huddle together to wait out the storm. Next, after the rain had stopped and the activities had resumed, an electrical failure plunged everyone into the dark. Soon several people drove their cars to the perimeter of the area and, with the car engines clattering and headlights shining, flooded the area with beams of light so that the entertainment could continue. The cozy area of light and laughter, surrounded by the dark of night, defined an informal space within which groups seemed to feel at ease with one another.

Huahine was the last to perform and did so to great acclaim. As a friend from Huahine told me, "We're always asked to go last because everyone knows that Huahine is 'thunder' and that when Huahine dances, everything explodes." And "explode" it did, with Huahine winning first prize (even with Richard and me as part of the procession and dance competition). After the festivities were over, and after most people had retired for the night, many of the group from Huahine continued singing, dancing, and laughing under the sagging tarp. As the night wore on, they slowly made their way to bed. The hot, humid night, which felt even more oppressive inside the schoolrooms, was an excuse for people to stay outdoors and visit with friends, and to work on their dance paraphernalia for the morning program, which was to welcome the government dignitaries.

I was awakened at 5:30 the next morning by a loud call telling us that coffee was being served. Within minutes people were up and in line for breakfast, which consisted of baguettes, processed canned meat with the brand name of Pâté Zwan, processed canned cheese, and *i'a ota*, a much-loved preparation of raw fish marinated in lime juice and garnished with coconut cream. The breakfast, like each meal the *matahiapo* received, had been prepared by the government's new cooking arrangement—Cuisine Centrale. In the late 1990s, as another effort to invest in public service, the government established a Cuisine Centrale on each island, a physically flexible "kitchen" that employed students from the local trade schools as cooks and servers to provide food for the schools on the island and for various island events— such as this one. Efficient as this plan might appear, it conflicted with an important Tahitian custom concerning food by replacing the village women with government employees. Before the Cuisine Centrale, the women of a village (usually those who had some connection to the event) would join together to donate, prepare, and serve the food, activities that are important ways for Tahitians to communicate respectful and caring behavior toward one another. With the Cuisine Centrale, however, the government purchased the food and paid students to cook and serve it.

It was interesting for me to see, however, that although this government initiative took the preparation of food away from the local women, the *matahiapo* subversively undermined the government program and refashioned the food preparation into something of their own, using food-related activities to create a counter-space. For example, the *matahiapo* from Huahine (and they alone) had brought various foods with them and, after breakfast from the Cuisine Centrale was finished, started preparing these (green coconuts, papaya, bananas, watermelons, and baked manioc pudding) in their traditional ways to present to the government dignitaries—a gesture loaded with meaning. They carefully divided the food into eight baskets (each basket representing one of the eight villages of Huahine) woven from coconut leaves brought from Huahine (fig. 6.3). This was a way of communicating their place-based identity and the rich meaning of their island, their land, and its foods. Within the boundaries of this government-sponsored event, and of the Cuisine Centrale in particular, they created their own counter-space through reference to their land. Although the government fed them with baguettes and Pâté Zwan, they, in turn, were going to offer the government dignitaries coconuts, bananas, and manioc pudding. At first I wondered why the *matahiapo* (many of whom were opposed to the pro-French government) were giving the government officials such a powerful traditional welcome (fig. 6.4). Later I realized that it was a forceful and respectful way for them to claim their space and communicate the power of their identity rooted in *te fenua*. By presenting local foods, they were turning a gesture of welcome—ostensibly inclusionary—into one of resistance. You give me your (French) food, but I give you my (Ma'ohi) food.

The activities that morning were devoted to welcoming government officials: among them, the vice president of French Polynesia, the minister

Fig. 6.3 *Matahiapo* women preparing to offer their baskets of food. Photo by Richard Taylor, 2001.

Fig. 6.4 Government dignitaries with the food from Huahine displayed in front of them. Photo by Richard Taylor, 2001.

of culture, the minister of land, the mayor of Taha'a, and the main representative from the Service des Affaires Sociales of the Leeward Islands. The meeting began promptly at 8:00 AM, and the atmosphere was suddenly quite formal. Welcoming speeches, prayers, and a brief presentation by each island group opened the event. The *matahiapo* from Huahine presented their food, accompanied by an eloquent speech (in Tahitian) about the food they were offering and how it came from their land.

Following this, Édouard Fritch, then the vice president of French Polynesia, gave the main—and an overtly political—speech. He started by saying, "In French Polynesia, people have become politically divided. . . . Don't listen to those who oppose the government." The main focus then turned to the importance of tourism. He described the government's plans for tourism over the next few years, especially the attraction of the cruise ships, and emphasized the important role tourism played in the Territory's economy. I noticed a marked drop in the audience's level of attention during his speech (even though he spoke in Tahitian). Some people left and went to sit near the sea. Of those who stayed in their seats, several engaged in conversations in hushed tones. Still others looked at the speaker with blank expressions on what otherwise would have been expressive faces. When he finished, the applause was polite but weak. People were then asked to move outside for the final government-related event—a flag-raising ceremony.

Outside the tarp-covered area to which Huahine's "flag of resistance" had been carried the evening before, several *gendarmes* began to raise two flags—one for France and one for French Polynesia (fig. 6.5). Like all flag-raising ceremonies, this one was much more than a fleeting act. It was a way for the government of French Polynesia to state its presence, claim its space, and communicate its power over land and inhabitants.

After the flags had been raised and were fluttering in the breeze, several of the Huahine *matahiapo* walked away and formed a circle of their own under a tree nearby—and began playing their ukuleles and guitars and singing songs (most of which were about Huahine and its land), again creating a counter-space, this time through music (fig. 6.6). Whereas the presence of the two flags marked the French and Tahitians as two distinct groups, the Ma'ohi songs the group was now singing seemed to unite them as one people from Huahine (and in opposition to the French). The government, as usual, staked its claim to Tahitian land by raising flags, but the Tahitians from Huahine staked their claims to *te fenua* and to their Ma'ohi identity through embodied actions involving food, music, and song.

Fig. 6.5   Raising the French and French Polynesian flags, 2001.

Fig. 6.6   *Matahiapo* from Huahine making music and singing, 2001.

Throughout the meeting, I kept noticing how group identities were defined spatially. Sometimes this was through physical elements, such as one's clothing pattern, sleeping quarters, a tarp over an area, or a banner identifying one's island. At other times it was through embodied acts, such as picking up a guitar to make music on the sidelines, getting up to dance, offering someone food, laughing, or shedding tears. These group boundaries of inclusion were forever colliding with boundaries of exclusion, which can only be resisted, but never crossed, as was evident in the distinction between the government officials (representing France) and the *matahiapo* (representing *te fenua*)—each with its own flag, foods, clothing, and seating areas.

In the evening (after the government officials had left), there was one last *soirée* at which the *matahiapo* from the different islands entertained one another with lively comedy skits and dancing. One of the highlights of the evening occurred when an elder from Taha'a did a hilarious imitation of a "famous" French singer. He crooned in a nasally, high-pitched voice, mimicking songs about upper-class life and romance in Paris. The audience was in stitches. At one point the master of ceremonies interrupted the singer to say that he had seen a beautiful young girl standing at the edge of the crowd watching the evening's entertainment. But after hearing this "French" singer, the girl had run off, fleeing quickly to "get away from the unbearable noise."

Vine Deloria has said that one of the best ways to understand a people is to know what makes them laugh. "Laughter encompasses the limits of the soul. In humor life is redefined and accepted. Irony and satire provide much keener insights into a group's collective psyche and values than do years of research" (Deloria 1969, 146).

Mikhail Bakhtin has provided specific insight into people's laughter, especially in festival settings, where people gather together as equals for communal entertainment. "Here, in the town square [or at the Taha'a *soirée*], a special form of free and familiar contact reigned among people who were usually divided by the barriers of caste, property, profession, and age" (Bakhtin 1993, 10). In these festival settings, with their altered sense of space and time, individuals can temporarily assume the persona of someone else to reverse social roles and communicate political messages, which helps to create a heightened awareness of the group's unity and sense of community. In these settings, satire, irony, and parody work to confound meanings, convey resistance, and provide a sense of rejuvenation for the group. "It matters that power seems to be everywhere, but wherever we look, power is open to gaps, tears, inconsistencies, ambivalences, possibilities for inversion, mimicry, parody and so on; open, that is, to more than one geography of resistance" (Pile and Keith 1997, 27).

Communicating political messages through the humorous inversion of language is an especially important means of interaction in the Pacific Islands, where clowning is often an essential element of important events.[14] The role of humor and clowning is especially critical in relations between people of differential power. "Although clowning and comedy 'remind us of the existence of the rule,'[15] they also remind us that such rules do not exist without support. The rules are rules as long as we obey them. Clowning has the potential to effect change" (Hereniko 1995, 77). Through parody and burlesque, clowning breaks the normal frames of expected behavior to instruct, criticize, and transform (W. Mitchell 1992). A clown's use of innuendo and puns allows for multiple translations and meanings according to the thoughts of the audience. "The clown's outrageous antics and bawdy language remind us of a part of ourselves we continually suppress in day-to-day interactions in order to appear respectable and acceptable to the majority" (Hereniko 1995, 7). A counter-space imitates existing space but, in parodying it, indicates its limitations. In her eulogy for Henri Hiro, writer and artist Michou Chaze also noted the importance of his laughter, saying,

Good-bye, Henri Hiro. It seems that we must say good-bye to you. But you remain with us. Your voice and your laughter will always resonate in the valley of Arei in Huahine, and echo from mountain to mountain. And in the same way that the low winds at the base of the valley rise, your voice [and laughter] will spread over the whole of Maʻohi Polynesia. (Stewart, Mateata-Allain, and Mawyer 2006, 81)

Before the *matahiapo* departed the following day, the workers at the Cuisine Centrale prepared the last lunch. Once again, the Tahitians reconfigured the event to turn it into something of their own. I noticed that each of the elders had brought a shell necklace to the lunch (Marietta handed one each to Richard and me). At the end of the meal the *matahiapo* from Huahine expressed their heartfelt thanks to the cooks and servers in a very Tahitian way. Some of the elders asked the helpers to come up to the front, and several of the *matahiapo* then talked about how hard the cooks and servers had worked and how well cared for the *matahiapo* had felt during the weekend. Then Marietta's husband picked up his ukulele and, with others following his lead, created joyful music in the dining area. One by one, each of us went up and thanked the cooks by kissing them on both cheeks (in French/Tahitian style) and placing our shell necklaces around their necks. Several of the *matahiapo* began dancing with the cooks and with one another. Uproarious laughter broke out as several *matahiapo* mimed the lyrics of the songs. Later, as the dancing and singing continued, and as tears of empathy began to stream down many cheeks, word arrived that the buses were outside, waiting to take the *matahiapo* from Huahine and Raiatea to the wharf at Tapuamu, where the *Tahiti Nui* was waiting for everyone to board the ship for the return voyage.

On the way home, the *Tahiti Nui* first stopped at Raiatea for passengers from that island to disembark. As we approached Raiatea, with its main town of Uturoa growing larger in front of us, I could see its new wharf in all its grandeur—yet another example of the constant tension between dominant spaces created by the government and Tahitian spaces that fight to survive. I had heard about the recently built wharf in Uturoa, a project funded by the Territorial government that would allow the *Renaissance* cruise ships to dock on-shore when they came to Raiatea (the "tourism future" that Vice President Fritch had promoted in his speech on Taha'a).

Neither I nor any of the Huahine *matahiapo* had seen the recent changes, and we moved to one side of the ship for a better view. While the *Tahiti Nui* was being tied up at the wharf, we had time to scrutinize the renovated space. Previously there had been small family-run stores and makeshift lean-tos for selling crafts. Now there was a wide esplanade covered with shimmering paving stones, punctuated at regular intervals by Parisian-style street lamps. Next to the new lavish visitor center was a two-story commercial center, with a roof of red tiles and with columned porticos that led to shops selling black pearl jewelry and designer clothing (fig. 6.7). Leaning over the railing for a better view, people immediately launched into playful commentary.

"We should call it Hollywood now, not Uturoa!"

"Look at those paving stones, they sparkle!"

"It's just like Paris now."

Contributing to the sense of dissonance was that the *Renaissance* cruise line had gone bankrupt within months of the wharf's inauguration. The wharf was indeed a false front. Just beyond the new wharf, not immediately visible from the ship, was the town of Uturoa, careworn and neglected as always, with very few changes evident since I first saw it in 1993. A short distance from the glistening new wharf was the poorly maintained and staffed hospital to which I had come from Huahine (where there is no hospital) three

Fig. 6.7 New wharf in Uturoa, Raiatea, 2001.

years earlier, after having broken my arm, and where I had spent a painful night in a dingy room, waiting eighteen hours for medical assistance. During his visit to Taha'a, Vice President Fritch had not talked to the *matahiapo* about health care or other services that might be relevant to their lives—only about how they should support the government and its efforts to increase tourism—the spaces of other people's pleasures. President Flosse's decision to build a wharf at Uturoa in an effort to impress the cruise ship passengers when they arrived was dependent on the erasure of local space—local businesses, livelihoods, history, and memories. I had seen this same erasure at Tahua Vaiete in Pape'ete, at the *marae* and the Fare Pote'e in Maeva, and in more embodied ways during the weekend at Taha'a when people were eating, dancing, singing, mimicking, and laughing. I saw it now at the wharf in Uturoa, which soon receded from view as our ship sailed on to Huahine.

The sun was setting when we approached Huahine. The wharf at Fare was filled with people who had come to pick up their family members. In the crowd I could see our daughter on her bicycle awaiting our return after spending the weekend with a friend. People disembarked, located their bags, greeted their families, said their good-byes, and went home.

During the next few days, a vibrant energy rippled throughout Huahine as many of the *matahiapo* talked about the trip, sharing memories with one another and regaling their families with entertaining stories. When I asked some of the elders about the trip, their responses were unanimously and overwhelmingly enthusiastic. Their reasons for enjoying the trip were many. Almost all of their explanations involved some form of crossing boundaries and communicating identities.

"The meeting brought us together as one group from Huahine."

"The trip brought us together with other groups from the Leeward Islands."

"This was the first time many of us had gone to another island with a big group like that."

"We loved the spontaneous entertainment by the different groups; all the singing and dancing and music were a lot of fun."

"It gave us the opportunity to do traditional things we don't otherwise do very much anymore, like the traditional welcome and the offering of the traditional foods."

"Some of the dances we performed were from our youth, things we hadn't done in a long time."

"Taha'a welcomed us generously."

"There was an abundance of food."

"People on Taha'a, like the people on Huahine, are still close to the land and connected to the past."

"We also enjoyed having you and Richard with us because it was the first time *popa'a* [white people] were with *matahiapo* and sat with us and did what we did."

And, most meaningfully for me, "It was fun to finally see two *popa'a* acting like Tahitians rather than always seeing Tahitians trying to act like *popa'a*."

I tried to probe more deeply about the political aspect of the gathering and how individual *matahiapo* viewed the dominant space of government politics. But one elder, Rere Teururai, summed things up concisely. "Politics is really not a concern for the old people. We didn't pay any attention to it."

"But what about the welcome by Vice President Fritch?" I asked. "What did you think about that speech?"

"I wasn't listening," she said. "My friends and I didn't even look at him when he talked. I couldn't tell you a word of what he said."

"What about tourism?" I persisted. "He said tourism is French Polynesia's future."

"All the changes that have happened because of tourism don't affect my life at all; that's their life, not mine," she insisted.

She then told me a story from her past, when, in 1989, the hotel down the road from her house first opened. Her story gave me a glimpse into yet another creative space of resistance—and one that, for her, has survived "under the radar" for a very long time:

> Even though the hotel was built at the end of the road down at the beach many years ago, and tourists drive up and down in front of my house all day, it doesn't matter to me. It doesn't affect my life. When the hotel first opened, my daughter and I were asked to make shell necklaces for the tourists. A Frenchman drove up in his car and came into my house and talked to me in French. I hated that. He jabbered on in French about "Oh, can you make so many shell necklaces for the hotel?" My daughter told him I didn't speak French, to which he responded, "But everyone speaks French!" She told me to just say "Oui" to everything he asked me. But of course, I refused to speak any French. Pouvana'a O'opa had told us never to let a French word come out of our mouths. So instead of saying "Oui" I just said "Vi" [which in Tahitian means "mango" but also happens to mean "subjugated" or "tamed"]. The Frenchman only paid me sixty CFP Francs [about 50 cents U.S. in 1989] for a necklace. But I knew the price for a necklace in the store was three hundred CFP Francs, or sometimes even five hundred. I made necklaces for about a month and then I decided to quit. I felt liberated when I stopped. (Rere Teururai, personal communication, 2001)

WHARVES, SHIPS, AND SPATIAL TACTICS

Thinking back on these two events—the day trip to the *Renaissance II* with the group of Tahitians and the weekend trip to Taha'a with the *matahiapo*—it seems that wharves and ships lend themselves well to exploring spaces of resistance. Wharves (like those at Maroe Bay, Fare, and Uturoa) mark borders between *te fenua* (the land) and *te miti* (the sea), between home and elsewhere, and often between feeling comfortable and feeling dislocated. It is at wharves that global capitalism most blatantly confronts local culture. As zones of contact and transition, wharves are borders we cross and places through which we move. Lefebvre thought that "the places through which we pass and where we meet—the street, the café, or the station [or the wharf]—are more important and truly more interesting than our homes and our houses, the places which they link" (Lefebvre 2002, 309). At the wharf at Maroe Bay, tourists were ferried back and forth between their pleasure outings and the buffet tables, and Tahitians were carried back and forth between their homes and their own adventures on the cruise ship. On a different day, the wharf at Maroe Bay was cordoned off and guarded by *Club Med II* attendants in white uniforms talking authoritatively into their walkie-talkies to maintain boundaries. At the wharf in Fare, the *matahiapo* excitedly boarded the *Tahiti Nui* for their trip to Taha'a and, three days later, returned to their families with stories about their trip and the fun they had. At the wharf in Uturoa, fancy new buildings and sparkling paving stones imported from France were erected in an attempt to divert attention from the careworn town in the rear.

Foucault has said, "In civilizations without boats dreams dry up" (1986, 27). Boats take people to new places and spaces. Crossing boundaries in the process, they carry people who dream of many things: more pampering, more fluffy towels, more lobster, more pizza for their family, more tourism, more flag raising, and more *matahiapo* trips. Ships can be excellent examples of heterotopias. Foucault has described a ship as "a floating piece of space, a place without a place, that exists by itself, that is closed in on itself and at the same time is given over to the infinity of the sea; and from port to port, from tack to tack, from brothel to brothel, it goes as far as the colonies in search of the most precious treasures" (Foucault 1986, 27).

Counter-spaces that are pleasurable, subtle, and subversive can take many forms. Some of these occur within the parameters of dominant power, as happened when the Tahitians onboard the *Renaissance II* took as much food as they could, or when an elder on Taha'a mimicked French singing. Others take place on the edges, as occurred when the *matahiapo* from Huahine walked away from the flag-raising ceremony and went to sing their own songs about Huahine. Still other counter-spaces are created when people simply refuse to conform, as illustrated by Rere Teururai's refusal to speak French. Different as these various styles of resistance may be, they are similar in the way they exist outside the knowledge of those who exercise power:

> Resistance cannot be understood as a face-to-face opposition between the powerful and the weak, nor as a fight that takes place only on grounds constituted by structural relations—because other spaces are always involved: spaces which are dimly lit, opaque, deliberately hidden, saturated with memories, that echo with lost words and the cracked sounds of pleasure and enjoyment. . . . Resistance does not just act on topographies imposed through the spatial technologies of domination, it moves across them under the noses

of the enemy, seeking to create new meanings out of imposed meanings, to re-work and divert space to other ends. . . . Resistance, then, not only takes place in place, but also seeks to appropriate space, to make new spaces. (Pile and Keith 1997, 16)

Tahitians create spaces of enjoyment in many spontaneous, creative, and bold ways, expressing resistance with their bundles of food taken from the cruise ship under full knowledge of the staff, with their coconut frond baskets of home-grown food offered to those who seek to dominate, with comic skits and laughter about French singers, with their ukuleles and guitars when making their own music, with blank stares and conversations whispered to neighbors while the vice president is speaking about government loyalty, and with utterances of "Vi" instead of "Oui" in response to French demands. Surrounded by a sea of dominant power, Tahitians create islands of resistance—refusing to feel subjugated—not even listening to the *Universal Soldier* video, with its messages about compliant citizens. No matter how many flags are raised or speeches given about the benefits of tourism or baguettes and cans of Pâté Zwan served, the dominant forces cannot easily control—and often cannot even "see"—the Tahitians' embodied actions—their sharing, feeding, eating, singing, dancing, speaking, not speaking, laughing, and shedding of empathetic tears.

CHAPTER SEVEN

E Aha Atu Ra? What Will Happen?

Anthropologists who study place have, for the most part, looked at those aspects that are physical, tangible, and geographical—landscapes, plazas, markets, spatial forms in the built environment, houses and ideas about home, maps, images, tourist sites, recreated settings, urbanism, and even ruins. My own earlier work in Wamira, where I looked at stones and their histories, movements, and meanings, is such an example (Kahn 1990, 1996). In Papua New Guinea, Wamirans provided me with place-related information with little effort on my part. They readily told me stories about the stones, making sure I recorded the details accurately, and even asked me to create a map of the stones and have it printed on rugby shirts. At the time, I thought that researching "place" was an uncomplicated endeavor.

When I wanted to learn about "place" in Tahiti, I found it far more challenging. My preconceived ideas about the topic led me to think that simply asking people about "place" would provide insight. I soon learned that this was not the case. I was not able to learn about it by merely paying attention to, and inquiring about, what seemed to be its "usual" indicators. Tahitians went about their daily lives paying little or no attention to the Tahiti of the Western imagination, and did not talk about "place" in ways that were understandable to me. I began to wonder how I could make sense of things.

One avenue, adopted here, is to use Lefebvre's approach that sees place emerge from the intertwined effects of power relationships. In French Polynesia, tourism and the nuclear testing program were obvious—although not the only—areas to explore. Power, and especially its tremendous imbalances, expresses itself noticeably in these areas. Hiro's work is valuable in articulating a Tahitian perspective on place, the spiritual and practical value of *te fenua*, and resistance to dominant power through the creation of counter-spaces. Insights gained from Hiro's perspective sheds light on the often subtle, and sometimes obvious, ways that Tahitians cope with and respond to the actions of the colonizer. Bringing the two perspectives together has been critical for an understanding of the intertwined complexities of place.

In spite of their differences, Hiro and Lefebvre also had much in common. Both saw the world as an interrelated whole, and both were political activists. Hiro said, "I refuse to think in opposites; even opposite colors are called complementary and produce harmony" (Hiro 2004, 83).[1] For him, the principal unity was between Ma'ohi people and the land, as well as between traditions of the past and how people live in the present. All was unified by, and rooted in, "the source"—*te fenua ma'ohi*—where the essence of people, land, genealogy, and identity were intertwined and mutually defined. Placentas become fertile islands in an oceanic world from which all life springs. "For Polynesians, man was created from sand, which is another way of saying earth. . . . Polynesian people are not separate from the earth, and the earth does not exist without people" (Raapoto in Saura 2002b, 9).

The unity, for Lefebvre, was between *l'espace conçu* and *l'espace perçu*. He linked the conceptual to the tangible, and theoretical ideas to everyday life. Space, for him, was the sum of everything—the physical, mental, and social—and can only be fully grasped by understanding how its various parts are related and how they generate one another:

> Space has now become something more than the theatre, the disinterested
> stage or setting, of action. Space can no longer be looked upon as an "essence,"
> as an object distinct from the point of view of "subjects," as answering to logic
> of its own. Is space a medium? A milieu? An intermediary? It is doubtless
> all of these, but its role is less and less neutral, more and more active, both
> as instrument and as goal, as means and as end. The production of space is a
> generative process, with variations, pluralities and multiplicities, disparities,
> disjunctions, imbalances, conflicts and contradictions. (Lefebvre 1991, 410–11)

Space is fluid, interconnected, and generative. A space constantly collides with other spaces, always in the process of becoming. These interpenetrations get layered upon one another to create a *present* space (Merrifield 2000, 171),[2] itself still always in transformation. "Places carry multiple meanings and are the sites of numerous overlapping, contradictory, synergistic activities, brought into being through, and productive of, difference and inequality" (Raffles 2002b, 329). In the active transformation of place, power can be reversed, space redefined, and identity reclaimed. Such was the case with the changing forms and meanings of the Fare Pote'e, the Tahitian music-making at the edges of the *matahiapo* meeting at Taha'a, and the potholes left in the road that went through locally owned land leading to a hotel.

In his poetry, Hiro eloquently communicates his vision of political transformation through the reclaiming of place and identity. His poem *Oihanu e,* in which he evokes images about land and place-based sources of nourishment, provides a particularly powerful example. In the poem, Hiro portrays Oihanu, the deity of culture, as the seed of Ma'ohi essence, the thread of cultural continuity, and the redeemer of cultural traditions. Oihanu and the land are intertwined. When colonizers destroyed Oihanu and silenced his breath, it caused "vegetation to dry up" and "cycles of fertility to be reversed." When Hiro encourages Ma'ohi to rekindle Oihanu's spirit and reclaim their place and identity, he asks them to "glorify the land" and "sing the beauty of the valleys." Hiro believed that by reawakening Ma'ohi traditions about the land, Oihanu could be reborn. For him, the poem was an urgent "call to life" that represented "the breath of future generations." In discussing the poem, Hiro said, "Oihanu is about creating continuity between our traditional civilization and the way we live today. . . . From this encounter between the past and the present, something new will be born" (Hiro 2004, 79).[3] Hiro's vision, which acknowledges the dignity of the land, was a call for political resistance, social action, and spatial transformation. Pambrun underscored the power of Hiro's words and their connection to place when he said, "Ten years after his death it can be dangerous to honor the memory of Henri Hiro and especially to voice his words, each word of which tossed out onto Ma'ohi land contains the seeds of resistance" (Pambrun 2005).

FROM THE INTERSTICES

Bringing a Western interpretive framework together with a Tahitian one reveals the complexity of place—and especially a place that itself is a product of Ma'ohi traditions and beliefs, and Western colonial interventions. From this synergy, new possibilities emerge for the anthropology of space and place. We can begin to see place in ways that might escape us if we viewed it solely from one or the other perspective. Exploring the relationships and tensions between Ma'ohi understandings of place and predominantly Western mass-mediated representations of Tahiti reveals a lived space that is simultaneously real *and* imagined, immediate *and* mediated, always in process, and always political. Whether quietly coexisting, or passionately colliding (sometimes even violently), neither Ma'ohi perspectives nor Western perspectives are separate realms operating independently. *Te fenua ma'ohi*/Tahiti, like all places, exists in complex, intertwined, fluid ways—in the land, in cultural beliefs and customs, in personal identities, in bodily practices, and in the most ordinary of everyday details. In Tahiti I gradually learned that an understanding of place/*te fenua* could emerge from the observation of these details—behavior, beliefs, poetry, song, stories, casual conversations, and body language. Exploring place means paying attention to these phenomena in a way that understands their interconnectedness. Embracing juxtapositions and entanglements provides an understanding of how place appears in numerous forms and locations, how it gets complicated in the differing agendas of *ta'ata ma'ohi* and the outside (usually Western) world, and ultimately how it affects everyday lives.

The advantage of viewing place from different, yet intertwined, perspectives became crystal clear one day during a walk in Pape'ete. It was mid-December 2001, and my family and I, accompanied by two Tahitian friends, were taking an afternoon stroll through the city before going to the *roulottes* for dinner. We began by walking the length of boulevard Pomare along the waterfront. When we arrived at the post office—an imposing faux-colonial-style building—we turned inland to walk along avenue Bruat in the shade of the expansive canopies of the stately *marumaru* (rain) trees. We soon came upon one of the Territory's most important public buildings—La Présidence, the presidential palace and seat of the government of French Polynesia. A major restoration project had just been completed a few months earlier, which returned the palace to its nineteenth-century Gallieni style.[4]

We stopped to look more carefully at the restoration. La Présidence, in accordance with the season, was decorated for Christmas. Two large wreaths, threaded with red and green ribbons, adorned the wrought-iron gate in front (fig. 7.1). After admiring the building and its elegant décor, I turned around and was startled by a very different scene.[5] There was another gate, more akin

Fig. 7.1 The Presidential Palace, Pape'ete, 2001.

TERRAIN MILITAIRE
TAHUA FAEHAU
ACCÈS RÉGLEMENTÉ
TOMORAA FAAU TABU

Fig. 7.2 Military area with young men behind the fence, Pape'ete, 2001.

to prison bars, behind which was a group of young men who had scrambled over the tall iron fence to get into a large, barren field (fig. 7.2). On this gate was a sign that read (in French and Tahitian):

Terrain militaire
Tahua faʻehau
(Military area)

Acces réglementé
Tomoraʻa faʻau tabu
(Access strictly forbidden)

Struck by the contrast between these two scenes, I approached each gate, placing first my eyes—and then my camera—between the bars to get a better view. In one direction everything appeared orderly, embellished, and immaculate (fig. 7.3). In the opposite direction, the field was strewn with trash and spotted with mud puddles. The young men were using this space in their own way; they had set up a net and were getting ready to play volleyball (fig. 7.4).

On both sides of avenue Bruat were very different "gated" communities. One had recently been refurbished at great expense and was now tastefully decorated and securely locked. The other, owned by the government and with a clear warning against trespassing, was bare and desolate except for some young men needing a place to play. I had never expected to see—directly across the street from the center of power in French Polynesia—such an obvious space of resistance. These young men playing volleyball provided an unambiguous statement about the absence of appropriate spaces for them and their activities.

From my position in between—my view from the interstices—I suddenly recognized that these groups of people (and their spaces) were deeply entangled in spite of the gates. Both were equally part and parcel of *te fenua maʻohi*/Tahiti, their definition of themselves inextricably linked to the other's perception of them. As the quickly setting sun's lengthening rays cast long shadows on the scene, in my mind the essence of "the struggle" was suddenly thrown into sharp relief. Space, as Lefebvre has said, is the "ultimate locus and medium of struggle. . . . There is a politics of space because space is political" (Lefebvre 1973, 59). No one is untouched by the politics of space. "Just as none of us is outside or beyond geography, none of us is completely free from the struggle over geography" (Said 1993, 7). This struggle about power, as manifested in space and place-related phenomena, is complex and endlessly fascinating precisely because it permeates everything and affects everyone. It is not only visible in obvious forms of violence, such as exploding bombs, burning buildings, and urban riots, it is also embedded in the

Fig. 7.3 The Presidential Palace, Papeʻete, 2001.

Fig. 7.4 Young men playing volleyball in the empty field, Papeʻete, 2001.

most unobtrusive and ordinary beliefs, images, and desires, such as faith in a gate, festive holiday decorations, and the desire to play volleyball. How ironic to think that gates could actually keep worlds apart.

For me, my place in between—between gates, cultures, languages, and places—provided an especially revealing view. Boundaries can turn into crossings, rivers into bridges, and fences (or gates) into "ensembles of interstices through which one's glances pass" (de Certeau 1984, 128). That day, my glance rested on places that looked contrary and disconnected. But I saw, for the first time with clarity, that they were both subtle aspects of the powerful coproduction of place, where "the 'outside' of place is always already 'inside'" (Braun 2001, 17–18).

Space, as an evolving practice and process, provides endless possibilities. Maʻohi people have the ingenuity to resist and overturn colonial politics and alter the production of space. Indeed, avenue Bruat was renamed as just such a symbol of the open possibility of space. The street was originally named to honor the French admiral Armand Joseph Bruat, who convinced Queen Pomare to let her realm become a French protectorate in 1842. In 2006, responding to political pressure, the government changed the name to avenue Pouvanaʻa Oʻopa to pay homage to the advocate of Tahitian independence who, in 1958, announced a plan for Tahiti to secede from France and form an independent republic. The Temaru government announced that this change "was just the beginning of a process of 'name decolonization'" (Gonschor 2007, 221).[6] The renaming of the street reminds us that the spirit of the Maʻohi people, like the young men who had defied the "access strictly forbidden" warning and had climbed the fence, continues to resist containment and assert itself.[7] Likewise, there have been several (albeit unsuccessful) attempts to come up with a more Tahitian name for French Polynesia. As Oscar Temaru vehemently said, "This is not French Polynesia. This is French-occupied Polynesia. We need our own name" (Oscar Temaru, personal communication, 2010).

SHIFTING THE BALANCE OF POWER

Recently, Pacific Islanders, working in both scholarly and popular realms, have been writing, filming, and performing in ways that have begun to shift the balance of power.[8] Several Pacific Islander scholars have asked anthropologists to recognize indigenous philosophies, sensibilities, and values. The leading Maori scholar of decolonization theory, Linda Tuhiwai Smith, has critiqued Western positivist perspectives and has argued that there are more culturally appropriate research methodologies and epistemologies for indigenous peoples (1999). Her approach includes both Maori knowledge and European perspectives to steer away from academic research that perpetuates cultural imperialism. Fijian scholar Unaisi Nabobo-Baba notes that research and the creation of knowledge, themselves, are about relations of power, and demands an end to the silencing of Pacific Islander voices in research and an acceptance of indigenous ways of seeing "with the eyes, soul, heart and stomach" (2004, 2006). She says, "The deriving of power in many instances has happened through the dominating of spaces to create knowledge, and the adjudicating of which knowledges and ways of knowing are valid and therefore legitimate. Domination happens in both implicit and explicit ways for Pacific peoples" (Nabobo-Baba 2004, 21).

Several Western anthropologists have responded and have argued for perceiving the world as simultaneously natural and cultural, or "naturalcultural," rather than divided into dichotomous, disarticulated categories of nature/culture, local/global, material/discursive, and rational/emotional.[9] They choose to focus on the congruence of place making and identity making, rather than the boundaries between them. Places "are spatially and temporally discontinuous, always in process, always in motion, always connected, and always in-the-making through historical sedimentation, naturalcultural practice, and the effectivities of the really real" (Raffles 2005, 377). Paige West cautions about the dangers of environmental anthropology and political ecology because they often overlook local beliefs and assume that "the environment is a commodified matter to be used rationally and neutrally or as if it were a 'resource' provided by nature" (West 2005, 639). Approaching place simply from a Western perspective creates the danger of "failing to understand and demonstrate the nuances of how people come to know, produce, and be a part of environments as well as missing aesthetic practices that may well be important political claims with material consequences" (West 2005, 639).

In their popular culture, Pacific Islanders have contested colonial imagery by turning the old clichés "inside out and upside down by . . . re-inventing these images on their own terms. Rather than working against the images of the 'dusky maiden' or the 'jolly-polys' these images are presented in different contexts to point to the very nature of their construction" (Taouma 2004, 35). Motivated by a desire to "re-picture" the Pacific, Pacific Islanders have created new images from their perspectives as dancers, jewelry and fiber artists, clothing designers, video and multimedia performance artists, and members of production teams for Pacific Islander television. Some have curated museum exhibits, such as Pasifika Styles (University of Cambridge Museum of Archaeology and Anthropology, Cambridge, 2006–8) and eth-Knocentrix: Museums Inside the Artist (October Gallery, London, 2009). In Living Photographs (and other exhibits), Shigeyuki Kihara, a visual and performance artist of Samoan and Japanese descent, has reoccupied the gaze (Metropolitan Museum of Art, New York, 2008–9). She accomplishes this through the creative use of Western technology, nineteenth-century colonial photography, and contemporary Pacific beliefs, thus recreating deep and meaningful spaces in Pacific Islanders' lives. Tamaira has deconstructed and reconstructed the image of the "dusky maiden," one of the most intoxicating, sexist, and racist icons of the Pacific Islands (2010). She does this by integrating strands from several perspectives: academic research, creative media, and her own fiction writing. Gradually, through these and other efforts and representations, there is new room for indigenous spaces, narratives, images, and identities.

BEYOND TAHITI

These insights—based on ideas about "place" in Tahiti / French Polynesia—have much to tell us about the world beyond Tahiti. Understanding the complexity of "place" from multiple perspectives, each with its unique representations, desires, politics, and meanings, is crucial in today's geographically fluid, intertwined world.

Climate change, environmental uncertainties, and changes in peoples' geographical locales wreak havoc on people's lives. Recently tsunamis have inundated coastal villages, and droughts have produced devastating famines, resulting in populations having to move to spaces occupied by others. In Melanesia, people from Carteret Islands and Takuu Island are being called the world's first refugees due to contemporary climate change, as rising sea levels cover their land and they are forced to find a new home (S. Gupta 2007). Relocated to Bougainville Island, they now live in urban squatter settlements in a place with a radically different rainforest environment. People on the Polynesian atolls and reef islands of Tuvalu face rising sea levels, increasing sea surface temperatures, ocean acidification, and extreme storms and droughts (Lazrus 2009). The government of Tuvalu, while trying to preserve cultural integrity and promote island development, now has to consider the possibility of relocating the entire population to places such as New Zealand.

"The impacts of a changing climate arrive along vectors of vulnerability that map structural and historical inequalities as much as they outline hazardous environments" (Lazrus 2009, 2). The aftermath of hurricane Katrina in New Orleans has erased any doubt one might have had about the intertwined relationships among natural disasters, power, and place.

Weapons testing and its profound environmental and human consequences continue today. The Hawaiian island of Kauai, a prime tourist destination, is also home to the Pacific Missile Range Facility (PMRF). It is the world's largest testing and training missile range, and the only one in the world where submarines, ships, aircraft, and space vehicles can operate and be tracked simultaneously. The U.S. military benefits from its relative isolation, year-round tropical climate, and intrusion-free environment. Indeed, the land adjacent to the base is aggressively fought over—the military wanting to preserve its use for agricultural purposes so as not to interfere with the missile range facility.[10] Cabeza Prieta National Wildlife Refuge in the Sonoran Desert of southwestern Arizona, one of the largest national wildlife refuges in the United States, shares a border with the Barry M. Goldwater Air Force Range and, as a result, is closed to the public at times due to bombing exercises. The refuge also borders Mexico, creating an interesting entanglement and coevolution of the U.S. military, wildlife conservation, Homeland Security, and the war on immigration (Meierotto 2009).

The movement of people across political borders and into different cultures—whether in hopes of escaping oppression or finding better economic opportunities—is ever more frequent and complicated. The resettlement of people to places already occupied by others, and the contested geographies that result, is now commonplace, with the numbers of refugees increasing each year. At the end of 2008, there were forty-two million displaced people in the world, more than one-third of them political refugees.[11] The Dadaab refugee camps in Kenya, the largest in the world, originally designed to hold 90,000, now have a population of about 300,000, most of whom are camel and goat herders from neighboring Somalia. Having housed refugees for more than fifteen years, Dadaab experiences daily crises in food, water, and sanitation, as well as periodic drought and severe flooding. The Israeli-Palestinian conflict in the Middle East is rooted in disagreements about land, the current Israeli occupation of Palestinian land, and the four million Palestinians who are refugees. Conflicts over border security, land rights, water rights, access to Jerusalem, and the legal status of refugees are mediated by violence and terrorism.

Tourism, the largest service industry in the world, results in the movement of about one billion people annually, making their way to every corner of the world.[12] Tourists visit impoverished *favelas* in Brazil to get a taste of "poverty" and "danger," ride camels in the Sahara and then sleep in "comfortable, clean Berber tents with sprung mattresses to experience 'exoticism,'"[13] and cruise on 3,000-passenger ships to small fishing villages in Alaska, where "you don't have to rough it to see all that Alaska offers."[14] Venice, the most heavily touristed city in the world, attracts on average more visitors in a day than there are permanent residents (Davis and Marvin 2004). With the sea rising, buildings deteriorating, and Venetians leaving, the number of tourists still continues to increase. Compared to other places in the world, the tourism industry in French Polynesia is a mere fleck in the global economy.

These contemporary situations, each with its own complex history, are often rooted in conflicting understandings of, political unrest in, and fantasized images of place. They result in the exercise of power in place-related ways, whether these are plans to move Tuvaluans to New Zealand, orders to close visitor access to Cabeza Prieta while missiles fly overhead, efforts to shelter increasing numbers of Somali refugees at Dadaab, or decisions to constantly increase the price of a gondola ride in Venice. In today's world, the movement of people, whether voluntary or obligatory, is escalating. Places and their politics become increasingly interconnected. The proliferation of place-related imagery, especially through the Internet, increases the speed and range of how ideas about place travel. Thus, it might benefit us all, as global citizens of the twenty-first century, to have a better understanding of the ways in which power manifests itself in the everyday details of place and affects the everyday lives of people. In his poem *E aha atu ra?* (What Will Happen?), Hiro provides inspiration when he prays for the nourishment of his homeland so that the land, in turn, can take care of future generations:

Eiaha na pai!
Te here o to'u ai'a i tavai ia u mai te hi'i mai i apiti
Mai i to'u nei tino tahuti.
E, ia vai a, e ia vai a!
E, ia vai a, e ia vai noa atu a!
Ei para ha'amaitai i to'u ai'a tumu,
Ia ruperupe, e ia hotu te hua'ai,
No to'u nei ai'a.

This is a prayer!
Oh, the love of my homeland,
Where the endless waves bathed me during my tender youth,
That it should again soothe my mortal body.
Oh, let this love live!
Live! Live! Live again and forever!
That my natal land can breathe and be nourished
So that the children of this land, my homeland, can thrive and prosper.
(Hiro 2004, 63)

Notes

1   Chapter 3 discusses this more fully and provides references.

2   In 2004 the term was changed from Overseas Territory to Overseas Collectivity.

3   A family friend, who was a high-level functionary at the United Nations, had obtained the apartment for us.

4   See Bonnemaison (2005); Keller and Kuautonga (2007); Stürzenhofecker (1998); and Wiessner and Tumu (1998).

5   See Hijikata (1973); Layard (1942); Parmentier (1987); Riesenfeld (1950); and Roe and Taki (1999).

6   I wanted to stay in the Pacific, where I felt comfortable with the customs, and where the Austronesian languages seemed relatively easy for me to learn. Yet I also wanted a setting where social and political life would be less village-centered than it had been in Papua New Guinea, reflecting the changing nature of anthropology and the world in the 1990s. I particularly wanted to do research in a place where I would have to search out my data in more strategically planned ways as it traveled in a globally connected world.

7   See Kahn (2000, 2003).

8   See Saura (2004, 2008) for an insightful exploration, based on extensive linguistic research, of the history of the political constructions around the use of the terms "Tahitian" and "Ma'ohi."

9   This terminology is common across the Pacific. For example, the phrase for human being in Maori is *tangata maori* and in Hawaiian is *kanaka maoli*.

10   On islands other than Tahiti, people usually prefer to use the name of their

own island to designate who they are, thus employing *ta'ata Tahiti* (a person from Tahiti), *ta'ata Mo'orea* (a person from Mo'orea), and so on. In general, however, a person has several options for self-reference, depending on the context. For example, someone from Huahine might refer to him- or herself as *ta'ata Huahine, ta'ata Tahiti,* or *ta'ata Ma'ohi.*

11   Boas's brand of "historical particularism" put an emphasis on the relationship between cultural behavior and different environments. See also Kuper (1972) for an early study of the contested nature of place among the Swazi.

12   See, for example, Massey (1984) and Massey and Allen (1984).

13   For two excellent annual review articles on space and place, see Gieryn (2000) and Lawrence and Low (1990).

14   See Basso (1988, 1996); Feld and Basso (1996); Fernandez (1984); Hirsch (1995); Morphy (1995); and Myers (1991).

15   See Duranti (1992); Fernandez (1988); Low (2003b); Munn (1996); and Pandolfi (1990).

16   See Brown (2000); Massey (1994); and H. Moore (1986).

17   See Low (2003a) and Sieber (1993).

18   Arnold (2006); Braun (2001, 2002); Raffles (2002a, 2002b, 2005); and West (2005, 2006).

19   See Appadurai (1996); Davis (2005); A. Gupta (1992); Low (1996, 2001, 2003a); McDonogh (1991, 1992); and D. Moore (1998).

20   See Appadurai (1991); Bestor (2004); Hannerz (1996); MacCannell (1992); and Ong (1999).

21   See Johnson and Murton (2007); Louis (2007); R. Martin (2001); Pablo (2001); and Taliman (2002).

22   My firsthand knowledge about Tahiti/French Polynesia and Tahitians was gained over several trips. In 1976 I was on Tahiti and Mo'orea as a tourist for several days; in 1993 I spent a week exploring options for a new field site; in 1994 I lived in Fetuna on the island of Raiatea for six months; in 1995 I lived in Faie on the island of Huahine for five months; in 1996 I attended the opening of the Fare Pote'e on Huahine for two weeks; in 1998 I was responsible for bringing a group of eighteen dancers to Seattle for two weeks; in 2001 I lived in Fare on Huahine for five months; and in 2010 I spent a month on Tahiti and Huahine. In addition, friends from Huahine came to Seattle to visit us in 1996, 1999, and 2010. I also spent six months in France in 2002, where I conducted both field and archival research related to French colonialism, French Polynesia, and French tourism to Tahiti.

23   The original name for Fare (pronounced "Fah-ray") was Fare Nui Atea ("great spacious house").

24   Grönlund (1999) influenced my diagram.

25 Lefebvre's application of the three-way trialectic owes much to Nietzsche (1966) and Heidegger (1971).

26 The term "thirdspace" has also been used, but in different ways, by others. bell hooks (1990) employs the term to understand ideas about marginality and radical openness. Homi Bhabha (1990, 1994) uses the concept to circumvent binaries and to understand how identities, hybridities, and cultural differences are produced. Steve Pile (1994) uses the term to explore the gendered nature of the relationship between power and knowledge, and to avoid the dualisms that mark and maintain supposedly fixed divisions between the powerful and the disempowered.

27 Most Western scholars make a deliberate distinction between "space" and "place." On the whole, they tend to think of "space" as abstract and of "place" as tangible, with an understanding that space takes on meaning through the specifics of place (Low and Lawrence-Zuñiga 2003, 13). Others, however, take the opposite approach, saying that "place" is primary and gets transformed into "space" through meaningful human action (Casey 1996; de Certeau 1984). Lefebvre tends to collapse this distinction, whereas David Harvey (1997) maintains that we need both approaches to construct our arguments. I have chosen not to engage with this debate, which is tangential to my central theme. It is a weighty topic of its own, about which much has been written.

28 This Lefebvre-based literature wrestles with his theories about various topics, including urbanism (Castells 1977; D. Harvey 1973); postmodernism (Gregory 1997; D. Harvey 1989; Jameson 1991; Soja 1989); bodies and sexuality (Blum and Nast 1996; Brown 2000; L. Stewart 1995); space (Gottdiener 1993; Merrifield 1993, 2000; Shields 1991; Soja 1996); the state (Brenner 2001; Elden 2001); and others, to name only a few (see Brenner and Elden 2001 for a more complete list). Some people have traced the connections between Lefebvre and other intellectuals, such as Nietzsche (Merrifield 1995); Lacan (Blum and Nast 1996; Gregory 1997); and Jameson (Dear 2000). Shields (1999) provided the first thorough work on Lefebvre in English, and there have since been three others (Elden 2004; Goonewardena et al. 2008; Merrifield 2006). To the best of my knowledge, only two people have produced major works that apply Lefebvre's ideas about space to specific places, namely D. Harvey (1974) for Baltimore and Soja (1996) for Los Angeles.

29 A few exceptions exist, for example, Low (2000); Munn (1996); Rodman (2001); Rotenberg (1995); Rotenberg and McDonogh (1993); and West (2005, 2006).

30 Hiro was adopted, which is a common practice in Polynesia. It underscores the belief that every Polynesian is able to care for another Polynesian, a custom that guards against individualism and egotism (Hiro 2004, 8).

31 Translated in Stewart, Mateata-Allain, and Mawyer (2006, 77).

32   Translated in Stewart, Mateata-Allain, and Mawyer (2006, 77).

33   Hiro wrote deliberately only in Tahitian, the language in which he was most at ease and that he deeply loved. He also saw this as a way to preserve and valorize the Tahitian language. He did, however, participate in the translation of his poems and texts (Do Carlson, personal communication, 2009).

34   Translated in Stewart, Mateata-Allain, and Mawyer (2006, 74).

35   Mead noted this custom in Samoa (1928, 21); G. Harvey in Aotearoa/New Zealand (2005, 121–22); Andreassen in Rapa (2008, v and 12); and Levy (1973, 144), Oliver (1974, 422), and Saura (2000, 2002a, 2002b) in French Polynesia. See also Bonnemère (2000); Hanson (1970, 39); Merrett-Balkos (1998); Panoff (1964, 118–19); and Strathern (1982) for variations and other interpretations of this practice throughout Oceania.

36   Tongan anthropologist Tevita Ka'ili discusses the existence of a similar cosmology in Tonga, where *"Fonua* [the Tongan equivalent of Tahitian *fenua*] is an integral part of Tongan genealogy and sense of place. The link between land and people is embedded in the Tongan concept of *fonua*—land *and* its people" (Ka'ili 2005, 93). "Within this mutually beneficial reciprocal relationship, people take care of (*tauhi*) their land, and in return, the land nourishes its people. . . . In Tonga the mother's placenta, land (and its people) and one's grave are all called *fonua*" (Ka'ili 2005, 93).

37   Translated in Stewart, Mateata-Allain, and Mawyer (2006, 80–81).

38   This particular poem was part of a show called Mana'o, which was put on stage at the cultural center in Pape'ete (Do Carlson, personal communication, 2009).

39   Using an indigenous analytical framework can help challenge any number of Western dichotomies and assumptions, as Kirsch (2006) demonstrates for the division between nature and culture.

NOTES TO CHAPTER ONE

1   *Pape* means "water" and *ete* refers to a carrying container of pandanus or bamboo.

2   Ironically, these colonial renderings of place are the prototypes of the maps I use in this book.

3   Europeans, of course, were not the only people making maps. As experienced seafarers, Tahitians had their own mental maps of the Pacific "sea of islands." The best known is the map that the Tahitian priest Tupaia, who joined the *Endeavor* in 1769, drew for Captain Cook. Although the original map has been lost, several copies remain (see Forster 1778). Tupaia's map covered more

than forty degrees of longitude and twenty degrees of latitude, and included islands that ranged from Tonga, Samoa, and Fiji in the west to the Marquesas in the northeast (a distance of more than 2,500 miles). In all, he named 130 islands (Jolly 2007, 534). Tupaia had only been to some of these islands, but knew about the rest from his father and grandfather. Not only did he know their names but he also knew their relative sizes, their geological formations, and whether or not they were inhabited (Dening 2006).

4   The Spanish explorer Alvaro de Mendana visited Fatu Hiva in the Marquesas in 1595 but did not make any attempt to trade with or colonize the islands. In 1606 the Portuguese navigator Pedro Fernandez de Quiros visited the Tuamotu Archipelago. In 1722 the Dutchman Jacob Roggeveen sailed across the Tuamotu Archipelago to Maupiti in the Society Islands. In 1765 the English admiral John Byron completed the charting of the remaining Tuamotu Islands. In 1772 the Spanish captain Domingo de Boenechea landed at Tahiti and claimed it for Spain. Spanish explorers also visited Tahiti in 1774, landing at Tautira (Corney 1915; Rodriguez 1996). All in all, these various explorations had little lasting effect on Tahiti.

5   Charles de Brosses is also credited with having coined the term "Polynesia" in 1756 (from the Greek *polus,* "many," and *nesos,* "island").

6   For an excellent and detailed account of the European discovery of Tahiti, see Salmond 2010.

7   Cultural misunderstandings entered the accounts as well. See Tcherkézoff (2003, 58) for an account of the confusion around the presentation of cloth to visitors, which in Polynesia is done as a gesture of respect to acknowledge a person's status.

8   The transit of Venus occurs when Venus passes between the sun and the Earth and, in doing so, eclipses a small spot on the sun.

9   Occasionally the name appears as Vaitepiha Bay.

10   For more about *marae,* see de Bovis (1976); Oliver (1974, 95–106, 177–93); and Saquet (2001, 48–53).

11   In general, the produce from the land, rather than the land (or sea) itself, was the guide to values set on particular areas of subsistence (Beaglehole 1961, 1796; Newbury 1980, 25).

12   For a thoughtful rereading and analysis of the relationship between Queen Pomare and the French colonial authorities, see O'Brien (2006b).

13   For the most part, "Tahitians remained divided between the small pro-French party created by Moerenhout and the anti-French chiefs and officials alienated from the new government" (Newbury 1980, 116).

14   Outside of Europe, France possesses both Départements d'Outre-Mer and

Territoires d'Outre-Mer (DOMs and TOMs). They are strategically scattered around the world in the Atlantic, Caribbean, Pacific, and Indian oceans, as well as in Antarctica. The DOMs (French Guiana, Guadeloupe, Martinique, and Réunion—all in the Atlantic) are legally as much a part of France as Paris. The TOMs (French Polynesia, New Caledonia, and Wallis and Futuna—all in the Pacific) are legally part of the French Republic but have somewhat greater autonomy (see Aldrich and Connell 2006, 1).

15 See T. Mitchell (1988) and Scott (1998), who discuss similar situations for Egypt, Russia, Brazil, and Tanzania.

16 The area in Paris was named after Henri III, who had been King of Poland briefly before his ascendancy to the throne of France.

17 In 2006 the pro-independence French Polynesia Council of Ministers voted to rename it avenue Pouvana'a O'opa, paying tribute to the first leader of the movement for an independent Tahiti.

18 See Berrong (2003) for a gay reading of Loti's work. Berrong traces what he sees as Loti's homosexual identity and, because of the constraints of the time, the approaches he used to talk about homosexuality covertly so it would remain hidden from the general audience in France.

19 The competition for these exhibitions was especially intense between Paris and Marseilles, which at the time was France's largest port, through which two-thirds of France's trade with its empire (most notably its African colonies) passed.

20 One visitors' guide "told industrialists and traders that they would find presented 'as complete an inventory as possible of the resources offered to your enterprise;' artists would discover 'new methods, new colors, new harmonies;' workers would feel great solidarity with fellow laborers across the seas; France's youth would perhaps be inspired with colonial vocations" (Aldrich 1996, 261).

21 During this period the images most often portrayed at the fairs were those of colonized peoples who were thought to be wild and savage—those who were seen as being most in need of French rule and influence—rather than those who were seen as gentler and nobler. Thus, the Pacific Islanders who were most prominently displayed were the dark-skinned indigenous people of France's penal colony of New Caledonia, rather than those of the envisioned paradise of Tahiti (Boulay 2001).

22 See Lindstrom (2007) for a discussion of postcards from Vanuatu, which portray local people as sexual, decorated, good-looking, and naturalized, thus positioning Vanuatu as an "exotic locale on the global tourist circuit" (Lindstrom 2007, 257).

23 According to Mathur, the representation of European women on the post-cards as symbols of leisure carried ambiguous meanings:

> [The postcards] reveal the anxieties that were generated by the uncertain place of white women in the colonies. The Victorian woman's proximity to "the natives" was a constant threat to the colonial patriarchy intent on protecting her perceived sexual purity. These postcards assured their mass audiences "at home" that European women were being properly managed within the precarious relations of race and gender that structured the colonial public order (Mathur 1999, 108).

24 Eisenman (1999) offers a reading of Gauguin's work that presents a complex understanding of Gauguin's sexuality.

25 Teha'amana, in fact, was not Tahitian but Tongan or Rarotongan (see Teaiwa 1999, 254).

26 For example, both the Metropolitan Museum of Art in New York (2002) and the Boston Museum of Fine Arts (2003) staged exhibits that brought this to the fore.

NOTES TO CHAPTER TWO

1 See Imada (2004); O'Dwyer (2004); and Teaiwa (1994, 1999, 2001) for other Pacific examples of the strategic links between tourism and militarism. Teaiwa has coined the term "militourism" to refer to "a phenomenon by which military or paramilitary force ensures the smooth running of a tourist industry, and that same tourist industry masks the military force behind it" (Teaiwa 1999, 251). Not surprisingly, militourism is especially common in places that are still negotiating colonial relationships, such as Hawai'i, Guam, New Caledonia, and French Polynesia (Teaiwa 1999, 251).

2 This is similar to what others have described—for example, Basso (1996) for the Western Apache, Bastien (1985) for the Aymara Indians of Bolivia, Dominy (1995) for the Maori, and Fernandez (1988) for Andalusia.

3 This interpretation is slightly different from that of Saura, who says that the *pu fenua* is planted near a tree "so that the substance that nourished the foetus nourishes the tree" (Saura 2002a, 127).

4 A 1997 study of 192 births at the public hospital of Mama'o in urban Pape'ete showed that 50 percent of mothers took the placenta home with them to bury in the ground. In rural hospitals on outer islands the proportion of placentas kept by the mothers is 80 to 90 percent (see Saura 2000; 2002a, 141; 2002b).

5 This is an English translation of the original *L'île des rêves écrasés* (Spitz 1991).

6 One-third of all court cases in Pape'ete pertain to land (Tetiarahi 1987, 46).

7   See http://www.magicmoorea.com/Sheraton (accessed 2010).

8   The sea is often thought of as one large *marae* (Oliver 1974; Spitz 2007, 30).

9   *Journal officiel de la Polynésie française,* February 29, 1964, deliberation #64-27.

10   See Regnault (1993) for a detailed documentation of the testing program in French Polynesia.

11   There had been antinuclear protests in French Polynesia as far back as 1950 "when Tahitian nationalist Pouvana'a O'opa collected signatures for the Stockholm Peace Appeal" (Maclellan 2005, 364; see also B. and M.-T. Danielsson 1986).

12   In 2006, Florent de Vathaire, a radiation expert from the National Institute for Health and Medical Research (INSERM) of France, presented a study of thyroid cancer in French Polynesia. The study "demonstrated a correlation between exposure to above-average radiation and the increase in cases of thyroid cancer, making him the first agent of a French government office to confirm the harmfulness of the tests" (Gonschor 2008, 223).

13   Others cite slightly different numbers. Regnault, for example, says there were 41 atmospheric tests and 140 underground tests (Regnault 2005).

14   Today French Polynesia still has an extremely high cost of living.

15   Salaries for expatriate French civil servants are augmented over the metropolitan standard by an additional 84 percent, which accounts for the French civil servants' nickname of "84 percenters."

16   Most were American Matson Line ships.

17   This contrasts significantly with tourists' abilities to travel to Hawai'i, which had an airport as early as 1927 and where ship travel was much more available.

18   Di Castri says that there were no more than 700 tourists each year in the 1950s (di Castri 2002, 261).

19   Pape'ete's Hotel Tahara'a Intercontinental (owned by Pan American's hotel subsidiary) had most of its décor (including a twenty-foot, five-and-a-half-ton tiki) carved in Whittier, California, because "many of the natives are employed in other jobs, such as at French atomic plants" (*Whittier Daily News* 1968, 3).

20   In spite of tourism's grand scale in French Polynesia's budget, the numbers of tourists are actually quite low, especially compared to other Pacific islands. For example, in 2000, Hawai'i received about seven million tourists, Guam more than one million, and Fiji about 300,000. During that same year, only about 233,000 tourists visited French Polynesia (di Castri 2002, 261). Another way of envisioning these numbers is to say that the MGM Grand in Las Vegas has roughly twice as many rooms as all of the hotels in French Polynesia combined.

21 See Imada (2004) for a comparison with Hawai'i, where hula troupes circulated throughout the United States to promote tourism during this same period.

22 Compared with other tourist destinations in the Pacific, this number is small. In Hawai'i, for example, tourism brings in more than $10 billion annually (State of Hawai'i, Department of Business, Economic Development and Tourism, 2009). See http://hawaii.gov/dbedt (accessed 2009).

23 See http://www.thebrando.com (accessed 2009).

24 See http://www.dooyoo.co.uk/food/bounty-bar/reviews (accessed 2007).

25 These days, of course, the Internet has enabled the global and instant circulation of the "postcard" image, which has further entrenched the myth. Not only do prospective tourists view images on sites that promote tourism but they also surf the Net looking for more personal images (and information) on travelers' blogs. Not surprisingly, these personal images and comments, which often center on the beauty of the landscape and the dreamlike amenities of the hotels, are very similar to those on the tourism sites.

26 Teva Sylvain has also produced postcards of men, especially men with tattoos. But these seem less important than those of women. On his current Web site he has 150 postcards of women, but only two of men, for sale. See http://www.tahitisouvenirs.com (accessed 2010).

27 Johnston describes a similar mind-set for Edward Steichen when he created his tourist advertisements for the Matson Line and Hawai'i in the 1940s. Doveline "Tootsie" Notley, who was "full-blooded Hawaiian," was "keenly aware of the racial implications of her selection as the Matson Girl." This could only happen, however, once there was "greater acceptance of fully Native Hawaiian women in advertising" (Johnston 2002, 212).

28 Smaller antinuclear protests had occurred in Pape'ete in 1973 and 1989 (see B. and M.-T. Danielsson 1986; Firth 2005).

29 This is similar to the phrase Chantal Spitz uses when she says "the concrete wombs nurturing the missiles [were] hideous objects implanted after the rape of the belly of the Land" (Spitz 2007, 94).

30 Jacques Brel is a French singer from Belgium who settled in the Marquesas in 1966. Paul-Émile Victor is a French arctic ethnologist, who, in his later years, pursued his childhood dream by settling on a deserted island near Bora Bora.

NOTES TO CHAPTER THREE

1 Tahiti's iconic beach at Matavai Bay, where Cook landed in 1769, has black sand. The color of the sand surprised Marlon Brando when he came to Matavai to film *Mutiny on the Bounty*. He ordered hundreds of tons of white sand from New Jersey to be transported to Matavai to cover up the black sand, thus

portraying what he thought was the idyllic Pacific white-sand beach for the film's audiences (Dening 1992, 179).

2   The dependence on mythical imagery for the promotion of tourism is certainly not unique to Tahiti. Yet adherence to the myth does seem unusually pronounced. For example, when tourists arrive at the Honolulu airport, they usually get a rental car and are free to go where they want. In Pape'ete, on the other hand, tourists are immediately confronted with a composed setting that creates a specific sense of place. They are greeted by attractive women bearing flowers, a Tahitian string band playing island music, and hotel vans rather than easily available rental cars for them to drive away in on their own.

3   This phrase appeared in Island Cruises and Travel (2009), Robinson Travel Service (2007), Tahiti Legends (2004), and Tahiti Travel (2008).

4   See http://www.GoToTahiti.com (accessed 2004).

5   See http://www.Tahiti-invest.com (accessed 2003).

6   See http://www.airtahiti.com (accessed 2005).

7   See, for example, Baré (2002); Bolyanatz (2004); Claessen (1994); Connell (2003); Cowell (1999); d'Hauteserre (2005); Edmond (1997); Faessel (2006); Geiger (2007); Hall (1998); Johnson (2006); Jolly (1997); Lansdown (2006); Liebersohn (2006); Margueron (1989); Matsuda (2005); Nicole (1993, 2001); O'Brien (2006a); Rennie (1995); Sturma (2002); Tcherkézoff (2004); Vibart (1987); and L. Wallace (2003). See also Saura (1998) for a counter viewpoint; i.e., not only how the French perceive the Tahitians but also how the Tahitians perceive the French.

8   This group was officially dissolved in 2006.

9   As one GIP worker told me, about 70 percent of them were ex-convicts who were unable to find other work, thus making them loyal to their boss, President Flosse.

10   GIE stands for *groupement d'intérêt économique* or "economic interest group."

11   The tourism positions available for unskilled workers, which are the jobs held by average Tahitians, are among the lowest-paid positions in the Territory. Of fifteen job categories listed by the government on their Web site, those at the very bottom of the salary scale were jobs in the hotel industry. See www. Tahiti-invest.com.

12   When I attended the conference in 2001, Thailand, Singapore, Hong Kong, and Taiwan were not yet included.

13   The tikis that were carved for the Hotel Tahara'a in Pape'ete in the 1960s were not only made in Whittier, California, but were also modeled after Maori tikis from New Zealand.

14   See http://www.GoToTahiti.com.

15   See Tahiti Tourisme North America (2008, 47).

16   At the 2007 Conférence des Représentants de GIE Tahiti Tourisme, similar images held sway. "By the end of the day, it was clear that the islands of Tahiti are perceived as pristine, beautiful, unique, untouched and authentic, to mention a few of the adjectives that were used to describe the natural beauty of the destination throughout the world." See http://start.emailopen.com/ttnanews/newsC5110.htm.

17   Foster's work is based on the ideas of Kevin Roberts, CEO of Saatchi and Saatchi Advertising, who defined the term as a brand that possesses a "special emotional resonance" (Roberts 2004, 74).

18   This book, while attempting to move beyond the surface of the images, is still yet another instance and image in the ongoing making of place, not unlike the many examples I discuss within its pages. Not only am I caught in the tangled web of other people's fantasies about Tahiti, but I now also continue to spin more threads and to twist them into the never-ending intricacy of a place. As an anthropologist, I both hover outside the web and am lost within it. "Ethnography . . . a situated practice, situated among and within, co-producing and co-produced by, a complex of other situated practices . . . is always already complicit in the narratives that it produces" (Raffles 2005, 377).

19   The Internet is slightly different from other forms of communication because many Pacific Islanders have access to it and use it to promote their own agendas, as seen in the case of promoting family-run guest houses.

20   As I had previously learned from Suzanne Lau Chonfont, who managed statistics at the Office of Tourism, prior to the events of September 11, tourism had generated US$250 million annually for the Territory from a tourism promotion budget of roughly US$10 million. This helped explain why more than half of the Office of Tourism's annual budget was devoted to advertising and marketing.

21   This is consistent with the ideas of both Plato and Lacan, who argued that desire was constituted as a lack, and was impossible to fulfill other than in dreams.

22   This is in sharp contrast to the situation in Tahiti, where most Tahitians, having learned French language, geography, and history in school, know a lot about France.

23   Statistics indicate that, when making travel arrangements, people rely increasingly on the Internet and less on travel agents. Between 1996 and 2008, the percent of people depending on the Internet increased from 5 percent to 95 percent (Tahiti Tourisme North America 2008, 50).

24   See http://investinyourlove.com (accessed 2010).

25   These examples are taken from http://www.lonelyplanet.com/travelblogs (accessed 2009).

26   American tourists who go to Tahiti spend significantly more on this trip than they do when they go to other destinations. "The average Tahiti trip costs almost $11,000; more than double the amount spent when traveling to the Caribbean and Mexico" (Tahiti Tourisme North America 2008, 32).

NOTES TO CHAPTER FOUR

1   This desire to stay in the world of the myth was revealed once when I was talking to a tourist and mentioned the topic of nuclear testing. Her instant response was, "Don't tell me about those things, I'm on vacation and don't want to know about them."

2   I did not tape or take notes from this conversation, but recorded the details, to the best of my recollection, immediately after the couple left.

3   See, for example, Balme (1998) and Harkin (2003).

4   See http://www.ispf.pf/ISF/Home.aspx (accessed 2008).

5   There are some exceptions, such as Moʻorea.

6   See http://www.letahaa.com (accessed 2009).

7   See http://www.boraboraspa.intercontinental.com (accessed 2009).

8   These sources are Air Tahiti, which is French Polynesia's domestic airline (30 percent); Moana Nui, which is the company that opened the first Continent supermarket (a well-known chain in France) in Papeʻete (25 percent); Banque Socredo, one of the three banks in the Territory (25 percent); Caisse de Prévoyance Sociale (CPS), the government agency that deals with social security and welfare (12 percent); and Brasserie de Tahiti, the producer of all of French Polynesia's beers and soft drinks (8 percent). *Les nouvelles de Tahiti* 2001, 25.

9   Loi Pons and Loi Paul are tax exemption laws initiated in 1986, and renamed in 2001, that encourage foreign investment in tourism projects in France's overseas departments and territories.

10   Although the lecture was given in 1967, it was not published until 1986.

11   A number of works have examined this divergence between sign and object, for example, Gable and Handler (1996); Herzfeld (1993); and Low (2001, 2003a).

12   See Rotenberg (1995) for an excellent study of Viennese gardens as heterotopias.

13   See also Hibbard (2006) on resort hotels.

14   See http://www.Tahiti-invest.com (accessed 2003).

15   Recent work on Pacific masculinities has emphasized the ways in which colonialism and tourism have sexualized Polynesian men as surfers, beach boys,

or fire-knife dancers "whose body and physical prowess are highlighted in an economy of pleasure" (Tengan 2008, 8, referencing work by Desmond 1999; Ferguson and Turnbull 1999; and Trask 1987).

16   See Desmond (1999) and Trask (1987) for examples of similar situations in Hawai'i.

17   Dancers I knew on Huahine usually earned about US$15 per person per performance.

18   This is an old warrior dance.

19   The blowing of a conch shell is still practiced (although rarely) in French Polynesia to announce that an event will soon begin.

20   Interestingly, Tahitians have borrowed and transformed some customs (for example, they have adapted fire dancing from Samoa, changed dance steps, and altered the length of the dance when performing in hotel floor shows), but not others.

NOTES TO CHAPTER FIVE

1   Even though people on Huahine call this a *motu*, it technically is not one because it is attached to the main island.

2   These fish traps are made from coral blocks that are placed side by side across the lake and arranged in the water in a V-shape, the point of which leads to a circular enclosure. At each of these enclosures is a small thatched shelter where people who are fishing can find protection from the sun or rain, and where they keep their fishnets.

3   The reenactment of rituals for the benefit of tourists is done at *Marae Arahurahu* on the island of Tahiti (much to the disapproval of many Tahitians).

4   She said she could tell by the way people dressed and by their general body language.

5   A formal organization was needed in order to receive public funds.

6   Dorothy relayed the following information about the visit to me.

7   Dorothy told this to me.

8   This is the branch of the Office of Tourism that deals with promoting touristic activities within French Polynesia.

9   The Taputapuatea *marae* on the island of Raiatea is thought to be the center of spiritual power in Polynesia and thus the most important *marae* in French Polynesia. In 1994 the government restored it, making it the main tourist attraction for Raiatea.

10   Friends on Huahine had asked me to write to Hawaiian Airlines and request these prizes.

11   These comments in the guestbook were written in French and English.

12   It is common for the meaning of tourist sites to be contested among local residents, government officials, and tourists (see, for example, Bender 1993, 1998; and Bruner 1996).

13   In response to people's complaints, the *unu* were moved outdoors in 2002.

14   More recently, as a result of the post-2004 changes in the government, public recognition of Henri Hiro has greatly increased. For example, two major events in 2010 commemorated the twentieth anniversary of his death. The Musée de Tahiti et ses Îles (Museum of Tahiti and Her Islands) featured a special exhibit about his life, his spiritual beliefs, and his political activism. Also, the July Heiva festivities opened with an evening that paid tribute to him through a focus on older Tahitian chanting, music, and dances, as well as a short film about him.

15   This is reminiscent of Smith's description of the Mataatua, a carved Maori house built in 1875 as a wedding gift from one tribal group to another, which was then sent to the British Empire Exhibition at Sydney in 1879, where it was completely transformed for the purpose of being assimilated into the exhibition. Smith presents the story of the Mataatua, which continued to be sent to various other museums and exhibitions around the world, as an example of "the colonization of an indigenous architectural space and indigenous spatial concepts" (L. T. Smith 1999, 52).

16   This behavior is an excellent example of what de Certeau has called "tactics," and what he distinguishes from "strategies." "Strategies" (weapons of the strong), which he links to institutions and structures of power, assume a place that can be circumscribed. "Tactics" (weapons of the weak), on the other hand, are the responses used by individuals to create space for themselves in environments defined by the powerful (de Certeau 1984, 34–39).

17   The mayor of Huahine has since requested and received government funds to help get young people involved in the *marae* and the Fare Pote'e by cleaning the area and maintaining the trails to the archaeological sites in the hills. Slowly, the people were again showing interest in learning about, and sharing, their cultural heritage (Yoshi Sinoto, personal communication, 2009).

NOTES TO CHAPTER SIX

1   Translated in Stewart, Mateata-Allain, and Mawyer (2006, 80).

2   Ironically, this is the same *pareu* that has now become one of the main souvenirs tourists buy—along with their aloha shirts—to remind them of their trip to Tahiti.

3   Lefebvre's approach differs from that of Foucault, who was also interested in the ways in which power was "actualized" but rarely examined specific forms

of resistance. Foucault, in contrast to Lefebvre, views modern space as dispersed and anonymous, and something to be understood mainly as an architectural grid for confining the human body.

4   See Haraway (1991) and Low (2003b) for similar ideas.

5   Translated in Stewart, Mateata-Allain, and Mawyer (2006, 77).

6   In 2001 the cruise cost approximately US$2,000.

7   See http://en.allexperts.com/q/Renaissance-Cruises (accessed 2005).

8   Due to rough seas, the ship had been unable to stop at Mo'orea before coming to Huahine.

9   For example, see Kahn (1986); Manderson (1986); Pollock (1992); Whitehead (2000); and Young (1971).

10   In 2002, Princess Cruises purchased the *Renaissance* vessels, which then joined their fleet as the *Pacific Princess* and *Tahitian Princess*. In 2009 the *Pacific Princess* was still stopping at Huahine, and a group of Tahitians was still going on board (and was still being paid in food).

11   These were the Service des Affaires Sociales and the Ministère de la Solidarité et de la Famille.

12   Richard and I stayed in a classroom with Marietta and her family.

13   Huahine did not surrender to the French until 1898, which was eighteen years after the rest of the islands surrendered.

14   See, for example, Hereniko (1995); W. Mitchell (1992); and Strathern (1975).

15   Here Hereniko is quoting Eco (1984, 6).

NOTES TO CHAPTER SEVEN

1   Translated in Stewart, Mateata-Allain, and Mawyer (2006, 78).

2   This is similar to what Hugh Raffles says about his experiences in Amazonia: "I came to understand places best when I saw them as formed by the movement of people and ideas and as constituted by traces of pasts and futures; when I thought in terms of place-making rather than of ready-made places" (Raffles 2002b, 329).

3   Translated in Stewart, Mateata-Allain, and Mawyer (2006, 72).

4   This is a reference to French Army marshal Joseph-Simon Gallieni, who was governor of Paris in 1914 and was active as a military commander in the French colonies. He promoted a similar style of architecture throughout France's colonies (see Wright 1991).

5   This scene has since changed. The lot is still empty, but has been cleaned up, with a row of new trees planted to shield the empty lot from view.

6   The following month, Oscar Temaru "inaugurated a monument to the victims of French nuclear testing in another park in Pape'ete" (Gonschor 2007, 221).

7　In a much-repeated, but also disputed (see Saura 2004, 2008), attempt to etymologically decipher the word *ma'ohi,* Turo Raapoto divided it into *ma* (clean, noble) and *ohi* (a sprout that has taken root) to indicate that Tahitians can be seen as indigenous fruit of the earth. In this vein Raapoto said, "Once again, it is not a question of having, but of being. Today, tomorrow and in the sprout (*ohi*) that will climb, our thirst for being, for being Ma'ohi will assert itself" (Raapoto 1980, 5).

8　See, for example, the writing of Tamaira (2010) and Taouma (2004); the filmmaking of Hereniko (2004) and Urale (1996); and the artistic work of Shigeyuki Kihara, Sue Pearson, and Rosanna Raymond. Lyons (2006) devotes the final chapter of *American Pacificism* to contemporary Pacific literature and the ways in which indigenous authors have contested Pacificist imaginings.

9　See, for example, Raffles (2002a, 2002b, 2005) and West (2005, 2006).

10　See http://www.globalsecurity.org/military/facility/pmrf.htm (accessed 2009).

11　See http://www.unhcr.org/4a375c426.html (accessed 2009).

12　"Tourism is the world's largest industry on the basis of its contribution to global gross domestic product (GDP). It generates about 10 percent of total world GDP and employs over 10 percent of the global workforce, and it's still growing" (World Tourism Organization, 2007). See http://www.unwto.org/index.php (accessed 2007).

13　See http://iguide.travel/Merzouga/Hotels_and_Accommodation (accessed 2009).

14　See http://cruises.about.com/cs/alaskacruises/a/alaskacruises.htm (accessed 2009).

References

Aldrich, Robert. 1990. *The French presence in the South Pacific, 1842–1940*. London: Macmillan Press.

———. 1993. *France and the South Pacific since 1940*. Honolulu: University of Hawai'i Press.

———. 1996. *Greater France: A history of French overseas expansion*. London: Macmillan Press.

Aldrich, Robert, and John Connell. 1998. *The last colonies*. Cambridge: Cambridge University Press.

———. 2006. *France's overseas frontier: Départements et territoires d'outre-mer*. Cambridge: Cambridge University Press.

Alloula, Malek. 1986. *The colonial harem*. Trans. Myrna Godzich and Wlad Godzich. Minneapolis: University of Minnesota Press.

Andreassen, Olaug Irene Røsvik. 2008. *When home is the navel of the earth: An ethnography of young Rapa Nui between home and away*. PhD diss., University of New South Wales.

Appadurai, Arjun. 1988a. Introduction: Place and voice in anthropological theory. *Cultural Anthropology* 3 (1): 16–20.

———, ed. 1988b. Theme issue: Place and voice in anthropological theory. *Cultural Anthropology* 3 (1).

———. 1991. Global ethnoscapes: Notes and queries for a transnational anthropology. In *Recapturing Anthropology*, ed. R. Fox, 191–210. Santa Fe: School of American Research.

———. 1996. *Modernity at large: Cultural dimensions of globalization*. Minneapolis: University of Minnesota Press.

Ariyoshi, Rita. 2001. Tahiti: The French Polynesian islands are the spot for romance. *Modern Bride Magazine*. February/March, p. 882.

Arnold, David. 2006. *The tropics and the traveling gaze: India, landscape and science, 1800–1856*. Seattle: University of Washington Press.

Association Opu Nui. 1995. Valorisation des sites historiques, village de Maeva, Huahine, Raro Mataʻi. Contrat de développement état-territoire, 1994–98. Huahine.

Auckland City Art Gallery. 1977. Two worlds of Omai. Auckland: Auckland City Art Gallery. Exhibit.

Bacchet, Philippe. 1999. *Îles et lumières*. Papeʻete: Au Vent des îles.

Bakhtin, Mikhail. 1993. *Rabelais and his world*. Trans. Hélène Iswolsky. Bloomington: Indiana University Press.

Ball, Martin. 2002. "People speaking silently to themselves": An examination of Keith Basso's philosophical speculations on "sense of place" in Apache cultures. *American Indian Quarterly* 26 (3): 460–78.

Balme, Christopher. 1998. Staging the Pacific: Framing authenticity in performances for tourists at the Polynesian cultural center. *Theatre Journal* 50 (1): 53–70.

Banks, Joseph. 1896. *Journal of the right honorable Sir Joseph Banks during Captain Cook's first voyage*. Ed. Sir Joseph D. Hooker. London: MacMillan and Company.

Baré, Jacques. 2002. *Le malentendu pacifique: Des premières rencontres entre Polynésiens et Anglais et de ce qui s'ensuivit avec les Français jusqu'à nos jours*. Paris: Éditions des archives contemporaines.

Barrillot, Bruno. 2002. *L'héritage de la bombe: Sahara, Polynésie 1960–2002*. Lyon: Centre de Documentation et de Recherche sur la Paix et les Conflits.

———. 2003. *Les irradiés de la république: Les victimes des essais nucléaires français prennent la parole*. Brussels: Éditions GRIP.

Barrillot, Bruno, and John Taroanui Doom. 2005. Response to Regnault. *The Contemporary Pacific* 17 (2): 373–77.

Barthes, Roland. 1977. The photographic message. In *Image—music—text*, trans. S. Heath, 15–31. New York: Hill and Wang.

Basso, Keith. 1988. "Speaking with names": Language and landscape among the Western Apache. *Cultural Anthropology* 3 (2): 99–130.

———. 1996. *Wisdom sits in places: Landscape and language among the Western Apache*. Albuquerque: University of New Mexico Press.

Bastien, Joseph. 1985. *The mountain of the condor: Metaphor and ritual in an Andean Ayllu*. Prospect Heights: Waveland Press.

Baston, Guillaume. 1790. *Narrations d'Omai, insulaire de la mer du sud, ami et compagnon de voyage du Capitaine Cook*. Rouen: Chez le Boucher le Jeune.

Baudrillard, Jean. 1988. *America*. London: Verso.

Beaglehole, John, ed. 1961. *The journals of Captain James Cook on his voyages of discovery.* Vol. 2. Hakluyt Society, Extra Series, no. 35. London: Cambridge University Press.

Bender, Barbara. 1993. Stonehenge—Contested landscapes (medieval to present day). In *Landscape: Politics and perspectives,* ed. B. Bender, 245–80. Providence: Berg.

———. 1998. *Stonehenge: Making space.* Oxford: Berg.

Benjamin, Walter. 1999. *The arcades project.* Ed. Roy Tiedemann. Trans. Howard Eiland and Kevin McLaughlin. Cambridge, MA: Harvard University Press.

Berger, John. 1991. *About looking.* New York: Vintage Books.

Berman, Marshall. 1983. *All that is solid melts into air.* London: Verso.

Berrong, Richard. 2003. *In love with a handsome sailor: The emergence of gay identity and the novels of Pierre Loti.* Toronto: University of Toronto Press.

Bestor, Theodore. 2004. *Tsukiji: The fish market at the center of the world.* Berkeley: University of California Press.

Bhabha, Homi K. 1990. The third space. In *Identity, community, culture, difference,* ed. J. Rutherford, 207–21. London: Lawrence and Wishart.

———. 1994. *The location of culture.* New York: Routledge.

Bionne, Henry. 1880. *Bulletin de la Compagnie du Canal Interocéanique,* no. 30.

Blum, Virginia, and Heidi Nast. 1996. Where's the difference? The heterosexualization of alterity in Henri Lefebvre and Jacques Lacan. *Environment and Planning D: Society and Space* 14:559–80.

Bolyanatz, Alexander. 2004. *Pacific romanticism: Tahiti and the European imagination.* London: Praeger.

Bonnemaison, Joel. 2005. *Culture and space: Conceiving a new cultural geography.* London: I. B. Tauris.

Bonnemère, Pascale. 2000. Le traitement du placenta en Océanie. Des sens différents pour une même pratique. *Sciences Sociales et Santé* 22:29–36.

Boorstin, Daniel. 1964. *The image: A guide to pseudo-events in America.* New York: Harper.

Boston Museum of Fine Arts. 2003. Impressions of light: The French landscape from Corot to Monet. Exhibit.

Bougainville, Louis-Antoine de. 1771. *Voyage autour du monde par la frégate du roi La Boudeuse et la flute L'Étoile en 1766, 1767, 1768 & 1769.* Paris: Chez Sailland & Nyon.

———. 1772. *A voyage round the world.* Trans. Johann R. Forster. London: J. Nourse.

Boulay, Roger. 2001. *Kannibals et vahines: Imagerie des mers du sud.* Paris: Réunion des Musées Nationaux.

Bourdieu, Pierre. 1988. Social space and symbolic power. *Sociological Theory* 7:18–26.

————. 1990. *The logic of practice.* Polity Press.

Braun, Bruce. 2001. Place becoming otherwise. *BC Studies* 131:14–24.

————. 2002. *The intemperate rainforest: Nature, culture and power on Canada's west coast.* Minneapolis: University of Minnesota Press.

Breckenridge, Carol. 1989. The aesthetics and politics of colonial collecting: India at world fairs. *Comparative Studies in Society and History* 31 (2): 195–216.

Brenner, Neil. 1997. Global, fragmented, hierarchical: Henri Lefebvre's geographies of globalization. *Public Culture* 10 (1): 135–67.

————. 2001. State theory in the political conjuncture: Henri Lefebvre's "Comments on a new state form." *Antipode* 33 (5): 783–808.

Brenner, Neil, and Stuart Elden. 2001. Henri Lefebvre in contexts: An introduction. *Antipode* 33 (5): 763–68.

Brown, Michael. 2000. *Closet space: Geographies of metaphor from the body to the globe.* New York: Routledge.

Bruner, Edward. 1996. Tourism in Ghana: The representation of slavery and the return of the black diaspora. *American Anthropologist* 98 (2): 290–304.

Carroll, Rick. 2005. *Huahine: Island of the lost canoe.* Honolulu: Bishop Museum.

Casey, Edward. 1996. How to get from space to place in a fairly short stretch of time: Phenomenological prolegomena. In Feld and Basso, *Senses of place,* 13–52.

Castells, Manuel. 1977. *The urban question.* London: Edward Arnold.

————. 1983. *The city and the grassroots: A cross-cultural theory of urban social movements.* Berkeley: University of California Press.

Chiang, Albert. 2005. The living lagoon. *Islands Magazine,* July/August, p. 21.

Claessen, Henri J. M. 1994. Tahiti and the early European visitors. In *European imagery and colonial history in the Pacific,* vol. 19, ed. T. van Meijl and P. van der Grijp, 14–31. Nijmegen Studies in Development and Cultural Change. Vol. 19. Saarbrucken: Verlag für Entwicklungspolitik Breitenbach.

Clark, Thomas Blake. 1941. *Omai, first Polynesian ambassador to England.* San Francisco: Colt.

Clifford, James. 1988. *The predicament of culture: Twentieth-century ethnography, literature, and art.* Cambridge, MA: Harvard University Press.

Connell, John. 2003. Island dreaming: The contemplation of Polynesian paradise. *Journal of Historical Geography* 29 (4): 554–81.

Corney, Bolton Glanville, ed. 1915. *The quest and occupation of Tahiti.* Vol. 2. London: Cambridge University Press.

Covit, Bernard. 1968. *Official directory and guide book: Tahiti.* Papeʻete: L'imprimerie du Gouvernement.

Cowell, Andrew. 1999. The apocalypse of paradise and the salvation of the West: Nightmare visions of the future in the Pacific Eden. *Cultural Studies* 13 (1): 138–60.

Danielsson, Bengt, and Marie-Thérèse Danielsson. 1986. *Poisoned reign: French nuclear colonialism in the Pacific.* Victoria, Australia: Penguin. English translation of *Moruroa, mon amour* (1977).

———. 1993. *Moruroa, notre bombe coloniale: Histoire de la colonisation nucléaire de la Polynésie française.* Paris: Éditions L'Harmattan.

Dann, Graham. 1996. The people of tourist brochures. In *The tourist image: Myths and myth making in tourism,* ed. T. Selwyn, 61–81. Chichester: Wiley.

Davis, Jeffrey S. 2005. Representing place: "Deserted isles" and the reproduction of Bikini Atoll. *Annals of the Association of American Geographers* 95 (3): 607–25.

Davis, Robert, and Garry Marvin. 2004. *Venice, the tourist maze: A cultural critique of the world's most touristed city.* Berkeley: University of California Press.

Daws, Gavan. 1980. *A dream of islands: Voyages of self-discovery in the South Seas.* Honolulu: Mutual.

Dear, Michael. 2000. Postmodern bloodlines: From Lefebvre to Jameson. In *The postmodern urban condition,* 47–69. Oxford: Blackwell.

de Bovis, Edmond. 1976. *Tahitian society before the arrival of the Europeans.* Trans. Robert Craig. Laie, HI: Institute for Polynesian Studies.

de Brosses, Charles. 1756. *Histoire des navigations aux terres australes.* Paris: Durand.

de Certeau, Michel. 1984. *The practice of everyday life.* Berkeley: University of California Press.

Deloria, Vine. 1969. *Custer died for our sins: An Indian manifesto.* New York: Macmillan.

———. 1994. *God is red: A native view of religion.* Golden, CO: Fulcrum Publishing.

Dening, Greg. 1992. *Mr. Bligh's bad language: Passion, power and theatre on the Bounty.* Cambridge: Cambridge University Press.

———. 2006. Looking across the beach—both ways. Paper presented at Cook's Pacific Encounters symposium, National Museum of Australia, July 28.

Deroo, Eric, Gabrielle Deroo, and Marie-Cécile de Taillac. 1992. *Aux colonies: Où l'on découvre les vestiges d'un empire englouti.* Paris: Presses de la Cité.

DeRoo, Rebecca. 2002. Colonial collecting: French women and Algerian *cartes postales.* In *Colonialist photography: Imag(in)ing race and place,* ed. Eleanor Hight and Gary Sampson, 159–71. London: Routledge.

Deschanel, Paul. 1884. *La politique française en Océanie.* Paris: Berger-Levault et Cie.

Desmond, Jane. 1999. *Staging tourism: Bodies on display from Waikiki to Sea World.* Chicago: University of Chicago Press.

Despoix, Philippe. 1996. Naming and exchange in the exploration of the Pacific: On European representations of Polynesian culture in late XVIII century. In *Mul-*

ticulturalism and representation, ed. J. Rieder and L. E. Smith, 3–24. Honolulu: University of Hawai'i Press.

d'Hauteserre, Anne-Marie. 2005. Maintaining the myth: Tahiti and its islands. In *Seductions of place: Geographical perspectives on globalization and touristed landscapes,* ed. Carolyn Cartier and Alan Lew, 193–208. London: Routledge.

di Castri, Francesco. 2002. Diversification, connectivity and local empowerment for tourism sustainability in South Pacific Islands—A network from French Polynesia to Easter Island. In *Tourism, biodiversity and information,* ed. F. di Castri and V. Balaji, 257–84. Leiden: Backhuys.

Didier, Chantal. 1995. Pour relancer le tourisme en Polynésie: Promotion de 545 millions CFP! *La dépêche de Tahiti,* November 30, p. 21.

Dominy, Michelle. 1995. White settler assertions of native status. *American Ethnologist* 22 (2): 358–74.

Druick, Douglas, and Peter Kort Zegers. 2001. *Van Gogh and Gauguin: The studio of the south.* Amsterdam: Thames and Hudson.

Duff, Wilson. 1975. *Images, stone, B.C.: Thirty centuries of Northwest Coast Indian sculpture.* Saanichton, B.C.: Hancock House.

Duranti, Alessandro. 1992. Language and bodies in social space: Samoan ceremonial greetings. *American Anthropologist* 94 (3): 657–91.

Eco, Umberto. 1980. Function and sign: The semiotics of architecture. In *Signs, symbols, and architecture,* ed. G. Broadbent, R. Bunt, and C. Jencks, 11–69. New York: John Wiley and Sons.

———. 1984. The frames of "comic freedom." In *Carnival,* ed. Thomas Sebeok, 1–9. Berlin: Mouton.

———. 1986. *Travels in hyper-reality.* London: Picador.

Edmond, Rod. 1997. *Representing the South Pacific: Colonial discourse from Cook to Gauguin.* Cambridge: Cambridge University Press.

Edwards, Elizabeth. 1996. Postcards—Greetings from another world. In *The tourist image: Myths and myth making in tourism,* ed. Tom Selwyn, 197–221. New York: John Wiley and Sons.

Eisenman, Stephen. 1999. *Gauguin's skirt.* London: Thames and Hudson.

Elden, Stuart. 2001. Politics, philosophy, geography: Henri Lefebvre in recent Anglo-American scholarship. *Antipode* 33 (5): 809–25.

———. 2004. *Understanding Henri Lefebvre.* London: Continuum International Publishing Group.

Ellis, William. 1829. *Polynesian researches, during a residence of nearly six years in the South Sea islands.* London: Fisher, Son, and Jackson.

———. 1969. *Polynesian researches: Society Islands, Tubuai Islands and New Zealand.* Rutland, VT: Charles E. Tuttle Co.

Estienne, Charles. 1953. *Gauguin.* Paris: Éditions d'Art Albert Skira.

Faessel, Sonia. 2006. *Visions des îles: Tahiti et l'imaginaire européen.* Paris: l'Harmattan.

Feld, Steve, and Keith Basso, eds. 1996. *Senses of place.* Santa Fe: School of American Research.

Ferguson, James, and Akhil Gupta, eds. 1992. Theme issue: Space, identity, and the politics of difference. *Cultural Anthropology* 7 (1).

Ferguson, Kathy, and Phyllis Turnbull. 1999. *Oh, say, can you see? The semiotics of the military in Hawai'i.* Minneapolis: University of Minnesota Press.

Fernandez, James. 1984. Emergence and convergence in some African sacred places. *Geoscience and Man* 24:31–42.

———. 1988. Andalusia on our minds. *Cultural Anthropology* 3 (1): 21–34.

Firth, Stewart. 2005. A comment on "the nuclear issue in the South Pacific." *The Contemporary Pacific* 17 (2): 359–62.

Firth, Stewart, and Karin Von Strokirch. 1997. A nuclear Pacific. In *The Cambridge history of the Pacific Islander,* ed. Donald Denoon, et al., 324–58. Cambridge: Caimbridge University Press.

Fitzpatrick, Brenda. 1995. *For God's sake . . . no! The churches and nuclear testing in the Pacific.* Geneva: World Council of Churches.

Forster, Johann Reinhold. 1778. *Observations made during a voyage round the world on physical geography, natural history, and ethic philosophy.* London: G. Robinson.

Foster, Hal. 1983. Postmodernism: A preface. In *The anti-aesthetic: Essays on postmodern culture,* ed. Hal Foster, ix–xvi. Seattle: Bay.

Foster, Robert. 2007. The work of the new economy: Consumers, brands, and value creation. *Cultural Anthropology* 22 (4): 707–31.

Foucault, Michel. 1966. *The order of things: An archaeology of the human sciences.* New York: Random House.

———. 1979. *Discipline and punish: The birth of the prison.* Trans. A. Sheridan. New York: Vintage.

———. 1980. Questions on geography. In *Power/knowledge,* ed. C. Gordon, 63–77. New York: Pantheon.

———. 1986. Of other spaces. *Diacritics* 16:22–27.

Frémy, Marc. 1995. Retrouver la croissance après la crise. *La dépêche de Tahiti,* November 30, p. 20.

Gable, Eric, and Richard Handler. 1996. After authenticity at an American heritage site. *American Anthropologist* 98 (3): 568–78.

Gallant, Mavis. 1968. *Paris notebooks: Essays and reviews.* New York: Random House.

Gauguin, Paul. 1949. *Paul Gauguin: Letters to his wife and friends,* ed. Maurice Malingue. Cleveland: World Publishing.

Geiger, Jeffrey. 2007. *Facing the Pacific: Polynesia and the U.S. imperial imagination.* Honolulu: University of Hawai'i Press.

Gieryn, Thomas F. 2000. A space for place in sociology. *Annual Review of Sociology* 26:463–96.

G.I.P. 2001. *G.I.P. Te toa arai: Revue d'information du groupement d'intervention de la Polynésie.* Pape'ete: L'imprimerie du Gouvernement.

Gluckman, Ron. 1995. No boom boom here. *Asiaweek* 21 (August).

Gonschor, Lorenz. 2007. French Polynesia. *The Contemporary Pacific* 19 (1): 213–22.

———. 2008. French Polynesia. *The Contemporary Pacific* 20 (1): 222–32.

———. 2009. French Polynesia. *The Contemporary Pacific* 21 (1): 151–62.

Goonewardena, Kanishka, Stefan Kipfer, Richard Milgrom, and Christian Schmid, eds. 2008. *Space, difference, everyday life: Reading Henri Lefebvre.* New York: Routledge.

Gottdiener, Mark. 1993. A Marx for our time: Henri Lefebvre and the production of space. *Sociological Theory* 11 (1): 129–34.

Grace, Patricia. 1986. *Potiki.* Honolulu: University of Hawai'i Press.

Greenhalgh, Paul. 1988. *Ephemeral vistas: The "expositions universelles," great exhibitions and world fairs, 1851–1939.* Manchester: Manchester University Press.

Gregory, Derek. 1997. Lacan and geography: The production of space revisited. In *Space and social theory: Interpreting modernity and postmodernity,* ed. Georges Benko and Ulf Strohmayer, 203–31. Oxford: Blackwell.

Grönlund, Bo. 1999. Bo Grönlund on Henri Lefebvre: Urbanity: Lived space and difference. http://homepage.mac.com/bogronlund/get2net/Lefebvreindlaeg_21_3_97v2.html (accessed 2005).

Gupta, Akhil. 1992. The song of the nonaligned world: Transnational identities and the reinscription of space in late capitalism. *Cultural Anthropology* 13 (3): 63–79.

Gupta, Akhil, and James Ferguson. 1992. Beyond "culture": Space, identity and the politics of difference. *Cultural Anthropology* 7 (1): 6–23.

Gupta, Sanjay. 2007. Pacific swallowing remote island chain. CNN, July 31.

Guth, Christine. 2004. *Longfellow's tattoos: Tourism, collection, and Japan.* Seattle: University of Washington Press.

Hall, C. Michael. 1998. Making the Pacific: Globalization, modernity and myth. In *Destinations: Cultural landscapes of tourism,* ed. Greg Ringer, 140–53. London: Routledge.

Hannerz, Ulf. 1996. *Transnational connections: Culture, people, places.* London: Routledge.

Hanson, Allan. 1970. *Rapan lifeways: Society and history of a Polynesian island.* Boston: Little, Brown and Co.

Haraway, Donna. 1991. *Simians, cyborgs, and women: The reinvention of nature.* New York: Routledge.

Hargreaves, Alec. 1981. *The colonial experience in French fiction*. London: Macmillan.

Harkin, Michael. 2003. Staged encounters: Indians and tourism. *Ethnohistory* 50 (3): 573–83.

Hart, Gillian. 2006. Denaturalizing dispossession: Critical ethnography in the age of resurgent imperialism. *Antipode* 38 (5): 977–1004.

Harvey, David. 1973. *Social justice and the city*. London: Edward Arnold.

———. 1974. Class-monopoly rent, finance capital and the urban revolution. *Regional Studies* 8:239–55.

———. 1989. *The condition of post modernity: An inquiry into the conditions of cultural change*. Oxford: Blackwell.

———. 1993. From space to place and back again: Reflections on the condition of modernity. In *Mapping the futures: Local cultures, global change,* ed. J. Bird et al., 3–29. London: Routledge.

———. 1997. *Justice, nature, and the geography of difference*. Oxford: Wiley-Blackwell.

———. 2000. *Spaces of hope*. Berkeley: University of California Press.

———. 2003. *Paris, capital of modernity*. New York: Routledge.

Harvey, Graham. 2005. Performing identity and entertaining guests in the Maori diaspora. In *Indigenous diasporas and dislocations,* ed. G. Harvey and C. D. Thompson, 121–34. Surrey: Ashgate.

Heidegger, Martin. 1971. Building dwelling thinking. In *Poetry, language, thought,* trans. A. Hofstadter, 141–61. New York: Harper Colophon Books.

Henrique, Louis. 1889. *Exposition coloniale de 1889*. Vol. 4, *Les colonies française*. Paris: Maison Quentin.

Henry, Teuira. 1928. *Ancient Tahiti*. Bulletin 48. Honolulu: Bernice P. Bishop Museum.

Hereniko, Vilsoni. 1995. *Woven gods: Female clowns and power in Rotuma*. Honolulu: University of Hawaiʻi Press.

———. 2004. *The land has eyes*. Directed by Vilsoni Hereniko. Produced by Vilsoni Hereniko and Jeannette Paulson Hereniko.

Herzfeld, Michael. 1993. *A place in history: Social and monumental time in a Cretan town*. Princeton: Princeton University Press.

Hess, Rémi. 1988. *Henri Lefebvre et l'aventure du siècle*. Paris: Éditions A. M. Métailié.

Hetherington, Kevin. 1997. *The badlands of modernity: Heterotopia and social ordering*. London: Routledge.

Hibbard, Don. 2006. *Designing paradise: The allure of the Hawaiian resort*. Princeton: Princeton Architectural Press.

Hijikata, Hisakatso. 1973. *Stone images of Palau*. Guam: Micronesian Area Research Center.

Hiro, Henri. 2000. *Message poétique.* Papeʻete: Tupuna Productions.

———. 2004. *Pehepehe i taʻu nunaa: Message poétique.* Tahiti: Haere Po.

Hirsch, Eric. 1995. Introduction. In *The anthropology of landscape: Perspectives on place and space,* ed. E. Hirsch and M. O'Hanlon, 1–30. Oxford: Clarendon Press.

hooks, bell. 1990. *Yearning.* Boston: South End Press.

Imada, Adria. 2004. Hawaiians on tour: Hula circuits through the American empire. *American Quarterly* 56 (1): 111–49.

Inglis, Fred. 1977. Nation and community: A landscape and its morality. *Sociological Review* 25:489–514.

Ista, Danielle. 2002. Que cesse le silence et les secrets qui ensevelissent nos morts. In *Les essais nucléaires et la santé,* ed. Marie-Claude Beaudeau, 34–35. Lyon: Centre de Documentation et de Recherche sur la Paix et les Conflits.

Jacobs, Jane. 1996. *Edge of empire: Postcolonialism and the city.* London: Routledge.

Jameson, Fredric. 1983. Postmodernism and consumer society. In *The anti-aesthetic: Essays on postmodern culture,* ed. Hal Foster, 111–25. Seattle: Bay.

———. 1991. *Postmodernism, or, the cultural logic of late capitalism.* Durham, NC: Duke University Press.

Janz, Bruce. 2005. Walls and borders: The range of place. *City and Community* 4 (1): 87–94.

Johnson, Jay, and Brian Murton. 2007. Re/placing native science: Indigenous voices in contemporary constructions of nature. *Geographical Research* 45 (2): 121–29.

Johnson, Sarah. 2006. Missionary positions: Romantic European polynesias from Cook to Stevenson. In *Travel writing in the nineteenth century,* ed. Tim Youngs, 179–99. London: Anthem Press.

Johnston, Patricia. 2002. Advertising paradise: Hawaiʻi in art, anthropology, and commercial photography. In *Colonialist photography: Imag(in)ing race and place,* ed. Eleanor Hight and Gary Samspon, 188–225. London: Routledge.

Jolly, Margaret. 1997. From Point Venus to Bali Hai: Eroticism and exoticism in representations of the Pacific. In *Sites of desire, economies of pleasure: Sexualities in Asia and the Pacific,* ed. M. Jolly and L. Manderson, 99–122. Chicago: University of Chicago Press.

———. 2007. Imagining Oceania: Indigenous and foreign representations of a sea of islands. *The Contemporary Pacific* 19 (2): 508–45.

Journal officiel de la Polynésie française. 1964. Papeʻete: L'imprimerie du Gouvernement.

Judd, Dennis. 1999. Constructing the tourist bubble. In *The tourist city,* ed. Dennis Judd and Susan Fainstein, 35–53. New Haven: Yale University Press.

Kahn, Miriam. 1986. *Always hungry, never greedy: Food and the expression of gender in a Melanesian society.* Cambridge: Cambridge University Press.

———. 1990. Stone-faced ancestors: The spatial anchoring of myth in Wamira, Papua New Guinea. *Ethnology* 29:51–66.

———. 1995. Heterotopic dissonance in the museum representation of Pacific island cultures. *American Anthropologist* 97 (2): 324–38.

———. 1996. Your place and mine: Sharing emotional landscapes in Wamira, Papua New Guinea. In Feld and Basso, *Senses of place,* 167–96.

———. 2000. Tahiti intertwined: Ancestral land, tourist postcard, and nuclear test site. *American Anthropologist* 102 (1): 7–26.

———. 2003. Tahiti: The ripples of a myth on the shores of the imagination. *History and Anthropology* 14 (4): 307–26.

———. 2007. Every action is a human interaction: The reciprocal nature of field methods. In *Pulling the right threads: The ethnographic life and legacy of Jane C. Goodale,* ed. Laura Zimmer-Tamakoshi and Jeanette Dickerson-Putman, 77–91. Champaign: University of Illinois Press.

———. 2011. Stepping onto the stage: Tourism and the transformation of Tahitian dance. In *Changing contexts, shifting meanings: Transformations of cultural traditions in Oceania,* ed. Elfriede Hermann. Honolulu: Honolulu Academy of Arts.

Ka'ili, Tevita. 2005. Tauhi vā: Nurturing Tongan sociospatial ties in Maui and beyond. *The Contemporary Pacific* 17 (1): 83–114.

Kay, Robert. 1997. *Hidden Tahiti and French Polynesia.* Berkeley: Ulysses.

Keller, Janet Dixon, and Takaronga Kuautonga. 2007. *Nokonofo kitea: We keep on living this way (myths and music of Futuna, Vanuatu).* Honolulu: University of Hawai'i Press.

Kincaid, Jamaica. 1988. *A small place.* New York: Farrar, Straus and Giroux.

King, Anthony, ed. 1980. *Buildings and society: Essays on the social development of the built environment.* London: Routledge.

Kirsch, Stuart. 2006. *Reverse anthropology: Indigenous analysis of social and environmental relations in New Guinea.* Stanford: Stanford University Press.

Kramer, Hilton. 1982. The high art of primitivism. *New York Times Magazine,* January 24, pp. 18–19, 62.

Krauss, Bob. 1988. *Keneti: South Seas adventures of Kenneth Emory.* Honolulu: University of Hawai'i Press.

Krizancic, Catarina. 2009. *Tahiti royale: Divine kings disguised as a rising French colonial elite.* PhD diss., University of Chicago.

Kuper, Hilda. 1972. The language of sites in the politics of space. *American Anthropologist* 74 (3): 411–25.

La dépêche de Tahiti. 1995a. Les poissons étaient bien du lagon! *La dépêche de Tahiti,* July 20, pp. 16–17.

———. 1995b. Retombées des émeutes: Le tourisme sinistré. *La dépêche de Tahiti,* September 13, pp. 1, 22–25.

————. 1995c. Jacques Ihorai inquiet par l'argent des essais. *La dépêche de Tahiti,* September 27, p. 21.

————. 2001a. Le "Tikehau Pearl Beach Resort": Inauguré: Luxe, calme et consensus. *La dépêche de Tahiti,* October 22, pp. 1, 36.

————. 2001b. "Tikehau Pearl Beach Resort": Le pari de l'autonomie. *La dépêche de Tahiti,* October 26, pp. 53–54.

————. 2001c. Conférence GIE Tahiti tourisme: Établir une stratégie de promotion internationale. *La dépêche de Tahiti,* December 4, p. 32.

Lansdown, Richard, ed. 2006. *Strangers in the South Seas: The idea of the Pacific in Western thought.* Honolulu: University of Hawai'i Press.

Lawrence, Denise, and Setha Low, eds. 1990. The built environment and spatial form. *Annual Review of Anthropology* 19:453–505.

Layard, John. 1942. *Stone men of Malekula: Vao.* London: Chatto and Windus.

Lazrus, Heather. 2009. *Weathering the waves: Climate change, politics, and vulnerability in Tuvalu.* PhD diss., University of Washington.

Lefebvre, Henri. 1939. *Le matérialisme dialectique.* Paris: Alcan.

————. 1973. *Espace et politique.* Paris: Éditions Anthropos.

————. 1974. *La production de l'espace.* Paris: Éditions Anthropos.

————. 1978. *De l'état: Les contradictions de l'état moderne.* Vol. 4. Paris: Union Générale d'Éditions.

————. 1979. Space: Social product and use value. In *Critical sociology: European perspective,* ed. J. Freiberg, 285–95. New York: Irvington Publishers.

————. 1991. *The production of space.* Trans. Donald Nicholson-Smith. Oxford: Blackwell.

————. 2002. *Foundations for a sociology of the everyday.* Vol. 2 of *Critique of everyday life.* Trans. John Moore. London: Verso.

Le Journal de Tahiti. 1969. La 3eme base du CEP est achevée à Totegegie. *Le Journal de Tahiti,* March 8, pp. 4–5.

Leney, Richard. 1995. Greenpeace vessel SV *Rainbow Warrior.* Diary, June 28.

Leslie, Esther. 2006. Walter Benjamin and commodity capitalism. *Socialist Worker.* July 8. See http://www.socialistworker.co.uk/art.php?id=9150.

Les nouvelles de Tahiti. 2001. Le 6me hôtel de la chaîne Pearl Beach Resort inauguré: Le luxe polynésien à visage humain. *Les nouvelles de Tahiti,* October 23, pp. 24–25.

Levy, Robert. 1973. *Tahitians: Mind and experience in the Society Islands.* Chicago: University of Chicago Press.

Lewandowski, Susan. 1984. The built environment and cultural symbolism in post colonial Madras. In *The city in cultural context,* ed. John Agnew, John Mercer, and David Sopher, 237–54. London: Allen and Unwin.

Lewis, Ben. 2005. *Blowing up paradise.* Film. First Run Icarus Films.

Liebersohn, Harry. 2006. *The travelers' world: Europe to the Pacific.* Cambridge, MA: Harvard University Press.

Lindstrom, Lamont. 2007. A body of postcards from Vanuatu. In *Embodying modernity and post-modernity,* ed. S. Bamford, 257–82. Durham, NC: Carolina Academic Press.

Lisle, Debbie. 2004. Gazing at ground zero: Tourism, voyeurism and spectacle. *Journal for Cultural Research* 8 (1): 3–21.

Lockwood, Victoria. 1993. *Tahitian transformation: Gender and capitalist development in a rural society.* Boulder: Lynne Rienner Publishers.

Loti, Pierre. 1880. *The marriage of Loti.* London: Routledge and Kegan Paul, 1986.

———. 1891. *Le roman d'un enfant.* Paris: Calmann Lévy.

Louis, Renee. 2007. "Can you hear us now?" Voices from the margin: Using indigenous methodologies in geographic research. *Geographical Research* 45 (2): 130–39.

Low, Setha. 1996. The social production and social construction of public space. *American Ethnologist* 23 (4): 861–79.

———. 2000. *On the plaza: The politics of public space and culture.* Austin: University of Texas Press.

———. 2001. The edge and the center: Gated communities and the discourse of urban fear. *American Anthropologist* 103 (1): 45–58.

———. 2003a. *Behind the gates: Life, security and the pursuit of happiness in fortress America.* New York: Routledge.

———. 2003b. Embodied space(s). *Space and Culture* 6 (1): 9–18.

Low, Setha, and Denise Lawrence-Zúñiga, eds. 2003. *The anthropology of space and place: Locating culture.* Malden, MA: Blackwell.

Loyrette, Henri. 1992. Le tour Eiffel: Les lieux de mémoire. In *Realms of memory: The construction of the French past,* ed. Pierre Nora, trans. Arthur Goldhammer, 349–77. New York: Columbia University Press.

Luxembourg, Rosa. 1963. *The accumulation of capital.* London: Routledge and Kegan Paul.

Lyons, Paul. 2006. *American pacificism: Oceania in the U.S. imagination.* London: Routledge.

MacCannell, Dean. 1976. *The tourist: A new theory of the leisure class.* New York: Schocken Books.

———. 1992. *Empty meeting grounds: The tourist papers.* New York: Routledge.

MacDougall, David. 2006. *The corporeal image: Film, ethnography, and the senses.* Princeton: Princeton University Press.

Maclellan, Nic. 2005. The nuclear age in the Pacific Islands. *The Contemporary Pacific* 17 (2): 363–72.

Mahé, Patrick. 2002. *Bon voyage: Catalogue officiel: Salon mondial du tourisme.* Levallois-Perret: Hachette.

Mancoff, Debra N. 2001. *Van Gogh and Gauguin: The studio of the south.* Amsterdam: Van Gogh Museum.

Manderson, Lenore, ed. 1986. *Shared wealth and symbol: Food, culture and society in Oceania.* Cambridge: Cambridge University Press.

Margueron, Daniel. 1989. *Tahiti dans toute sa litterature.* Paris: Éditions l'Harmattan.

Marseille, Jacques. 1986. *L'Age d'or de la France coloniale.* Paris: Éditions Albin Michel.

Martin, Jean. 1987. *L'Empire renaissant, 1789–1871.* Paris. Denoël.

Martin, Rena. 2001. Native connections to place: Policies and play. *American Indian Quarterly* 25 (1): 35–40.

Massey, Doreen. 1984. *Spatial divisions of labour.* London: Macmillan.

———. 1994. *Space, place, and gender.* Minneapolis: University of Minnesota Press.

Massey, Doreen, and J. Allen, eds. 1984. *Geography matters!* Cambridge: Cambridge University Press.

Mateata-Allain, Kareva. 2005. Oceanic peoples in dialogue: French Polynesian literature as transnational link. *International Journal of Francophone Studies* 8 (3): 269–88.

Mathur, Saloni. 1999. Wanted native views: Collecting colonial postcards of India. In *Gender, sexuality and colonial modernities,* ed. A. Burton, 95–115. New York: Routledge.

Matsuda, Matt. 2005. *Empire of love: Histories of France and the Pacific.* Oxford: Oxford University Press.

Mbembe, Achille. 2001. *On the postcolony.* Berkeley: University of California Press.

McCormick, Eric Hall. 1977. *Omai: Pacific envoy.* Auckland: University of Auckland.

McDonogh, Gary. 1991. Discourses of the city: Policy and response in post-transitional Barcelona. *City and Society* 5 (1): 40–63.

———. 1992. Gender, bars, and virtue in Barcelona. *Anthropological Quarterly* 65 (1): 19–33.

McMullin, Dan Taulapapa. 2005. "The fire that devours me": Tahitian spirituality and activism in the poetry of Henri Hiro. *International Journal of Francophone Studies* 8 (3): 341–57.

Mead, Margaret. 1928. *Coming of age in Samoa.* New York: American Museum of Natural History.

Meierotto, Lisa. 2009. The co-evolution of nature conservation and militarization on the U.S.-Mexico border. Ph.D. diss., University of Washington.

Melville, Herman. 1846. *Typee: Narrative of a four months' residence among the natives of a valley of the Marquesas Islands; or, a peep at Polynesian life*. London: J. Murray.

Merleau-Ponty, Maurice. 1945. *Phenomenology of perception*. Trans. Colin Smith. London: Routledge, 1996.

———. 1968. *The visible and the invisible*. Evanston: Northwestern University Press.

Merrett-Balkos, Leanne. 1998. Just add water: Remaking women through childbirth, Anganen, Southern Highlands, Papua New Guinea. In *Maternities and modernities: Colonial and postcolonial experiences in Asia and the Pacific*, ed. M. Jolly and K. Ram, 213–38. Cambridge: Cambridge University Press.

Merrifield, Andrew. 1993. Place and space: a Lefebvrian reconciliation. *Transactions of the Institute of British Geographers*, n.s., 18 (4): 516–31.

———. 1995. Lefebvre, anti-logos and Nietzsche: An alternative reading of the production of space. *Antipode* 27 (3): 294–303.

———. 2000. Henri Lefebvre: A socialist in space. In *Thinking space*, ed. Mike Crang and Nigel Thrift, 167–82. New York: Routledge.

———. 2006. *Henri Lefebvre: A critical introduction*. London: Routledge.

Metropolitan Museum of Art. 2002. Gauguin in New York collections: The lure of the exotic. Exhibit.

Mitchell, Timothy. 1988. *Colonising Egypt*. Cambridge: Cambridge University Press.

Mitchell, William, ed. 1992. *Clowning as critical practice: Performance humor in the South Pacific*. Pittsburgh: University of Pittsburgh Press.

Moore, Donald. 1998. Subaltern struggles and the politics of place: Remapping resistance in Zimbabwe's Eastern Highlands. *Cultural Anthropology* 13 (3): 344–81.

———. 2005. *Suffering for territory: Race, place, and power in Zimbabwe*. Durham, NC: Duke University Press.

Moore, Henrietta. 1986. *Space, text, and gender: An anthropological study of the Marakwet of Kenya*. Cambridge: Cambridge University Press.

Morgan, Nigel, A. Pritchard, and R. Pride, eds. 2002. *Destination branding: Creating the unique destination proposition*. Oxford: Elsevier Butterworth-Heinemann.

Morphy, Howard. 1995. Landscape and the reproduction of the ancestral past. In *The anthropology of landscape: Perspectives on place and space*, ed. E. Hirsch and M. O'Hanlon, 184–209. Oxford: Clarendon Press.

Morton, Patricia. 2000. *Hybrid modernities: Architecture and representation at the 1931 colonial exposition, Paris*. Cambridge, MA: MIT Press.

Munn, Nancy. 1996. Excluded spaces: The figure in the Australian Aboriginal landscape. *Critical Inquiry* 22 (3): 446–65.

Musée National des Arts d'Afrique et d'Océanie. 2001–2. Kannibals et vahinés: Imagerie des mers du sud. Paris. Exhibit.

Myers, Fred. 1991. *Pintupi country: Pintupi self: Sentiment, place and politics among Western Desert Aborigines.* Berkeley: University of California Press.

Nabobo-Baba, Unaisi. 2004. Research and Pacific indigenous peoples: Silenced pasts and challenged futures. In *Researching Pacific and indigenous peoples,* ed. Tupeni Baba, 'Okusitino Mahina, Nuhisifa Willimams, and Unaisi Nabobo-Baba, 17–32. Auckland: Centre for Pacific Studies, University of Auckland.

———. 2006. *Knowing and learning: An indigenous Fijian approach.* Suva, Fiji: Institute of Pacific Studies, University of the South Pacific.

National Library of Australia. 2001. Cook and Omai: The cult of the South Seas. Exhibit. Canberra.

Newbury, Colin. 1980. *Tahiti nui: Change and survival in French Polynesia, 1767–1945.* Honolulu: University of Hawai'i Press.

Nicole, Robert. 1993. Images of paradise. In *Last virgin in paradise,* ed. V. Hereniko and T. Teaiwa, 59–64. Suva, Fiji: Mana Publications.

———. 1999. Resisting orientalism: Pacific literature in French. In *Inside out: Literature, cultural politics, and identity in the new Pacific,* ed. V. Hereniko and R. Wilson, 265–90. Boston: Rowman and Littlefield.

———. 2001. *The word, the pen, and the pistol: Literature and power in Tahiti.* Albany: State University of New York Press.

Nietzsche, Friedrich. 1966. The birth of tragedy. In *Basic writings of Nietzsche,* 1–144. New York: Random House.

Norris, Scott, ed. 1994. *Discovered country: Tourism and survival in the American West.* Albuquerque: Stone Ladder Press.

O'Brien, Patty. 2006a. *The Pacific muse: Exotic femininity and the colonial Pacific.* Seattle: University of Washington Press.

———. 2006b. "Think of me as a woman": Queen Pomare of Tahiti and Anglo-French imperial contest in the 1840s Pacific. *Gender and History* 18 (1): 108–29.

O'Connor, Kaori. 1986. Introduction. In *The marriage of Loti,* vii–xiv. London: Routledge and Kegan Paul.

O'Dwyer, Carolyn. 2004. Tropic knights and hula belles: War and tourism in the South Pacific. *Journal of Cultural Research* 8 (1): 33–50.

O'Keefe, John, and William Shield. 1785. *A short account of the new pantomime called Omai, or, a trip round the world.* London: T. Cadell.

Oliver, Douglas. 1974. *Ancient Tahitian society.* 3 vols. Honolulu: University of Hawai'i Press.

———. 1981. *Two Tahitian villages: A study in comparison.* Laie, HI: Institute for Polynesian Studies.

Ollman, Bertell. 1993. *Dialectical investigations.* London: Routledge.

Ong, Aihwa. 1999. *Flexible citizenship: The cultural logics of transnationality.* Durham, NC: Duke University Press.

O'Reilly, Patrick. 1975. *Tahiti au temps des cartes postales.* Paris: Société des Océanistes.

Pablo, Marcia. 2001. Preservation as perpetuation. *American Indian Quarterly* 25 (1): 18–20.

Pambrun, Jean-Marc Teraʻituatini. 2003. *Les parfums du silence.* Papeʻete: Le Motu.

———. 2005. Blog. http://blog.lecriturien.org/post/2005/03/06/22-henri-hiro-dix-ans-apres (accessed 2007).

Pandolfi, Mariella. 1990. Boundaries inside the body: Women's sufferings in southern peasant Italy. *Culture, Medicine, and Psychiatry* 14 (2): 255–74.

Panoff, Michel. 1964. *Les structures agraires en polynésie française.* Paris: Centre documentaire pour l'Océanie.

Parmentier, Richard J. 1987. *The sacred remains: Myth, history, and polity in Belau.* Chicago: University of Chicago Press.

Perloff, Nancy. 1995. Gauguin's French baggage: Decadence and colonialism in Tahiti. In *Prehistories of the future,* ed. E. Barkan and R. Bush, 226–69. Stanford: Stanford University Press.

Pile, Steve. 1994. Masculinism, the use of dualistic epistemologies and third space. *Antipode* 26 (3): 255–77.

Pile, Steve, and Michael Keith, eds. 1997. *Geographies of resistance.* London: Routledge.

Pollock, Nancy. 1992. *These roots remain: Food habits in islands of the Central and Eastern Pacific since Western contact.* Honolulu: University of Hawaiʻi Press.

Pritchard, George. 1983. *The aggressions of the French at Tahiti and other islands in the Pacific.* Auckland: Auckland University Press.

Prochaska, David. 1990a. *Making Algeria French: Colonialism in Bône, 1870–1920.* Cambridge: Cambridge University Press.

———. 1990b. The archive of Algérie imaginaire. *History and Anthropology* 4:373–420.

Puputauki, Léonard. 1998. *Magazine d'information du G.I.P.* Papeʻete: Groupement d'intervention de la Polynésie française.

Raapoto, Turo. 1980. Maʻohi: On being Tahitian. *Pacific perspective, Pacific cultures: Past and Present* 9 (1): 3–5.

Rabinow, Paul. 1982. Ordonnance, discipline, regulation: Some reflections on urbanism. *Humanities in Society* 5 (3–4): 267–78.

———. 1989. *French modern: Norms and forms of missionary and didactic pathos.* Cambridge, MA: MIT Press.

Rafael, Vince. 2000. *White love and other events in Filipino history.* Durham, NC: Duke University Press.

Raffles, Hugh. 2002a. *In Amazonia: A natural history.* Princeton: Princeton University Press.

———. 2002b. Intimate knowledge. *International Social Science Journal* 54 (173): 325–35.

———. 2005. Towards a critical natural history. *Antipode* 37 (2): 374–78.

Regnault, Jean-Marc. 1993. *La bombe française dans le Pacifique: L'implantation, 1957–1964.* Tahiti: Scoop Éditions.

———. 2005. The nuclear issue in the South Pacific: Labor parties, trade union movements, and Pacific Island churches in international relations. *The Contemporary Pacific* 17 (2): 339–57.

Relph, Edward. 1991. *Place and placelessness.* London: Pion.

———. 2001. The critical description of confused geographies. In *Textures of place: Exploring humanist geographies,* ed. Paul Adams et al., 150–66. Minneapolis: University of Minnesota Press.

Rennie, Neil. 1995. *Far-fetched facts: The literature of travel and the idea of the South Seas.* Oxford: Clarendon.

Rhodes, Lorna. 2004. *Total confinement: Madness and reason in the maximum security prison.* Berkeley: University of California Press.

Riesenfeld, Alphonse. 1950. *The megalithic cultures of Melanesia.* Leiden: E. J. Brill.

Roberts, Kevin. 2004. *Lovemarks: The future beyond brands.* New York: Powerhouse.

Robineau, Claude. 1975. The Tahitian economy and tourism. In *A new kind of sugar: Tourism in the Pacific,* ed. B. Finney and K. Watson, 61–76. Honolulu: East-West Center.

Rodman, Margaret. 1992. Empowering place: Multilocality and multivocality. *American Anthropologist* 94 (3): 640–56.

———. 2001. *Houses far from home: British colonial space in the New Hebrides.* Honolulu: University of Hawai'i Press.

Rodriguez, Maximo. 1996. *Les Espagnols à Tahiti.* No. 45. Trans. Horacio Belçaguy. Paris: Publications de la Société des Océanistes.

Roe, D., and J. Taki. 1999. Living with stones: People and the landscape in Erromango, Vanuatu. In *Shaping your landscape: The archaeology and anthropology of landscape,* ed. P. J. Ucko and R. Layton, 411–22. London: Routledge.

Rose, Deborah Bird. 1996. *Nourishing terrains: Australian Aboriginal views of landscape and wilderness.* Canberra: Commonwealth of Australia.

Rotenberg, Robert. 1995. *Landscape and power in Vienna.* Baltimore: Johns Hopkins University Press.

———. 2001. Metropolitanism and the transformation of urban space in nineteenth-century colonial metropoles. *American Anthropologist* 103 (1): 7–15.

Rotenberg, Robert, and Gary McDonogh, eds. 1993. *The cultural meaning of urban space.* Westport, CT: Bergin and Garvey.

Rousseau, Jean-Jacques. 1754. *Discours sur l'origine de l'inégalité parmi les hommes.* Paris: R. London and J. Dodsley.

Ryan, Tom. 2002. "Le président des terres australes": Charles de Brosses and the French enlightenment beginnings of Oceanic anthropology. *Journal of Pacific History* 37 (2): 157–86.

Said, Edward. 1993. *Culture and imperialism.* New York: Knopf.

Salmon, Tati. 1904. *The history of the island of Borabora and genealogy of our family from marae vaiotaha.* Pape'ete: Privately printed.

Salmond, Anne. 2010. *Aphrodite's island: The European discovery of Tahiti.* Berkeley: University of California Press.

Sancton, Thomas. 1995. Fallout in paradise. *Time* (international), September 18, pp. 2–27.

Saquet, Jean-Louis. 2001. *Te fenua: The Tahiti handbook.* Pape'ete Tahiti: Éditions Avant et Après.

Saura, Bruno. 1998. *Des Tahitiens, des Français, leus représentations réciproques aujourd'hui. Essai.* Pape'ete: Christian Gleizal Éditeur.

———. 2000. Le placenta en Polynésie française: Un choix de santé publique confronté à des questions identitaires. *Sciences Sociales et Santé* 22:1–23.

———. 2002a. Continuity of bodies: The infant's placenta and the island's navel in Eastern Polynesia. *Journal of the Polynesian Society* 3 (2): 127–45.

———. 2002b. Enterrer le placenta; l'évolution d'un rite de naissance en Polynésie française. Île en île. http://www.lehman.cuny.edu/ile.en.ile/pacifique/saura_placenta.html (accessed 2008).

———. 2004. Dire l'autochtonie à Tahiti. Le terme *ma'ohi*: Représentations, controverse et données linguistiques. *Journal de la Société des Océanistes* 119:119–37.

———. 2008. *Tahiti ma'ohi: Culture, identité, religion et nationalisme en Polynésie française.* Pirae, Tahiti: Au Vent des Îles.

Schjeldahl, Peter. 2002. French postcards: The wiles of Gauguin. *New Yorker,* July 29, pp. 82–84.

Scott, James. 1985. *Weapons of the weak: Everyday forms of peasant resistance.* New Haven: Yale University Press.

———. 1998. *Seeing like a state: How certain schemes to improve the human condition have failed.* New Haven: Yale University Press.

Segalen, Victor. 1890. *Essay on exoticism.* Durham, NC: Duke University Press, 2002.

Shackelford, George T. M., and Claire Frèches-Thory. 2004. *Gauguin Tahiti.* Boston: Museum of Fine Arts.

Shields, Rob. 1991. *Places on the margin: Alternative geographies of modernity.* London: Routledge Chapman Hall.

———. 1999. *Lefebvre, love and struggle: Spatial dialectics.* New York: Routledge.

Sieber, R. Timothy. 1993. Public access on the urban waterfront: A question of vision. In Rotenberg and McDonogh, *The cultural meaning of urban space,* 174–93.

Smith, Bernard. 1985. *European vision and the South Pacific.* New Haven: Yale University Press.

Smith, Linda Tuhiwai. 1999. *Decolonizing methodologies: Research and indigenous peoples.* New York: Zed Books.

Soja, Edward. 1989. *Postmodern geographies.* London: Verso.

————. 1996. *Thirdspace: Journeys to Los Angeles and other real-and-imagined places.* Oxford: Blackwell.

Sontag, Susan. 1976. Introduction. In *Portraits in life and death,* by Peter Hujar. New York: DaCapo Press.

————. 1979. *On photography.* New York: Picador.

Spitz, Chantal. 1991. *L'île des rêves écrasés.* Pape'ete: Les Éditions de la Plage.

————. 1999. J'irai cracher sur vos mémoires. Letter to the newspaper *La dépêche de Tahiti,* June 1999.

————. 2000. Rarahu iti e, autre moi-même. In *Bulletin de la société des études océaniennes: Supplément au mariage de Loti,* ed. Daniel Margueron, Robert Koenig, Christian Beslu, et al., 285–87. April-September. Pape'ete: Société des études océaniennes.

————. 2003. Héritage et confrontation: Où en sommes-nous cent ans après la question posée par Gauguin "D'où venons-nous? Que sommes-nous? Où allons-nous?" Paper read at the international conference Paul Gauguin (to mark the 100th year of Guaguin's death), Héritage et confrontations, L'Université de la Polynésie française, March 6–8. Available at http://www.lehman.cuny.edu/ile.en.ile/ (accessed 2006).

————. 2007. *Island of shattered dreams.* Trans. Jean Anderson. Wellington, NZ: Huia Publications.

Steiner, Christopher. 1999. Authenticity, repetition, and the aesthetics of seriality: The work of tourist art in the age of mechanical reproduction. In *Unpacking culture: Art and commodity in colonial and postcolonial worlds,* ed. R. Phillips and C. Steiner, 87–103. Berkeley: University of California Press.

Stevenson, Robert L. 1896. *In the South Seas.* New York: Charles Scribner's Son.

Stewart, Frank, Kareva Mateata-Allain, and Alexander Dale Mawyer, eds. 2006. *Varua tupu: New writing from French Polynesia.* Honolulu: University of Hawai'i Press.

Stewart, Lynn. 1995. Bodies, visions, and spatial politics: A review essay on Henri Lefebvre's *The production of space. Environment and Planning D: Society and Space* 13:609–18.

Stewart, Susan. 1984. *On longing: Narratives of the miniature, the gigantic, the souvenir, the collection.* Baltimore: Johns Hopkins University Press.

Stoler, Ann. 2002. *Carnal knowledge and imperial power: Race and the intimate in colonial rule.* Berkeley: University of California Press.

Strathern, Andrew. 1975. Veiled speech in Mount Hagen. In *Political language and oratory in traditional societies,* ed. M. Bloch, 185–203. New York: Academic Press.

———. 1982. Witchcraft, greed, cannibalism and death: Some related themes from the New Guinea Highlands. In *Death and the regeneration of life,* ed. M. Bloch and J. Perry, 111–33. Cambridge: Cambridge University Press.

Strokirch, Karin von. 1997. French Polynesia. *The Contemporary Pacific* 9 (1): 227–33.

Sturma, Michael. 2002. *South Sea maidens: Western fantasy and sexual politics in the South Pacific.* Westport, CT: Greenwood Press.

Stürzenhofecker, Gabrielle. 1998. *Times enmeshed: Gender, space and history among the Duna of Papua New Guinea.* Stanford: Stanford University Press.

Sylvain, Teva. 1994. *La legende des filles des mers du sud.* Tahiti: Pacific Promotion Tahiti S. A.

Tahiti Tourisme North America. 2008. *Tahiti Tourisme marketing plan.* El Segundo, CA: Tahiti Tourisme North America.

Tahiti Tourisme North America Travel Planner. 2001. *Travel planner 2001.* Papeʻete: GIE Tahiti Tourisme.

Taillemite, Étienne, ed. 1977. *Bougainville et ses compagnons autour du monde, 1766–1769.* 2 vols. Paris: Imprimerie Nationale.

Taliman, Valerie. 2002. Sacred landscapes. *Sierra* (November/December): 36–45.

Tamaira, A. Marata. 2010. From full dusk to full tusk: Reimagining the "dusky maiden" through the visual arts. *The Contemporary Pacific* 22 (1): 1–35.

Taouma, Lisa. 2004. Gauguin is dead. . . . There is no paradise. *Journal of Intercultural Studies* 25 (1): 35–46.

Tcherkézoff, Serge. 2003. On cloth, gifts and nudity: Regarding some European misunderstandings during early encounters in Polynesia. In *Clothing the Pacific,* ed. Chloë Colchester, 51–75. Oxford: Berg.

———. 2004. *Tahiti 1768: Jeunes filles en pleurs: La face cachée des premiers contacts et la naissance du mythe occidental.* Papeʻete: Au vent des îles.

Teaiwa, Teresia. 1994. Bikinis and other s/pacific n/oceans. *The Contemporary Pacific* 6 (1): 87–109.

———. 1999. Reading Paul Gauguin's *Noa Noa* with Epeli Hauʻofa's *Kisses in the Nederends:* Militourism, feminism, and the "Polynesian body." In *Inside out: Literature, cultural politics and identity in the new Pacific,* ed. Vilsoni Hereniko and Rob Wilson, 249–63. Boston: Rowman and Littlefield.

———. 2001. *Militarism, tourism and the native: Articulations in Oceania.* PhD diss., University of California, Santa Cruz.

———. 2006. On analogies: Rethinking the Pacific in a global context. *The Contemporary Pacific* 18 (1): 71–87.

Tengan, Ty P. Kawika. 2008. *Native men remade: Gender and nation in contemporary Hawai'i*. Durham, NC: Duke University Press.

Tetiarahi, Gabriel. 1987. The society islands: Squeezing out the Polynesians. In *Land tenure in the Pacific*, ed. R. Crocombe, 45–58. Suva, Fiji: University of the South Pacific.

———. 2005. French nuclear testing in the South Pacific, or when France makes light of its duty to remember. *The Contemporary Pacific* 17 (2): 378–81.

Tevane, Maco. 2000. "Ma'ohi" ou "Maori"? *Tahiti Pacifique Magazine* 116:15–18.

Thomas, Nicholas. 2003. *Cook: The extraordinary voyages of Captain James Cook*. New York: Walker and Company.

Toullelan, Pierre-Yves, and Bernard Gille. 1992. *Le mariage Franco-Tahitian: Histoire de Tahiti du XVIIe siècle à nos jours*. Pape'ete, Tahiti: Éditions Polymages-Scoop.

Trask, Haunani-Kay. 1987. *From a native daughter: Colonialism and sovereignty in Hawai'i*. Monroe, ME: Common Courage Press.

Travel and Leisure. 2003. Fifty romantic retreats. *Travel and Leisure* (February): 88–92.

Tsing, Anna. 2000. The global situation. *Cultural Anthropology* 15 (3): 327–60.

Turner, Louis, and John Ash. 1975. *The golden hordes*. London: Constable.

Tyerman, Daniel. 1831. *Journal of voyages and travels by the Rev. Daniel Tyerman and George Bennet, esq deputed from the London Missionary Society, to visit their various stations in the South Sea Islands*. London: Frederick Westley and A. H. Davis.

Urale, Sima. 1996. *Velvet dreams*. Directed by Sima Urale and produced by Vincent Burke and Clifton May. Top Shelf Productions.

Urry, John. 1990. *The tourist gaze: Leisure and travel in contemporary societies*. London: Sage.

———. 1995. *Consuming places*. New York: Routledge.

Vibart, Eric. 1987. *Tahiti: Naissance d'un paradis au siècle des lumières*. Brussels: Édition Complexe.

Vincendon-Dumoulin, C. A., and C. L. F. Desgraz. 1844. *Iles Tahiti. Esquisse historique et géographique précédée de considérations générales sur la colonisation française dans l'Océanie*. Paris: Imprimerie de Fain et Thunot.

Wallace, David. 1996. Shipping out: On the (nearly lethal) comforts of a luxury cruise. *Harper's Magazine* 292 (1748): 33–56.

Wallace, Lee. 2003. *Sexual encounters: Pacific texts, modern sexualities*. Ithaca: Cornell University Press.

West, Paige. 2005. Translation, value, and space: Theorizing an ethnographic and engaged environmental anthropology. *American Anthropologist* 107 (4): 632–42.

———. 2006. *Conservation is our government now: The politics of ecology in Papua New Guinea*. Durham, NC: Duke University Press.

Wheeler, Tony, and Jean-Bernard Carillet. 1997. *Tahiti and French Polynesia*. Oakland: Lonely Planet.

Whitehead, Harriet. 2000. *Food rules: Hunting, sharing, and tabooing game in Papua New Guinea*. Ann Arbor: University of Michigan Press.

Whittier Daily News. 1968. "Made in Whittier" tikis will greet tourists in Tahiti. *Whittier Daily News*, August 30, p. 3.

Wiessner, Polly, and Akii Tumu. 1998. *Historical vines: Enga networks of exchange, ritual, and warfare in Papua New Guinea*. Washington, DC: Smithsonian Institution Press.

Wright, Gwendolyn. 1991. *The politics of design in French colonial urbanism*. Chicago: University of Chicago Press.

Young, Michael. 1971. *Fighting with food: Leadership, values and social control in a Massim society*. Cambridge: Cambridge University Press.

Zukin, Sharon. 1995. *The cultures of cities*. Oxford: Blackwell.

Index